New Orleans
Pralines

PLANTATION SUGAR, LOUISIANA PECANS, AND THE MARKETING OF SOUTHERN NOSTALGIA

ANTHONY J. STANONIS

LOUISIANA STATE UNIVERSITY PRESS BATON ROUGE

Published by Louisiana State University Press
lsupress.org

Manufactured in the United States of America
First printing

DESIGNER: Barbara Neely Bourgoyne
TYPEFACE: Minion Pro
PRINTER AND BINDER: Sheridan Books, Inc.

JACKET ILLUSTRATIONS: First known photograph of a praline seller in New Orleans, late 1890s, by George François Mugnier (courtesy of the Louisiana State Museum, Museum Purchase, 09813.0022); praline photo, Adobe Stock/gridspot.

LIBRARY OF CONGRESS CATALOGING-IN-PUBLICATION DATA
Names: Stanonis, Anthony J. (Anthony Joseph), author.
Title: New Orleans pralines : plantation sugar, Louisiana pecans, and the marketing of Southern nostalgia / Anthony J. Stanonis.
Description: Baton Rouge : Louisiana State University Press, [2024] | Includes bibliographical references and index.
Identifiers: LCCN 2024010662 (print) | LCCN 2024010663 (ebook) | ISBN 978-0-8071-8248-2 (cloth) | ISBN 978-0-8071-8320-5 (epub) | ISBN 978-0-8071-8321-2 (pdf)
Subjects: LCSH: Praline—Louisiana—New Orleans—History. | Confectionery—Economic aspects—Louisiana—New Orleans—History. | Confectionery—Social aspects—Louisiana—New Orleans—History. | New Orleans (La.)—History.
Classification: LCC HD9330.C653 U5745 2024 (print) | LCC HD9330.C653 (ebook) | DDC 338.4/76641530976335—dc23/eng/20240405
LC record available at https://lccn.loc.gov/2024010662
LC ebook record available at https://lccn.loc.gov/2024010663

To my mother, Michaela Stanonis,
for moving from Germany to New Orleans.

.....

To my son, Charlie Stanonis,
for moving from Ireland to New Orleans.

CONTENTS

Acknowledgments

On mornings, I often stroll down the streetcar tracks of St. Charles Avenue to Audubon Park in New Orleans. Shaded by century-old live oaks draped in Spanish moss, the park provides a quiet space to ponder, to read, and to watch ducks, egrets, squirrels, and turtles around the lagoons.

This peaceful urban space belies its key role in the American sugar industry and the emergence of the praline. Audubon Park sits on Étienne Boré's plantation, where sugarcane was first successfully granulated in the United States in 1795. This achievement birthed a brutal slave regime and set American society on the path to an intensifying sugar-heavy diet. Soon after, sugar plantations along the Mississippi River from Baton Rouge to New Orleans would emerge as one of the wealthiest areas of the country. Boré became celebrated. He even was appointed as New Orleans's first mayor when the French colony transferred to U.S. rule after the Louisiana Purchase in 1803.

Although Boré's plantation now lies under an asphalt exercise track, a golf course, a zoo, playgrounds, and other features typical of an urban green space—including two universities—Louisiana's sugar plantation heritage remains part of living memory.

It was on a walk around Audubon Park's track one day in October 2022 that I encountered an African American woman, perhaps in her fifties or sixties, talking with a friend about her childhood. In a moment of serendipity, she passed me just as she was recounting how her father regularly took the family upriver to Edgard, Louisiana, to cut a few stalks of mature sugarcane. He even kept the cane knife he had used growing up on a sugar plantation to ensure that his family members never forgot their ancestral past.

Our understanding of history boils down to a blending of facts, memories, and, occasionally, outright fabrications. And it is the fabrications—how they emerged and why—that speak volumes about a time and a place. This book deals with one of the biggest myths in the complex history of New Orleans: that the praline, a confection central to the city's self-image and tourism industry, is a culinary creation inherited directly from France's aristocracy and cherished by its French Creoles.

My acknowledgments are rather short this time around. I had originally planned for this project to be an article but soon discovered that the research confronted me with numerous unexpected realizations. It had to be a book. I just did not have the time to write it until the pandemic lockdowns set in. Most of this book was written in the isolation of those long months.

First, I would like to thank my former colleagues at Queen's University Belfast for keeping alive a sense of community and engagement during those strange times in 2020. I especially thank Brian Kelly and Danny Kowalsky.

I also thank Bruce Baker, David Gleeson, Zoe Hyman, and Richard Follett for their work on Louisiana and their friendship during the years I lived in Northern Ireland.

Closer to home, I thank Mark Fernandez, Justin Nystrom, Lynnell Thomas, and Jen Wallach. In various ways, they kept me curious about New Orleans, tourism, and foodways in the American South while I lived abroad.

I also thank the staff at the Virginia Historical Society, the New Orleans Public Library, the Louisiana Collection at Tulane University, the Special Collections at the University of New Orleans, the Historic New Orleans Collection, and the Special Collections at Loyola University New Orleans.

The prodding of Jenny Keegan at LSU Press helped turn a rough manuscript into a publishable book. I thank her for keeping me focused. I also thank the two anonymous reviewers for their detailed and thoughtful comments.

Finally, I thank all my friends for keeping me sane during the pandemic and this writing process. I especially thank Ron Scalise, Peter Talluto, Daniel Brown, Rachel Wallace, John Nathan, and Jen Dubin.

New Orleans
Pralines

INTRODUCTION

THE PRALINE CITY

"Walk around the French Quarter today and you'll notice the barrage of touristy shops that hock hot sauce, beads, pralines, and crass T-shirts—the basic starter kit for getting arrested on Bourbon Street," proclaimed Gwendolyn Knapp for Eater.com in 2016. Her list highlighted conspicuous consumption New Orleans–style, a blending of the tacky with the tasteful. Of the items available, however, the praline stood out as a "symbol of a rich black culinary heritage and city tradition." In its simple combination of brown sugar and pecans, the praline represents New Orleans and its long history as a southern city. Yet Knapp concluded, "The praline is often overlooked as one of New Orleans's most storied foods."[1]

The millions of tourists who have gobbled pralines over the last 150 years may overlook the storied past of the candy that is synonymous with New Orleans, but the tasty treat offers an opportunity to explore the history of the Crescent City and its hinterland. Jules Weiss, proprietor of a French Quarter gift shop, commented on the popularity of the praline in 1974: "If I had to pick a 'most popular souvenir,' I'd have to say pralines, because they're inexpensive, can be used up and you don't have to find a place for them."[2] Such practicality only partly explains the success of the confection. Narratives built around the praline offered a version of New Orleans, particularly its Creole past, that resonated with many locals and tourists. Further, each ingredient told a tale. Historian Benjamin Cohen notes, "Talking about sugar always means talking about culture: plantations and slaves, colonialism and empire, taste, nutrition, diet, commodity economics, science, cultivation." The praline offers a complicated tale, at times brutal and shocking but, in other instances, uplifting and surprising.[3]

French explorers claimed the Gulf Coast for France in 1699; they established New Orleans in 1718. Along the banks of Louisiana's waterways, they encountered pecan trees. These trees had evolved to clasp their roots into the natural levees.

In the late 1700s, planters began sowing fields of sugarcane on the alluvial soil along rivers and bayous. Sugar plantations sent shipments to New Orleans's wharves to satiate the growing hunger for sweetness. The transformation of the port and urban area from a French colonial backwater into the third-largest city in the United States by 1840 was fueled largely by the profits reaped by sugar planters.

To produce and process cane, planters purchased humans forced to the New World from Africa. The enslaved planted, cut, and processed the cane. The work was grueling and deadly. At some point, most likely in a plantation kitchen or in a sugar mill, an enterprising soul mixed freshly cracked pecans with recently harvested sugar.

The word "praline" refers to Marshal du Plessis-Praslin, a French noble and experienced negotiator from the court of Louis XIV. Accounts credit the cook employed by du Plessis-Praslin as the inventor of the sugar-coated nut, almonds being preferred at the time. The cook named the confection "praline" in the marshal's honor. Though seemingly simple fare, the sugared almonds heralded imperial grandeur and the global reach of France under the Sun King: the praline celebrated the French Empire, with its far-off sugar colonies. European powers had only begun planting their flags on the sun-drenched Caribbean islands on which sugar plantations flourished. Martinique and other islands became crown jewels repeatedly fought over by the European empires. The candy also advertised royal wealth because the cost of sugar remained so high.[4]

As the embodiment of imperial France, pralines could even awe those who ate them. One account described how Marshal du Plessis-Praslin appeared to the people at Bordeaux, a citizenry in revolt against the monarchy, in 1649. The king's representative hosted rebellious city leaders at a sumptuous eight-course meal held during negotiations, where pralines were first served. The revolt ceased. Bordeaux's leaders had tasted royal power.[5]

Though these pralines were unlike those eventually popularized in New Orleans, Louisianans have long associated their pecan patty of brown sugar with the treats created for du Plessis-Praslin. A noble French lineage gave refinement to a candy sold as a common street food from the nineteenth century onward. Local chronicler Pie Dufour, like many others, directly linked the name to the nobleman when addressing tourists in 1955: "Have you eaten any of our pralines? They were named for the Duc de Praslin and as you doubtless know are a delicious confection made of pecans and sugar." The substitution of pecans for almonds seemed a no-brainer. Gaspar "Buddy" Stall, another popular historian of Louisiana, made the leap between Plessis-Praslin's treat and the New Orleans praline sound simple in his 1994 history of the city: "Since almonds were not readily available to early French inhabitants of Louisiana, the meat of the pecan was substituted. Presto! The pecan praline became the most popular confection of our area." It seemed that easy, except it was not.[6]

A close look at the etymology of "praline" within Louisiana complicates the narrative. The term "praline" evolved within the Francophone world of the eighteenth and nineteenth centuries. The French term describing sugar-coated nuts expanded to include less simple candies. The French labeled as a "praline" any confection typically consisting of nuts (usually almonds or hazelnuts), sugar, and chocolate mixed with cream. The word also crossed over into English. Anglo confectioners with an eye to marketing linked their treats to French haute cuisine. In the parlance of New Orleanians through the mid-nineteenth century, the term "praline" served as a generic reference akin to bonbon, rather than an exclusive name for the patty-shaped candy now so synonymous with the Crescent City.[7]

Advertisements from New Orleans around the time of the Civil War reveal how "praline" conformed to common French and English usage. Bochet and De Lamarres, a self-proclaimed "Southern Steam Chocolate Manufactory" on Chartres Street in the French Quarter, placed an advertisement in the *Daily Picayune* in April 1861. The firm employed "Parisian workmen of well known ability" who crafted "any variety of Confectionary, Sugar Plums, and Chocolate Bonbons, iced, with liquor, cream, pralines." The candymakers blended sugar-coated nuts with chocolate. In 1863, another steam-powered chocolate manufactory run by D. Lopez on Chartres Street offered a selection of "Cream Chocolate; Chocolate Pralines; Cordial Chocolate; Croquet Michelieu; a large assortment of Miniature Cordials; Cream Bonbons." J. Villarrubia's candy shop in 1870 similarly sold "Chocolate Pralines."[8]

Pralines as disks of brown sugar containing pecans were largely unknown to New Orleanians until the late nineteenth century. In fact, Louisiana's Creoles, meaning those residents of French ancestry dating to the mid-nineteenth century or earlier, used the term "plarine" to distinguish the sugary patty from a bonbon generically labeled "praline." "Plarine" derived from the French word "plat," meaning flat. This word and the confection circulated among the antebellum sugar plantations in Francophone areas, both likely arriving in New Orleans with African Americans escaping enslavement during the Civil War. Enslavers typically tasked their human property with cooking meals, an arduous process given Louisiana's heat.[9]

The earliest known reference to a plarine appears in a diary entry from a Confederate soldier, the eighteen-year-old Willie Barrow. Barrow had been born along the Mississippi River in St. Francisville, Louisiana. After the death of his parents, he spent his childhood on the sugar plantations of his politically connected uncle. Barrow enlisted as a private and served along the Gulf Coast before being captured at Shiloh. Like his fellow soldiers stationed in Berwick, Louisiana, in late 1861 and early 1862, he commented on chewing sugarcane, retrieving syrup from nearby plantations, and enjoying "some piccan candy."[10] On Saturday, December 7, 1861, he penciled, "We had a pretty good dinner, Roast beef, peas, rice, bread & molasses, and two bottles of claret. after dinner I went down town came back and eat some 'plarines' that D.B.G. had made; after that, I drank a punch after supper I went to the barroom and smoked a couple of cigars." The mention of plarines reflects the Civil War's role in mixing the culinary cultures of the American South, in this case introducing Barrow, an Anglo-Louisianan, to Franco-Louisianan customs along Bayou Teche. The fact that Barrow placed *plarine* in quotes suggests that the word was a French term foreign to him and that the confection was equally unfamiliar. For a man who frequented New Orleans, Barrow considered this candy made by a fellow soldier to be unusual. Local French terminology and this unique Louisiana treat had yet to cross into American vernacular and consumption beyond plantation districts like Bayou Teche where sugar and pecans abounded.[11] Locals during the twentieth century acknowledged that the pecan praline did not enter popular (white) New Orleans culture until the 1880s and 1890s.[12]

"Praline" largely eclipsed "plarine" in common usage among New Orleanians in the early twentieth century. A revealing debate over which term applied to the delicacy erupted in the *Daily Picayune* in 1911, a time when praline production and marketing shifted from homemade confections sold on the streets to mass-produced candies sold in stores. The early twentieth century also marked the passing of Creoles born within antebellum Francophone Louisiana. The popularization of the candy under the term "praline," with its linguistic link to French heritage even among English speakers, began to erode the more niche, Creole French term for the confection. Yet, some New Orleanians continued to use the "native-born" term "plarines." As the newspaper reported, "Plarine, signifying something flat ('plat'), was a word coined almost naturally by the Creole children of the Vieux Carre, so that 'plarine' may be called an original, native, local, unique appellation." One Creole native contended that "'pralines' are always 'almonds coated with burnt sugar,' and hence cannot be mistaken for pecan 'plarines.'" A self-described "old timer" in 1958 similarly recalled how, during his youth in the late nineteenth century, pralines were "then spelled plarines."

By World War I, however, widespread marketing efforts by local English-speaking candymakers and the rise of tourism centered on American travelers to New Orleans popularized the word "praline" as an exclusive reference to the brown sugar patty containing pecans. Ironically, the word "praline" for the brown sugar patty emerged during the twentieth century as an identifier of newcomers to New Orleans: locals pronounced "praline" as "prah-leen," the French pronunciation passed off as the word supposedly used by French Creoles, whereas English speakers might say "pray-leen."[13]

The story of the praline is the story of New Orleans. It is also the story of Louisiana, a backwater mercantile outpost transformed in the early nineteenth century into a sugar-producing powerhouse grounded on enslaved laborers of color. The sugar plantations, in turn, facilitated pecan production on an industrial scale by the late 1800s. Emancipated African Americans scavenged resources and, as will be seen, popularized the praline by combining the natural resources of the plantations with the commercial opportunities afforded by the shipping nexus of New Orleans. As sugar and pecans became more widely available, the American hunger for sweets—and nuts—grew. This growth not only marked a New South built on calls for the diversification of crops beyond cotton and sugar but also an expanding American empire hungry for new markets and resources. The rise of leisure travel during the late nineteenth and early twentieth centuries opened more opportunities to promote praline sales and, in doing so, to rewrite and reimagine the history of New Orleans via the praline.

The following chapters unpack three interwoven narratives about the praline: the history of women of color as entrepreneurial street peddlers in New Orleans, the production of sugarcane and pecans, and the depictions of street vendors of African descent created by white writers and businesspersons. These narratives are not easily untangled. Much of the evidence about praline vendors comes from white-authored sources rooted deep in nostalgia for the antebellum South. But when interrogated through census records, municipal records, and photographic evidence—as well as close readings of newspapers, novels, and tourist diaries, among other sources—the separate histories of praline peddlers, the praline, and popular imagery of African American vendors emerge.

This journey starts with a chapter on African American life in New Orleans during the Civil War and Reconstruction. The enslaved fled Louisiana's sugar plantations to seize freedom. New Orleans, occupied by Union troops in April 1862, became a beacon. Experienced with growing and harvesting sugarcane and pecans, the self-emancipated likely carried the praline to the Crescent City where the poor, hungry Black population swelled during the 1860s. The second chapter scrutinizes Louisianans' fixation with brown sugar by recounting the struggles of the sugar industry in the late nineteenth and early twentieth centuries. Foreign sugarcane, domestic beet sugar, and the rise of a corporate monopoly on refining all threatened the state's plantations, fostering celebrations of local sucrose. The third chapter turns to representations of New Orleans's praline peddlers by white writers, predominantly women, as Jim Crow laws in the 1880s and 1890s rolled back the rights gained by African Americans during Reconstruction. These authors imagined African American entrepreneurs as mammies loyal to former enslavers. In these tales, the vendors preserved Creole traditions out of a devotion to their former masters. The fourth chapter relates the rise of the pecan as a New South industry. Shelled pecans from farmed orchards replaced foraged pecans long used by African Americans for pralines. The abundance of quality pecans allowed candy companies to drive most Black praline hawkers from the streets in the early twentieth century. The final chapter traces the rise of the praline as the most popular souvenir within the New Orleans tourism trade during the twentieth century. Small tourist shops, many operated by white women, opened during the interwar years to exploit Americans' interest in the praline. To compete, these shop owners regularly used mammy imagery, often devising new ways to exploit racial stereotypes and making race integral to New Orleans's tourism industry into the early twenty-first century.

Foods ground identity and embody historical memory in New Orleans, where culture serves as a product marketed to tourists. Narratives about food, however, change with the times to reflect local concerns. Anthropologist David Beriss contends, "New Orleans's reputation is built on the reproduction and re-invention of a particular indigenous cuisine," that of the Creoles. Those involved in the city's food and tourism industries operate within the "mythology of New Orleans cuisine," with any personal twists to favored local recipes needing to be "both interestingly creative and still part of the culture of high Creole cooking." This certainly holds true for the praline. The small sugary patty became one of the most legendary Creole concoctions, despite the dubiousness of that claim. For many Americans after the Civil War, New Orleans was the "Praline City."[14]

When Mildred Cram arrived in New Orleans to research her book *Old Seaport Towns of the South* in 1917, she asked, "For what other purpose was the delectable praline, that sugar-cane and pecan concoction of surpassing delicacy and diabolical temptation, invented save to ravish the soul of the visitor?" This book responds to Cram's century-old question.[15]

1

Pralines, Madame?

Emancipation, Free Enterprise, and the Praline Seller

"The praline woman sits by the side of the Archbishop's quaint little old chapel on Royal Street, and slowly waves her latanier fan over the pink and brown wares," begins the 1899 vignette "The Praline Woman," by Alice Dunbar-Nelson. Words poured from the hawker. "Mais oui, madame, I know you étrangér. You don't look lak dese New Orleans peop'. You lak' dose Yankee dat come down 'fo' de war," she converses with one passerby. The vendor anticipates her customers' needs and desires while engaging in an inviting banter. To another, the woman queries, "Pralines, madame? You buy lak' dat? Dix sous, madame, an' one lil' piece fo' lagniappe fo' madame's lil' bébé. Ah, c'est bon!" A little extra—lagniappe—for the child of a customer fostered satisfaction and encouraged future sales. She immediately hustles the next pedestrian: "Pralines, pralines, so fresh, so fine! M'sieu would lak' some fo' he's lil' gal' at home? Mais non, what's dat you say? She's daid! Ah, m'sieu, 't is my lil' gal what died long year ago." Even when stumbling into tragedy, the shrewd seller shifts the conversation to create a shared sense of loss. And to the next, the woman asks, "Pralines, madame? I lak' you' face. What fo' you wear black? You lil' boy daid? You tak' one, jes' see how it tas.'" A dynamo of conversation, the hawker responds to questions about the production of pralines, gifts a praline to a passing priest, and exchanges barbs with an Irishman before the onset of rain drives her home to gather more pralines made by her dependents to sell the next day.[1]

Dunbar-Nelson, a pioneering African American writer, spent her childhood and adolescence in New Orleans. Her mother had been enslaved on a plantation near Opelousas, Louisiana, until fleeing to wartime New Orleans, where she worked as a seamstress. She soon met Dunbar's father, believed to be a white merchant marine. Their light-complexioned child, born Alice Ruth Moore, drifted into literary and social circles of Creoles of color. Occasionally, she passed as white to enter museums and performances barred to African Americans. Dunbar-Nelson left New Orleans shortly after publication of her second collection of stories, which included "The Praline Woman." She subtly subverted the racial clichés found in the mainstream literature of her day even as she, like the praline woman, accommodated whites' expectations to gain sales. Her short stories drew from her local experiences to make visible and humanize the marginalized working-class African Americans of New Orleans.[2]

What the reader sees in Dunbar-Nelson's account is not a praline-selling mammy loyal to a white family. Instead, she is a clever saleswoman striving to provide for herself and her dependents. The hawker engages passersby to attract attention. She offers samples of her goods but does so in the context of honoring a deceased child, giving a treat to a pedestrian to give to his spouse, and rewarding a priest for a blessing. She uses hard-to-ignore emotional gambits. Dunbar-Nelson's praline seller embodies the strivings of African Americans as they struggled to carve a life in post-emancipation New Orleans.

A CITY REBORN

As federal forces approached New Orleans in April 1862, panic spread. Businesses emptied as white men rushed to arms. In the offices of the *New Orleans Daily Crescent,* William Semple sat exasperated, because "every man in the Crescent office has gone to the war."[3] The conquering bluecoats deepened an economic depression that first broke across the levees with President Lincoln's election. Debates over secession led planters to hoard their harvests for fear of seizure. Louisianans also cut their spending. The British Consulate in New Orleans observed the depreciation in the "value of property of all kinds to a ruinous extent."[4]

Eighteen months of intensifying anxiety peaked with word that U.S. gunboats had successfully passed Confederate forts downriver; this news first reached the public via the city's markets as produce sellers arrived from outlying farms. A teenaged George Washington Cable later recounted the spreading panic among Confederate sympathizers: "Before the smart-stepping lamplighters were half done turning off the street lights, before the noisy market-houses all over town, from Camp Callender to Carrollton, with their basket-bearing thousands of jesting and dickering customers, had quenched their gaslights and candles to dicker and jest by day, or the devotees of early mass had emerged from the churches, Rumor was on the run."[5]

The infrastructure that supplied the city with sustenance then turned into vehicles of escape. Cable, who observed the Union's landing party before fleeing into Mississippi to join the Confederate cavalry, recounted, "Everywhere hacks, private carriages, cabs, wagons, light and heavy, and carts, frail or strong, carts for bread or meat, for bricks or milk, were bearing fugitives—old men, young mothers, grandmothers, maidens and children—with their trunks, bales, bundles, slaves and provisions—toward the Jackson Railroad to board the first train they could squeeze into, and toward the New and Old Basins to sleep on schooner decks under the open stars in the all-night din of building deckhouses." Across the color line, New Orleans native J. B. Jourdain was happy to see that, with the city's alarm bells ringing, the rebellious whites "threw their arms away, and went in every direction to get out of the way" of the advancing federals.[6]

The riverfront grew thick with smoke as the fleeing rebel army set torches to supplies left behind. "Along the entire sinuous riverside the whole great blockaded seaport's choked-in stores of tobacco and cotton, thousands of hogsheads, tens of thousands of bales—lest they enrich the enemy—were being hauled to the wharves and landings and were just now beginning to receive the torch, the wharves also burning, and the boats and ships on either side of the river being fired and turned adrift," recalled Cable. Even far upriver from New Orleans, panic spread. Kate Stone on her plantation near Vicksburg, Mississippi, interpreted the fall of New Orleans as a sign that "fair Louisiana with her fertile fields of cane and cotton . . . lies powerless at the feet of the enemy." Fellow planters believed the same. Stone noted, "As far as we can see are the ascending wreaths of smoke, and we hear that all the cotton of the Mississippi Valley from Memphis to New Orleans is going up in smoke."[7]

The plumes marking Confederate retreat signaled to the enslaved that freedom was at hand. Fear of an imminent slave revolt spurred by the presence of Union soldiers terrified local whites. The New Orleans teenager Clara Solomon confided in her diary, "I fear more the negroes than Yankees & an insurrection is my continual horror." But the feared insurrection turned into a mass exodus from the plantations to the big city: New Orleans became a refuge for the enslaved and for pro-Union sympathizers. The presence of federal troops, the anonymity provided by the large populace, and the prospect of social mobility within the commercial center beckoned. Younger, more daring enslaved people flocked to the city. From July through September 1862, large groups escaped from plantations along the Mississippi River carrying cane knives, clubs, and even old firearms to ward off Confederate patrols during their march to New Orleans. A few planters encouraged the most restless slaves to depart in hopes of controlling their more timid captives. By September 1862, more than ten thousand self-liberated African Americans crowded into and around New Orleans. Nevertheless, as late as March 1863, roughly 71 percent of slaves, even those living in rural parts of Orleans Parish, stayed put.[8]

General Benjamin Butler of the Union Army, an abolitionist who had pioneered the policy of freeing the enslaved under the legal guise of seizing enemy contraband, commanded New Orleans through the end of 1862. He announced that he had been reared "in the full belief that slavery is a curse to a nation." Despite his convictions, Butler, facing a food shortage in May 1862, prohibited runaway slaves from entering the city, though many of his troops and officers ignored the order. Most refugees from the plantations congregated at the outskirts of New Orleans, primarily along the perimeter of federal lines upriver at Camp Parapet, which was commanded by General John Phelps. Phelps clashed with his superior Butler by actively encouraging the enslaved to abandon nearby plantations. A Union officer reported from the camp during the summer of 1862 that "they drift hither in gangs every day from the plantations. They dot the fields in front of the rampart, women and children squatting in the wet grass under pouring rain, all waiting for liberty to remain here. The earlier comers have already built themselves huts of cane or of rails, leaky and wretched shelters enough, far inferior to the cabins they left." Such hardships paled compared to being in bondage.[9]

Within this initial wave of rural enslaved people to New Orleans came those persons most familiar with the local trade in foodstuffs, as highlighted by an incident in May 1862. One enslaver pleaded with Butler for the return of his human property from Phelps's encampment: "My negro Sam and his wife Mary left my farm, about 2 miles above Camp Parapet . . . before daylight. They took my mule and cart, several of my poultry, fodder, bed and blankets, clothing, and all their own goods." The enslaved couple had confiscated the property of their enslaver, purchased with the sweat of their labor, to launch a new life. Sam, the slaveowner admitted, was his "market man" responsible for transporting the plantation's vegetables to New Orleans and then selling these goods. Venturing to the encampment to retrieve his property, the master stood dumbfounded when a "man in uniform stepped up with my negro, claiming all the balance of the goods as the negro's property." In other instances, when news arrived of the enslaved being punished on nearby plantations, Union soldiers marched from the lines "immediately to liberate them," according to a captain in a Massachusetts regiment.[10]

Through their feet and the backing of federal arms, African Americans thus eroded the "peculiar institution" while stretching the resources managed by Butler. Yet, the official policy of the Lincoln administration kept slavery legal until the Emancipation Proclamation went into effect on January 1, 1863—and even then, it only applied to territory occupied by the Confederacy on that date. Attempting to control the self-emancipated and to appease hostile whites, Butler encouraged the unreformed municipal police to enforce the slave code, leading to the harassment of the city's long-standing free Black population and to clashes with recently arrived refugees from the plantations. When General Phelps organized African Americans near his encampment into military units and, in July 1862, requested equipment for them, Butler refused. Phelps promptly resigned. Yet the very next month, a shorthanded Butler, while rejecting the enlistment of contrabands, began recruiting free Black New Orleanians into the Louisiana Native Guard. Three regiments were organized by late November 1862. Still undermanned, Butler in late 1862 further eased restrictions on enlistment, allowing the enslaved of foreign nationals or known Confederate sympathizers to join the ranks. However, Butler simultaneously strengthened the pass system requiring all Blacks to carry permission from an employer or the U.S. military; failure to do so risked arrest for vagrancy.[11]

As the war progressed, so did the liberation of enslaved persons, the influx of rural African Americans into New Orleans, and the slow restoration of commerce. Gen. Nathaniel Banks replaced Butler in December 1862 and oversaw affairs in New Orleans through May 1864. He eased some of his predecessor's restrictions on locals known to harbor Confederate sympathies while more actively recruiting African Americans into the military. The new commander also instituted education programs and legal protections for people of color. Banks looked to stem the flow of African Americans off the plantations who were draining his supplies in New Orleans and heightening tensions with planters. He thus arranged contracts for plantation owners to hire Black workers within Union-occupied Louisiana. The labor arrangement restarted the agricultural economy and aided the federal war effort by bolstering sugar supplies. During military campaigns along Bayou Teche in 1863 and the Red River in 1864, Banks limited the seizure of rebel property to entice planters back into the Union. The enslaved nevertheless officially gained their freedom under the Emancipation Proclamation as the Union forces pressed deeper into Louisiana. An officer from New York who was marching along Bayou Teche toward New Iberia, Louisiana, in the summer of 1863 recounted reactions among the enslaved: "Some of them actually think they will never have to work again any more. The more intelligent portion seem to know that even if they are free they will suffer much want and degradation that they ever have known before they all learn to take care of themselves."[12]

By joining the Union Army, former bondsmen along with a sizable population of free persons of color centered in New Orleans assisted in the eradication of slavery while inspiring greater political engagement and a stronger entrepreneurial spirit. Black soldiers in blue uniforms understood their enlisting in the Union Army as a personal statement of defiance. An African American, parading with his regiment down Canal Street in October 1862 halted in front of the store owned by his former enslaver, a man who had enlisted in the Confederate military. An observer recalled that this soldier "shook his rifle at the name over the door, and shouted, 'Dat's de man *I* wants to meet on de field ob battle!'" All the Black soldiers knew that their acts stirred white New Orleanians' resentment as they proceeded past a "scowling line of white faces."[13]

Although reluctant to use Black troops in combat, the casualty toll by 1863 pressed Union commanders to throw African American units into battle. The Louisiana Native Guard became one of the first units of Black soldiers to see combat when ordered to mount an assault on the Confederate stronghold at

Port Hudson, Louisiana, on May 27, 1863. Captain André Cailloux, a native New Orleanian and Creole of color, became a martyr in the struggle for abolition after being mortally wounded. To replace the thinning ranks, Banks in August 1863 drafted all Black men without a visible means of support in New Orleans. Overzealous recruiters invaded African Americans' homes and arrested Black men on the streets. Banks suspended the draft temporarily when planters complained of the need for workers during the fall harvest season, though he insisted that all Black men register for future conscription. A widely reprinted article from the *New Orleans Era* in January 1864 declared, "Slavery could no more survive rebellion and martial law than a man can survive a stab through his heart."[14] Although the Emancipation Proclamation did not apply, Banks took steps to erode slavery. On December 26, 1863, he ordered signs advertising slave sales and pens removed. He suspended slavery by military order on January 11, 1864, reinforced by a state constitutional convention later that year and passage of the Thirteenth Amendment in 1865. After implementing these measures, Banks, worried about spies and lawlessness, in early 1864 instituted a 7:30 pm curfew on all Blacks in New Orleans and required permits for any meetings.[15]

The racialized politics and social upheaval that emerged from this revolutionary shift in labor and commerce inspired an entrepreneurial spirit among Black New Orleanians eager to enjoy their hard-won freedom. Charles Sauvinet, a lifelong New Orleanian and Creole of color, witnessed this transformation after embracing the arrival of Union troops as liberators. Fluent in French and English, he received an appointment as translator to the provost court, and when Black regiments were formed from the local population, his linguistic skills made him "one of the first sent for" to serve as an officer. Sauvinet noted the drive of the enlisted freedmen. He recalled that "as soon as they were free of their regular duties, they all had their books, and you could see them all day long trying to learn." The formerly enslaved men, having long been denied an education, learned quickly that education opened opportunities. Sauvinet marveled, "Out of my regiment I presume there are some 200 men that went in who were slaves before the war and who came out of the regiment knowing how to read passably."[16]

This entrepreneurial drive was heralded in June 1864 when French Creoles of color and others of African ancestry congregated at Congo Square—a site on the fringe of the French Quarter long used by the enslaved for Sunday gatherings, religious rituals, and trade—to celebrate the passage of emancipation by the free state convention the previous month. Francis Boisdore, a lifelong resident who was born free, spoke in French to the thousands of onlookers, among them sixteen Black veterans of the Battle of New Orleans: "The sweat of your brow now belongs to yourselves; no insatiable, inexorable man-masters to render accounts to! you [*sic*] are sure to reap the benefits of what you possess. Work with eagerness and emulation—give proof that you fully comprehend that liberty does not consist in idlenes, [*sic*] and laziness!" A subsequent awarding of prizes promoted the creations of Black New Orleans, both artistic and practical. These included a prize to Amy Temple for "sweet wafers," another to "baker" Charles Hughes for a "loaf of bread," and another to "confectioner" Lucinda Green for "ice cream."[17] Hard work and hustle became synonymous with freedom. Describing the difference between bondage and freedom, one Louisianan born into slavery succinctly explained this motivational spirit: "But them hard times we had sho make me preciate dis free liberty."[18]

Much of this hope was built on President Abraham Lincoln's push to restore Louisiana as a full member of the United States before the presidential election in November 1864. Louisiana therefore became a testing ground for early policies aimed at the racial reform of politics, economics, and society within a seceded slave state. Lincoln proposed that a new state government for Louisiana could be formed as soon as 10 percent of the male population swore loyalty oaths. The state also had to recognize the freedom of the enslaved. Louisiana delegates drafted a new constitution in 1864 abolishing slavery and extending the vote to some African Americans—those who had served in the Union Army, owned property, or were literate. The federal government in 1865 created the Bureau of Refugees, Freedmen, and Abandoned Lands, popularly known as the Freedmen's Bureau, to provide aid to the destitute across the defeated Confederacy and to oversee labor contract negotiations.[19]

The war wrought a significant shift in the population of New Orleans, creating a substantial market for a cheap but calorific treat of sugar and pecans. In 1860, the U.S. Census documented 144,596 whites and 24,074 persons of color, free and enslaved, in the city. The slaughter and the economic turmoil of civil war subsequently reduced the white population to 142,943, reversing decades of growth. The decline came despite the city incorporating the neighboring town of Jefferson, with 7,710 whites, and annexing Algiers, with 3,802 whites, located on the western bank of the Mississippi River. Many within this white population had experienced a chaotic decade as refugees. W. O. Hart, four years old when the war started, recounted living in exile after his family fled New Orleans on the last train before its occupation. They returned in 1868 after multiple moves through Mississippi and Alabama. Of the possessions left behind in the family home, "everything had disappeared." In contrast, the size of the population classed as colored reversed decades of decline. New Orleans in 1870 claimed 50,456 persons of color; the Black population more than doubled over the decade. Many of these African Americans had gained a most valuable possession: ownership of their own bodies. But many owned little, if anything, other than themselves.[20]

The end of slavery brought hope to African Americans, but emancipation did not bring tranquility or prosperity. Most whites fervently resisted efforts by people of color to claim social and political equality. Violence pervaded New Orleans in the decade after the Confederacy's collapse. The few whites who accepted the full incorporation of African Americans into society and were typically aligned with the Republican Party were vastly outnumbered by the staunchly white supremacist majority of the city, which had strong ties to the defeated Confederacy and the Democratic Party. This white majority worked to undermine the state government and any pro-Reconstruction policies. Clergyman Thomas Conway, who worked for the Freedmen's Bureau in New Orleans until the end of 1865, estimated that along with "two or three thousand white loyal men, there were twenty or thirty thousand black loyal men in New Orleans." These supporters of the federal government and its efforts faced constant hostility. Conway reported, "The police of New Orleans . . . were, nearly all of them, rebels, and inflicted violence and injury upon the freedmen almost without limit." Indeed, the election of March 1866 restored to power the former Confederate mayor John Monroe, who had been imprisoned for much of the war by Gen. Butler. Monroe promptly purged pro-Unionists from the police force, putting former police chief and ex-Confederate colonel Thomas Adams in charge. Confederate veterans soon dominated the police ranks. Conway elaborated, "The police, instead of arresting negroes quietly, would take their clubs and pound them on their heads, as if anxious to have the opportunity to maltreat them." O. J. Dunn, an African American born in New Orleans in 1826, witnessed a city repopulated by battle-hardened Confederate veterans; reporting on the Black experience, Dunn wrote, "We are insulted on every occasion, whenever they have an opportunity. In going through the streets it is a common thing to hear them say, 'These negroes think they have their own way now, but they are mistaken.'"[21]

When supporters of racial equality hosted a political gathering at the Mechanics Institute on July 30, 1866, a white mob surrounded the building and attacked everyone who tried to leave. More than forty African Americans and several white allies were murdered; over a hundred suffered wounds. Many of these African Americans were laborers. Taking time away from their jobs to secure their newly won suffrage, they understood the link between political and economic power. A *New York Times* correspondent noted that those present were "very evidently men who had suddenly left their work to join the procession, for they had the hooks that are used for turning cotton-bales, and one man had a saw, evidently a carpenter's." The reporter identified them as recently emancipated "freedmen."[22] Federal officials quickly responded with a congressional investigation and greater federal oversight of Reconstruction in Louisiana, which led to the election of Republican politicians sympathetic to African Americans and to the creation of a modernized police force and integrated schools, among other reforms. Most whites within the city, however, plotted to preserve the racial status quo. Charles Dallas, a Black editor at the *New Orleans Tribune,* summarized the massacre as "only a sequel to their rebellion." The congressional committee condemned the suffering of African Americans "persecuted by system, hunted like wild beasts, and slaughtered without mercy and with entire impunity from punishment."[23]

Conditions in the nearby sugar fields were more tumultuous than in New Orleans. For the emancipated, the promise of freedom dissipated in rural Louisiana more quickly than in the Crescent City, the state capital from 1864 until 1879. As the capital, New Orleans contained a garrison of federal troops who guarded the Republican government. The rural parishes of southern Louisiana where sugar plantations predominated lacked such a backstop. One traveler shortly after the Civil War observed, "The sugar-planters had all ostentatiously proclaimed that the Emancipation Proclamation had demoralized their labor and ruined their business. Some, through spite, others because they believed it, were absolutely abandoning the cane as it stood in their fields, on the ground that the negroes couldn't be trusted to make the sugar."[24] Other planters attempted to hire foreigners, including Germans, for the fieldwork, but these immigrants regularly fled because of the difficult labor conditions. African Americans who had stayed on the plantations now worked the sugar fields and mills for wages. "And so the business went on with Black engineers, Black crushers, Black filterers, Black sugar-makers,—all Black throughout,—but the sugar came out splendid in quantity and quality," remarked another visitor to Louisiana.[25]

Motivated by a spirit of civic activism within New Orleans during the late 1860s and early 1870s, some African Americans attempted to pressure the courts to put teeth into the racially egalitarian measures implemented during Reconstruction. Black civic leaders filed at least fourteen lawsuits for discrimination against saloons, soda shops, and theaters between 1869 and 1875. A court awarded Charles Sauvinet, now serving as the Orleans Parish civil sheriff, $1,000 in damages from a saloon for refusing to serve him in 1871. An 1874 case against the Academy of Music for ejecting a Black patron after he purchased a ticket also ended with a fine of $1,000. Although such cases attempted to uphold racial equality, the political and social winds quickly shifted by the late 1870s.[26]

In the aftermath of the New Orleans Massacre at the Mechanics Institute and a similarly vicious racial attack in Memphis in 1866, Congress passed the Reconstruction Act of 1867. It placed the former Confederate states into five military districts, each commanded by a Union general. Even though the Louisiana Constitution of 1864 advocated for African Americans' rights, white supremacists had swept the subsequent elections as vigilantes used violence to intimidate Black voters; these newly elected politicians then questioned the legitimacy of the 1864 constitution. With closer federal oversight provided by the Reconstruction Act, however, these former Confederates were driven out of the state government. A new constitution extending African Americans' rights was ratified in 1868. Republicans, led by Governor Henry Clay Warmoth, took possession of the state government in elections that year. The election of former Union general Ulysses S. Grant to the presidency further dampened efforts by former Confederates to overthrow the state government.[27]

During the 1870s, white supremacy did triumph, but the partial achievements of Reconstruction took time to recede in New Orleans. By 1872, political divisions emerged within the Republican Party. Some believed in staunchly defending African Americans' rights. Others believed in moderating racial views to attract more white voters. To make matters worse, elections in 1872 led to the creation of two state governments. Republican governor William Kellogg took office in New Orleans, while Democrat John McEnery formed his own government. Tensions rose across the state, most notoriously in a massacre of more than a hundred Black freedmen and state militia by white supremacists in Colfax, Louisiana, in April 1873. To defuse tensions, a group of white New Orleanians aligned with several Creoles of color to form the interracial Unification Movement. These whites, with Confederate General P. G. T. Beauregard as spokesperson, advocated that public places and schools be integrated and African Americans' political rights respected under the Louisiana constitution. They were less interested in racial progress, however, than in maintaining the peace as a means of fostering commerce throughout the city and attracting outside investment. When a backlash ensued, white participants abandoned the effort and joined virulently racist groups. Whereas the Democratic Party served as a legitimate political organization, militant whites formed the Crescent City White League as a paramilitary wing of the party in 1874. The White League temporarily overthrew the Republican government of Governor Kellogg in a pitched street battle in New Orleans on September 14, 1874, the so-called Battle of Liberty Place. Reinforcements of federal troops restored order and forced McEnery to concede his claim to the governorship. Yet racial tension seethed unabated.

Reconstruction ended in 1877. Republican presidential candidate Rutherford B. Hayes, succeeding Grant, conceded federal oversight of Louisiana in return for the state's electoral votes needed to win the White House. By the 1880s, white supremacists and Lost Cause apologists began stripping away Reconstruction-era protections of African Americans' political, social, and economic rights. Those rights would not be restored until the civil rights struggle of the mid-twentieth century.[28]

TASTE OF FREEDOM

Pralines reflected the reality of Black labor and African Americans' low status within the economy after the Civil War, even if their entrepreneurship evidenced their economic ambitions. By foraging pecans and using cheap sugar, likely procured from the docks through a thriving black market of stolen goods sold at a discount, poor Black women were able to carve out a new life after slavery. Historian Bruce Baker notes that the riverfront provided numerous means for "cashless self-provisioning." New Orleans's black market in sugar was especially robust among the poor hungering for calories in the late nineteenth century. Applying their domestic labor in the kitchen, praline sellers converted these high-calorie items into a delectable snack. A single patty, as opposed to loose pecans dusted in sugar, made the praline easier to market. Pralines and other street food energized the Black bodies powering commerce through postbellum New Orleans.[29]

Appreciating the role of pralines in New Orleans requires a brief look at the simultaneous origins of the king cake. White resisters to Republican rule took the offensive on the cultural front by cloaking their politics in the garb of Carnival festivities. Although the Mistick Krewe of Comus was formed in 1857 to bring order to street processions, other organizations, often called krewes, emerged during Reconstruction, including Rex (1872) and Momus (1872). Their parades of decorated floats adopted motifs that occasionally ridiculed Radical Republicans. Most infamously, Comus's parade carried the theme "Missing Links to Darwin's Origin of the Species" in 1873 with designs depicting President Grant as a tobacco grub and Congressman Benjamin Butler as a hyena; Butler was the former occupying general who had recently written the initial version of the Enforcement Act of 1871 authorizing the president to deploy the military against terrorist groups such as the Ku Klux Klan. Tellingly, this was also the first parade with floats that were entirely built in New Orleans, rather than with designs imported from France.[30] Organized by wealthy white families, the highly secretive krewes not only asserted control of the streets but also forged powerful links among families and businesses. Their parades showcased wealth seemingly unaffected by the war and its political, social, and economic aftermath. The faux royalty also heralded local white bloodlines. These Carnival organizations heavily influenced the practices and regalia of white supremacist groups across the former Confederacy.[31]

The krewes also popularized within their pageants a new confection, the king cake. The cake had evolved from the medieval French Catholic tradition of the *galette des rois,* translated as the "cake of the kings," prepared on the Epiphany on January 6. The date celebrated the arrival of the three Magi, or kings, at the birthplace of Jesus. French families along with other Catholic immigrants carried the tradition to New Orleans. During Reconstruction, however, wealthy white New Orleanians, many of them American Protestants, reimagined the king cake. The Twelfth Night Revelers, a secret organization formed in 1870, paraded on January 6 to the French Opera House in the French Quarter, mere blocks from the statehouse on Jackson Square. Once gathered inside, they served a king cake, containing a gold bean and several silver beans, to the young women of the club. Each year, the fortunate young woman who received the slice containing the gold bean became the queen; those receiving a slice with a silver bean became royal maids. By the late 1880s, elite social gatherings in New Orleans during Carnival occasionally incorporated a king cake as part of their private celebrations. One or more beans or pecans placed within the king cake randomly selected the guests of honor. By the 1910s, bakeries tapped into the popularity of the king cake to mass market the confection on Mardi Gras and, in later decades, throughout the Carnival season between the Epiphany and Mardi Gras. The mass-marketed king cake soon incorporated a white porcelain doll as a Carnival souvenir, replacing the bean. The local McKenzie's bakery chain popularized the inclusion of a pinkish plastic baby in the 1960s, reinventing a tradition that still survives in New Orleans. Though attempts have been made to racially diversify the baby or incorporate other emblems of the city within the cake, the whiteness of the king cake baby remains prominent and serves as a reminder of the confection's origins in Reconstruction politics.[32]

In contrast, the proliferation of the praline reflected the economic struggles of the poor, particularly African Americans. Even before the Civil War, the foundations of New Orleans's economy were crumbling. The rapid construction of railroads siphoned to northeastern ports agricultural goods that had traditionally floated downriver, a trend that intensified during the late nineteenth century. The massive migration of freedpersons to the city suppressed wages. A national depression and recurring yellow fever epidemics during the 1870s made survival even more difficult for poor New Orleanians.[33]

Skilled Blacks, particularly in the male-dominated building trades or along the riverfront where expertise was valued, could demand reasonable payment and work conditions. But only a very select few Black workers, such as cotton screwmen responsible for loading ships with bales, possessed such skills. Screwmen not only commanded the expertise to force concessions but also worked closely with whites in interracial unions. Shoemakers, tinners, printers, tailors, druggists, and other Black artisans used their skills and any connections to white benefactors to shield themselves and their families from the fickle economy and society. Historian John Blassingame notes that African Americans who were already laboring in these skilled careers as free persons of color before the Civil War dominated these occupations after the conflict. Whereas Blacks constituted roughly one-quarter of the city's population in 1870, they claimed 30–65 percent of the jobs as steamboatmen, masons, gardeners, barbers, cigarmakers, draymen, carpenters, bakers, and plasters. Blacks continued to be overrepresented in these positions in 1880, although their percentage declined to between 25 and 52 percent.[34] Their grip on these trades began to slip in the late nineteenth century.

For instance, Charles Hughes, an African American who arrived in New Orleans in 1849 at age 23 from Washington, DC, earned his livelihood by baking. He rushed to assist the Union occupation in 1862, working at various times during the war as a cook for a captain in the 30th Connecticut, a hospital steward, and a recruiter for Black regiments. In the late 1860s, he returned to baking, a demanding occupation given the hot temperatures within New Orleans for much of the year but one that afforded some independence from white oversight.[35]

Working-class African Americans—many of them formerly enslaved in rural Louisiana—found themselves in far more harrowing circumstances. The emancipated Elvira Garrett recalled that most enslaved Louisianans departed the plantations "practically naked." These poor conditions were worsened by white employers' tendency to hire working-class Blacks only for the most arduous jobs and to fire those who failed to heed their whims.[36]

Black men and women had limited opportunities to escape poverty. Some African Americans accepted dangerous jobs on railroads or steamboats. Others entered the service economy as cooks, porters, waiters, and bellhops. Thomas Harris, born in Norfolk, Virginia, had lived in New Orleans for nearly two decades by the end of the Civil War, when he gained employment as a porter in a police station. His daily routine included cleaning cells, tidying offices, and running errands. Many Black men found employment as drayage operators or longshoremen. German traveler Ernst von Hesse-Wartegg in 1879 observed "ragged Negroes" loading his steamboat. These laborers, he wrote, "sleep under the large roofs-without-walls on the levees or in one of the abandoned houses so plentiful in New Orleans. Bananas and oranges are inexpensive. There are leftovers from meals served on boats. They drink out of the Mississippi." The headwear used to scoop the water, like the rest of their clothes, were so filthy that a "practical farmer could put the hats to use on his fields, as manure."[37]

Dreams of economic independence clouded with the onset of an economic depression during the 1870s. Property values declined 50 percent over the decade, leaving real estate in 1880 stuck at 1860 values. This kept property affordable even if wages remained low and employment difficult to obtain. In 1870, African Americans owned a paltry 1.4 percent of the total amount of property in Orleans Parish. This jumped by 56 percent over the next decade, reaching 2.5 percent in 1880. Although the city contained a few large Black-owned businesses, the vast majority had one owner or were family-centered operations. Prospects for accruing wealth remained limited.[38]

Black women found opportunities as domestics, laundresses, and cooks, both for white families and for Black male laborers. For entrepreneurial African American women seeking to escape day labor, home-centered businesses were common in the late nineteenth century. Competition was fierce, further stoking the hustle of these workers. A visitor to New Orleans marveled at the bustle along the riverfront: "Negroes on the Levée swarm like black ants, dragging bales of cotton, rolling hogsheads of sugar, and trotting to and fro from the steamers, carrying rice and Indian corn in little square bags." Black women kept Black men fed as they toiled: "In and out through the stacks and bales came negresses with bright handkerchiefs round their heads, carrying baskets and basins containing dinners for the black ants." Not just feeding their husbands or relatives, these women also sold meals to hungry dockworkers.

Black women thus turned their domestic chores into income streams. Cooking skills provided economic opportunities. By laboring as laundresses or street peddlers, African American women negotiated the racialized economy. Such occupations somewhat insulated Black women from the demands of whites, because their white customers acted as clients rather than employers. Self-employed African American women still faced racism but retained the power to refuse services. They gained a greater degree of personal independence and economic freedom. The sight of African American women operating lunch carts or providing snacks from baskets became commonplace in southern cities of the late nineteenth century.[39]

For African Americans pressed to the economic margins, the abundance lining the New Orleans riverfront supplied a lifeline that also kept the port functioning. Travelers had long admired the variety and quantity of goods piled onto the riverbank. In January 1819, Benjamin Latrobe remarked, "Along the levee, as far as the eye could reach to the West & to the market house to the East [otherwise known as the French Market] were ranged two rows of market people, some having stalls or tables with a tilt or awning of canvass, but the majority having their wares lying on the ground, perhaps on a piece of canvass, or a parcel of Palmetto leaves." Latrobe spied for sale "wild ducks, oysters, poultry of all kinds, fish, bananas, piles of oranges, sugar cane, sweet & Irish potatoes, corn in the Ear & husked, apples, carrots & all sorts of other roots, eggs, trinkets, tin ware, dry goods, in fact of more & odder things to be sold in that manner & place, than I can enumerate." Latrobe also noted that "were it not for the vegetables & fowls & small marketing of all sorts raised by negro slaves, the city would starve."[40] African Americans, enslaved and free, raised and sold the goods that made New Orleans thrive—and they supplied the labor that powered the port's commerce. The extensive refurbishment of the levee undertaken in 1830 expanded the capacity for commerce, as numerous wharves and warehouses were added. A visitor in 1847 remarked that the "levee was alive with hundreds of negroes and teams at work moving freight; thousands and thousands of bales of cotton and hogsheads of sugar and tobacco and barrels of molasses and whiskey, huge piles of sacks of coffee, salt and corn and tiers of boxes of merchandise; the river bank, or levee, was crowded for miles up and down with big side-wheel steamboats . . . out in the stream were anchored many sailing ships . . . while 'broad-horn' flats and keelboats bridged the river half-way across in many places."[41]

In the postbellum years, the stockpiles of goods along the riverfront tempted those who were handling cargo for meager wages. New Orleans's economy depended heavily on a black market of stolen products taken from the docks to sustain its cheap workforce. It was tolerated by white businessmen who profited from paying low wages and who often colluded in schemes that ripped off insurers, passing on the costs to companies outside New Orleans. Bruce Baker, analyzing crime along the New Orleans riverfront, succinctly concluded, "Capitalists need criminals." Such was certainly true for the white power structure looking to maintain its grip over the city after the Civil War. The seasonal trade in cotton and sugar required a large reserve labor pool, made up of predominantly unskilled African Americans hired for a pittance and fired whenever convenient; these Blacks spent months unemployed when shipments slowed. In such an economy, the urban poor stole foodstuffs to survive and to outwit wealthy employers who disregarded their needs. Even those who did not steal from the docks benefited as thieves sold goods directly or through a fence, keeping food prices affordable. The fact that crime sustained workers via a black market in foodstuffs reinforced popular white misconceptions that racialized theft. Whites viewed theft as a character flaw endemic to people of color, not a result of starvation wages and racial bias in hiring.[42]

Political winds fanned the black market. Whereas Republicans reformed and strengthened the New Orleans police during Reconstruction, municipal leaders after Reconstruction slashed the force's size and kept salaries low. A newspaper editorialized, "The wonder is that thieves don't pick up the town and carry it off." Not until the 1890s did city leaders invest in modernizing the force. Yet corruption continued to thrive in the underfunded police department. The underground economy likewise grew until the late 1910s, when tightened security during World War I, mechanization along the docks, and further police reforms curtailed access to riverfront cargo.[43]

Whether purloining unsecured items along the shore or adventuring under the wharves, the rewards were substantial, as Henry Latham observed along the Mississippi River in 1867: "Under the Levée must be the paradise of rats; it is also frequented by thieves. The art of the Levée thief is to cut out a plank under a stock of costly goods above, coffee for instance, and to abstract the core of the pile, leaving the stack apparently intact." The practice lingered into the 1920s, inspiring writer E. Earl Sparling to incorporate a tale about a pair of thieves—a young, apprenticed Irishman and an aged, experienced Frenchmen—in his short story collection *Under the Levee* in 1925. Sparling writes, "There was no overhead; there was a fast turnover with high profit." Far from thieves, these men were understood to be financially shrewd capitalists. Sparling admired the daring of these so-called wharf rats: "No expensive and elaborate equipment did these business men of the wharves need. A sharpened *machette,* relic of some sugar plantation, and a close-mesh gunny sack; that was all." Prying or cutting away the boards of the wharf, the thieves then ripped into sacks, hogsheads, and other containers. "Coffee, Mexican beans, rice, sugar—it was all the same to them if it was salable loot," remarked Sparling.[44]

The riverfront wharfs and adjoining railroad warehouses were frequently raided by the poor, despite scrutiny from police and watchmen. Surviving police reports, mostly from 1910, show how thieves targeted food and other supplies passing through the port as a survival strategy. In January 1910, George Watt, an African American, was charged with breaking into a railroad car along the river to steal eight cans of Swift's Jewel lard, valued at $44. Each can weighed fifty pounds. He had attempted to sell one of the cans to an African American man working nearby as a cooper. Watt then hid four cans in a barrel, left another in the middle of a neutral ground on a major thoroughfare, and scattered the remaining cans in other parked railroad cars to retrieve later. A month later, four African Americans broke into an Illinois Central boxcar to steal fresh corn still in their shucks.[45]

The police reports hint at how essential theft was in keeping the city's laboring poor alive and working; they also suggest how municipal leaders turned a blind eye to the city's vital black market. In late February 1910, a group of seven white boys, ranging in age from 10 to 16, tossed ten barrels of coal off a railroad car. Such antics might seem like a prank or a result of teenage hormones run amok, but these acts were also practical, even necessary, for poor New Orleanians' survival. Just as Watt left a can of lard on the street for anyone to discover, the coal dumped by the boys gave New Orleanians access to the fuel needed to fire stoves and heat homes. It is striking when reading the extant applications for free peddling licenses by destitute widows and abandoned wives that so many received these permits to sell wood and coal, in addition to produce or homemade cakes, pies, and breads. Wood could be scavenged from the neighborhood or outlying areas. Fruits and vegetables could be obtained from piles of nearly spoiled goods discarded by merchants along the riverfront. Baked items added value to raw materials, such as flour and sugar, through labor. Coal, however, was a far more curious commodity for the extremely poor to sell: it points to theft and the black market it powered. What else explains how Antonia Retteo, a white woman with two children, could sell bread and coal from home on a free license given to her because of her poverty? Where did Providenzia Puccia, a destitute immigrant with seven children at home and a husband who "left for Italy," acquire the wood, coal, and fruit she sold? And how did Emma Morgan, an African American who also received a free license, maintain a "small wood and coal shop" to support her four children after her husband left for work in

New Iberia but "failed to send her any money"? Children's seeming mischief at the railyard and their targeting of coal barrels suggest where many New Orleanians with little money to spare obtained the fuel needed to heat pots, pans, and ovens. The black market provided the resources needed to keep New Orleanians alive. Significantly, the police reports remained silent on how these women got their supplies, even while detailing family circumstances and assets.[46]

African American women involved in trades such as praline selling navigated an urban society long imbalanced along gender lines. Under slavery, planters valued males as field hands: they were more capable than women of the physically hard labor of cultivating sugar and other crops. Auction prices for enslaved men were considerably higher than for enslaved women. Enslaved women predominated within New Orleans, where the white population sought their labor as domestic servants. Ownership of an enslaved person also served as a symbol of familial wealth. Further, enslaved women were perceived as less of a lethal threat to the slave regime than male slaves, a particular concern in an urban environment where enslaved persons moved in the streets with some anonymity as they ran household errands or marketed wares to profit their owners.[47]

Whether enslaved or free, some street vendors required a permit to work in New Orleans. A municipal ordinance from 1831 attempted to bring order to the growing commercial chaos: "No person shall hawk or peddle, or expose for sale, in public places, in any manner whatsoever, within the limits of the city of New Orleans, any produce, eatables, merchandise, or articles of trade generally, without having first obtained a license to that effect from the Mayor of the city." Licenses cost $10 per quarter. Yet a major loophole recognized the vital services provided by "marchandes," the local name given to women street peddlers. It exempted marchandes from having to obtain a license while also encouraging a focus on classes of exempted products. The antebellum ordinance declared that persons "selling only eatables, that have been baked, confectionary, fruit in baskets, or beer of the country, are not subject to the provisions of this ordinance." Baskets laden with sweets not just satisfied the sweet tooth of urbanites but also circumvented the costs and restrictions laid out by the municipal ordinance on street vendors.[48]

From antebellum days, Black women had worked the New Orleans streets as saleswomen. Most were free women of color earning a livelihood. Others were enslaved and sent into the streets by their enslavers but were typically allowed to retain some of the profit, which both encouraged their efforts and bolstered returns for their owner. The result struck one visitor to the city in the 1830s: "Many of the female slaves are *marchandes* during the week, and their shrill cries never cease from morning's dawn till *'le milieu de la nuit'—Marchande de tait; marchande des pâtés, tous chauds; marchande des oranges, douces tres douces; marchande des ooufs, Creoles, tous frais; marchande des galettes chauffe; marchande des plants; marchande des figues, douces et frais,* and *marchandes* in everything to eat and drink or use in a *small way,* for the Creoles buy everything in that way." These street vendors fed and supplied the population, proving essential to the flow of commerce.[49]

The city's marchandes even peddled their wares in the plantation districts. Eulalie Mandeville, a free woman of color recognized as one of the wealthiest women in New Orleans on her death in 1845, operated a dry goods business in which she employed free women of color on commission and used her several enslaved women to market cloth, lingerie, accessories, and various garments. These laborers hawked on the streets, visited homes of potential customers, and traveled to planters' mansions in surrounding parishes.[50]

The marchandes were especially noted for their homemade confections. A woman visiting New Orleans from New York during the 1850s remembered how the "Marchand Rabus would go through the streets, crying, '*Marchand rabus, oh rabus*'—a delicious Sunday morning breakfast cake. Women with great flat baskets on their heads would call out, '*Calas, Calas, belle Calas, toute chaude,*' which were cakes made of rice flour and fried and sold 'very hot.'" The vendors' calls echoed into the evening, their desserts tempting residents and bystanders: "The familiar cry at night was, 'crème a la glace, a la polka, crème a la glace, a la crocov'eme, a la mazurka.'" Rarely did a visitor to New Orleans fail to note the marchandes and their wares.[51]

The delivery services provided by the marchandes became particularly vital in a crisis. One New Orleanian in the late 1850s witnessed how yellow fever was decimating neighborhoods. But these epidemics also provided an opportunity to the brave and resourceful African American street vendors catering to an urban population too fearful or sick to leave their homes. For those weakened by disease, the refrain of the criers could torment: "To have a strong craving appetite, but a frame so weak it trembles with the raising of a hand; to hear the delicacies of the season cried by each passing *marchande* fresh, like her stock, from the St. Mary market, or the environs of Carollton [*sic*], but to know they are one and all tabooed articles . . . as you find yourself restricted to a wine-glass of ale per diem, fed out in hourly spoonfuls, and crackers in meat broth given you as sparingly; these are the real annoyances of the yellow fever." The marchandes represented a city persisting in the face of crisis. For those recovering or free of disease, the services of the street vendors provided a lifeline and a sense of normalcy.[52]

The Union occupation brought crisis and opportunity to the marchandes of New Orleans. The retreating Confederates either removed or destroyed food supplies before Union forces arrived. Eager to weaken the Union hold, trade with New Orleans from the Confederacy all but halted, cutting off vital food deliveries. An English steel merchant visiting the city in late 1862 stood in awe that "neither a bale of cotton, a hogshead of sugar, a bushel of corn, a packet of merchandise, or a man at work, could be seen from end to end of that levée, nearly nine miles long." Although commerce slowly resumed, the war marked a notable decline in trade through New Orleans. The influx of poor African Americans liberated from slavery lowered wages for laborers while expanding the number of hungry mouths eager for an affordable snack packed with calories and protein.[53] Food shortages erupted.

Black women's earnings played a key role within Black society. Low wages, precarious employment opportunities, and high mortality caused by poor health and dangerous work environments undermined the ability of Black men to sustain their families. Between 1860 and 1880, the annual death rate for Black New Orleanians fluctuated between 32 and 81 per thousand, whereas the figure drifted between 5 and 39 per thousand for whites. Average life expectancy for a Black child at age one was 36 years; a white child at age one could expect to live 46 years. In 1880, of the 12,452 African American families identified by census takers, roughly 18 percent of married male heads of household were unemployed, making the earnings of the matriarch a lifeline. Reflecting both the housing shortage endured by African Americans and the need for boarders to cover costs, the typical family dwelling contained an average of 6 residents, with an average of 2.2 nonfamily members within each household. Of the women heading Black households, more than 80 percent were widows. Neighborhoods with the highest percentage of enslaved persons in the Black population in 1860 had the lowest percentage of Black men heading households in 1880. Most of the rural African Americans who migrated to New Orleans crammed into tenements near the river. Black men provided cheap labor not only for the docks but also for the steamboats and other vessels: this reduced the population of Black men with firm roots in the city by creating a male population of what John Blassingame calls "floaters." The importance of women within the Black economy of New Orleans is further reflected in the statistical imbalance between men and women: for every 100 Black women between the ages of 15 and 45 in 1870, there were only 65 Black men of those ages. The imbalance remained stark a decade later: there were only 69 Black men for every 100 Black women.[54]

Selling cakes and other confectionary remained a key means for African American women to earn money after emancipation. However, the French-speaking marchandes, according to Lafcadio Hearn's sympathetic and astute observations of postwar Black life in New Orleans, initially fended away competition from the newly emancipated arrivals from rural plantations. Born in Greece in 1850 to a Greek mother and a British officer from Ireland, Lafcadio Hearn was educated in Ireland, England, and France before migrating to the United States at age 19. He settled in Cincinnati, Ohio, in 1872 and soon married a freedwoman. His employer, the *Cincinnati Daily Enquirer,* then fired Hearn for violating Ohio's anti-miscegenation law. He accepted a job with the rival *Cincinnati Commercial.* Hearn, divorcing after three years of marriage, traveled to New Orleans in 1877 to report on Louisiana politics. He stayed for the next decade, working as a journalist for the *Daily City Item* and later the *Times-Democrat.* The polyglot New Orleans appealed to Hearn, who appreciated the port's diverse cultural background. His keen eye captured in vignettes life among African Americans and Creoles. Over the next decade, Hearn immersed himself in the culture of the Crescent City's streets, recording urban life with fewer of the biases evidenced by his contemporaries. Often living on the verge of starvation during his time in the United States, Hearn keenly surveyed New Orleans's food culture. He even for a few weeks partnered in the operation of an eatery in New Orleans alternatively called the "Hard Times Restaurant" and "5 Cents Restaurant." In 1885, he would publish, anonymously, the first cookbook on New Orleans cuisine.[55]

Like some antebellum accounts, Hearn's sketch of urban life in September 1880 titled "Cakes and Candy" describes the skill of Black women in hawking their goods. He heralds the confections, writing that "she maketh them herself, and great be the cunning skill wherewith she prepareth the little dainties." He recognizes these sellers' long-standing presence on the streets, noting that some of "these ancient women have been selling dainties to little ones through two generations" and many of the "infants who trotted to them with five cents in their dimpled fingers are now grown-up men and women." Their staying power made African American confectioners aware of shifts in tastes and the peculiarities of their regular, multigenerational customers. Hearn notes how the "old woman knoweth much of the history of families and the vicissitudes thereof." That Hearn depicts these sellers as French speakers familiar with generations of white New Orleanians highlights the dominance of local Creoles of color, rather than the newly arrived freedwomen from the surrounding plantations, in maintaining the market for assorted sweets. Further, these shrewd businesswomen used their ties to white customers to limit competition by appealing to familiarity or by casting doubt on the products and skills of new confectioners. Their hold only began to give way during the 1880s and 1890s as age, intermarriages, and tourism opened opportunities for postwar arrivals to the city.[56]

One widely read tale published in 1891 by Cecilia Viets Jamison, now largely forgotten in New Orleans literary lore, reveals the sophistication of these praline hustlers. Jamison, a native of Nova Scotia, married a New Orleans lawyer after the Civil War. She rubbed elbows with fellow writers Lafcadio Hearn, George Washington Cable, and Mollie Moore Davis, all of whom mined local culture for their tales. Like these writers, Jamison anticipated the looming literary shift to realism in her desire to capture street life.

Her most popular novel, the internationally successful *Lady Jane* from 1891, recounts with admiration the tale of "Madelon, or 'Bonne Praline,' as she was called." Jamison deals deftly with race. Madelon is clearly Creole, but Jamison obscures her racial bloodlines both to intrigue white readers and to ensure they were not repelled by the positive depiction of a person of color. The Creole lived in a "tiny, single cottage" with a "tiny kitchen and yard, where Madelon made her pralines and cakes." Madelon, put simply, was a "merchant." The skilled cook maintained a "stand for cakes and pralines up on Bourbon Street, near the French Opera House, and thither she went every morning, with her basket and pans of fresh pralines, sugared pecans, and calas *tout chaud,* a very tempting array of dainties, which she was sure to dispose of before she returned at night." Madelon's household was a small factory for production of the sweet confection. A "half-grown darky . . . washed, cooked, and scrubbed" the house and wares. Madelon's daughter assisted in cracking and sorting the pecans. She placed them in "three separate piles, the perfect halves in one pile, those broken by accident in another, and those slightly shriveled, and a little rancid, in still another." These were put to different uses: "The first were used to make the sugared pecans for which Madelon was justly famous; the second to manufacture into pralines, so good that they had given her the sobriquet of 'Bonne Praline'; and the third pile, which she disdained to use in her business, nothing imperfect ever entering into her concoctions, were swept into a box, and disposed of to merchants who had less principle and less patronage." A single mantra guided the homemade production line. To Madelon and her daughter, "business was business, and pecans cost money, and every ten sugared pecans meant a nickel." Jamison's account, though fictional, reflects a reality of hard labor and careful preparation day in and day out for a select few skilled candymakers of color in the Crescent City.[57]

Jamison's *Lady Jane* not only captures a shrewd business operated by Black women within New Orleans but also broadcast the image of the praline seller across the globe. It was reprinted several times into the 1960s and enjoyed translations into German, French, Italian, and even Norwegian. The New Orleans praline seller was an international sensation, though the image of the industrious praline woman promoted by Jamison clashed with the more romanticized and more explicitly racial imagery crafted by the likes of Grace King and other local defenders of Jim Crow.[58]

A U.S. census taker in 1900 provided the lone record of an African American family-run praline operation from the late nineteenth century. Marie Albrier was a 58-year-old African American who rented a home on Dumaine Street. Her parents had come from Cuba. The 1860 and 1870 censuses show her father as a skilled tinsmith and list the family members as mulattos, suggesting that they blended into the local population of free persons of color before the Civil War. Marie Albrier was born in Louisiana. Only five of her twelve children remained alive, but all five resided in her home. Albrier listed her occupation as "praline maker"—the first and only appearance of praline production recorded as an occupation in census records for New Orleans until 1920. Her eldest child, the 44-year-old Ernestine, also appeared as a "praline maker." Although Albrier's only surviving son worked as a house painter, her 31-year-old daughter Medelenne labored as a "praline saleswoman," hawking the homemade confections. The two surviving daughters in their late twenties assisted as family servants, likely aiding with the praline business when not caring for the three young grandsons living in Albrier's home.[59]

Newspaper articles provide insight on other praline sellers of the late nineteenth century. New Orleanians in March 1908 mourned the passing of Elizabeth Carter, "another of the old parline [*sic*] vendors who was a familiar figure at the different railroad stations in this city." The *Item* described her as "among the last of the old timers whosold [*sic*] pralines." Carter had been a popular and ever-present figure in the neighborhoods around her small cottage at Villere Street and St. Bernard Avenue, where she "disposed of most of the candy she made herself." The newspaper eulogized her: "She was a typical mammy. She was polite and respectful to the white people." Of course, such catering to whites not only facilitated sales but also fostered important business connections. J. Adam Lautenschlaeger, a prominent grocer in the area and a former member of the city council, honored "Mammy Carter" for her skill and the quality of her goods. Carter had spent the last years of her life with relatives "over at McClellanville," a small community across the river near the McClellan Dry Docks. This departure from the streets occurred after more and more pralines were "manufactured by a number of concerns, forcing her to retire, one of the very last to 'step down and out,' as it were." Not that all praline sellers abandoned their posts. The article noted how "two or three are still engaged in the business that was very profitable years ago." This included a "surviving" praline hawker operating at the corner of Canal and Bourbon Streets, "a place she has occupied for years."[60]

The details provided about Carter on her death allow a rare opportunity to explore the life of a Black praline seller in New Orleans. Carter was born around 1846, making her roughly 62 years old at her passing.[61] Reconstructing Carter's life is difficult given her common name, name change at marriage(s?), and marginal life as an African American laboring through the tumult of a highly mobile society transitioning from slavery to war to Jim Crow. Her life as a popular praline seller, however, reveals the successes and hardships faced by these women.[62]

Because Carter was childless and divorced from her husband, her estate landed in court. Carter died with a remarkable savings of $620.61 held by the People's Savings, Trust, and Banking Company. Her sole debts were $18 for house rent and $26.50 for her funeral. Three surviving sisters, all divorced, filed to divide the inheritance. The children of a fourth sister, who had died in 1883 and had also divorced, joined the petition to the court. All the Carter sisters were illiterate, each marking the final decree with an "x." Born into a slave regime, the Carter sisters were prevented from learning to read and write. This changed for the next generation of African Americans—but slowly. The two nephews, born in 1864 and 1867, also signed with a mark; they worked as day laborers. Although schools had opened to African Americans and there even was a brief moment of integrated schooling in the early 1870s, the stresses of political violence, racial intimidation, and economic need to support the family likely cut short the education of these young men. A scant 43 percent of Black men older than 10 years old demonstrated literacy in 1870. The two nieces, born in 1874 and 1882, were able to sign their names. The elder, a day laborer, applied a stilted hand to the paper. The younger, a cook, pressed forward the pen with a smooth, confident signature. As time progressed, Black institutions of learning within New Orleans gained at least limited acceptance. Young Black women—unable to vote due to their sex, no matter their race, until ratification of the Nineteenth Amendment in 1920—were seen by white society as less threatening to the status quo. Education for young Black woman also sparked the hope of Black families eager for their children to gain better marriage prospects. The death of Carter therefore exposes not only the incredible achievement of this praline seller in building a financial nest egg through her marketing finesse but also the travails of Black working-class life in the late nineteenth century.[63]

Further insights into the economic life of praline peddlers can be gleaned from the popularly known Tante Clementine, who operated a stand on Chartres Street in the French Quarter from the 1870s into the 1920s. The writer G. William Nott romanticizes Tante Clementine in the last years of her life: "Everything in the neighborhood has undergone a change, everything except the stand of Tante Clementine." Readers seeking to commune with the "hospitality and good-fellowship of ancient days" of antebellum New Orleans needed only to visit this praline seller. Nott declares, "For those who like to turn back the pages of history and live a few moments in the past, nothing will give them more pleasure than a few moments chat with Tante Clementine."[64] Olga Kaufmann did just that. On a Sunday morning in 1924, Kaufmann encountered "Tante Clementine" speaking "negro French" outside the Ursuline Convent. She was sitting on a small stool with a basket filled with pralines and calas, "the kind of picture we have been accustomed to see only on postcards in recent years." Such nostalgia pervaded New Orleans while providing free advertising for the sellers.

The *States* voiced the widespread concern shared among readers when Tante Clementine disappeared in February 1925. The newspaper announced the news with a front-page headline, "Old Praline Woman Is Missing." Readers learned that "Clementine, the old colored praline woman, who has been selling pralines on Chartres and Ursuline streets, for fifty years, has disappeared from her home, 1320 Dauphine Street." Her daughter and friends searched in vain for the more than 90-year-old matriarch and pleaded with the community to find her.[65]

Press coverage of Tante Clementine's disappearance reveals the ways praline-selling women transcended their working-class status to forge links with even the most powerful New Orleanians. Although her disappearance sparked a police search and front-page headlines, her proper name remained unmentioned. We cannot recover who she was, but her disappearance exposed the layers of commerce linked through this praline seller across nationalities and races in New Orleans. Her address, 1320 Dauphine Street, was owned by a French family headed by Antoine Araguel, who came from Egypt with his wife near the turn of the century. They had purchased the property along with a retail grocery nearby on Esplanade Avenue in 1917. Antoine Araguel died in 1918, leaving his wife to support the family. City directories suggest that the Araguels rented out the house on Dauphine Street because the names of residents changed frequently, although no mention of a Clementine appears. Most residents were male. Did Clementine sublet the property or board in one of the rooms? Did Tante Clementine not only pay rent to the Araguels but also aid their retail grocery by hawking sweets?[66]

Curiously, despite the press stating that Tante Clementine's daughter and friends were searching frantically for her, the *Times-Picayune* and *States* both urged anyone with information to contact Joe Colin at 2635 Gravier Street. Colin was an African American, born in 1867, with a large family that had wide-ranging economic interests. His younger brother William Colin had trained in a bakery and, by the early 1900s, operated a retail business. Did Tante Clementine sell homemade pralines and other sweets made by the Colin household? For much of Joe Colin's marriage to Annette Colin, his mother-in-law Justine Bernard, born around 1840, resided with them. Was

Bernard the famed Tante Clementine? Had she moved out as the Colin family grew and aged, seeking opportunities within the burgeoning French Quarter tourist trade only a handful of blocks from the family home? Was Annette the dutiful daughter desperate to find her mother?[67]

Joe Colin worked as a valet to William R. Irby after laboring for him as a porter in a tobacco factory. Irby was a banking and tobacco magnate, one of the wealthiest men in New Orleans. After a major hurricane in 1915 damaged the St. Louis Cathedral and St. Louis Hotel in the French Quarter, Irby donated funds for restoration efforts. He also invested heavily in real estate in the historic neighborhood until his death by suicide in 1926. Did Tante Clementine serve the interests of Irby? By appearing as a praline seller, did she help cast the French Quarter as a historic remnant of a bygone era, boosting property values and making her a matter of citywide concern?[68]

Clearly, Tante Clementine earned enough to live on her own, even when she was around age 90. Her entrepreneurship captured locals' devotion that transformed into national attention as New Orleanians like G. William Nott celebrated her and her wares. She also cultivated economic links to a middle-class merchant, a well-connected African American family, and a major New Orleans powerbroker.

A CITYWIDE MARKET

Praline sellers like Tante Clementine turned major thoroughfares into improvised marketplaces. One wayfarer along Canal Street in the 1880s remarked on the "amber-hued turbaned dispensers of pink pralines and yellow stage planks with a rosebud for lagniappe." These hawkers competed with vendors of roasted chestnuts, French flower women, organ grinders, and other street peddlers of goods and entertainment. Such praline sellers could still be found on Canal Street during Mardi Gras into the 1920s. Nellie Conner McCay reported in 1927 on the "old 'praline woman,' a picturesque relic of slavery days" who greeted the "passing throngs with an humble smile, patiently displaying a tray of pink and white pralines, which she silently proclaims are for sale." Holidays such as Carnival that brought shoppers and revelers onto the streets proved a boon for praline sales.[69]

Praline peddlers frequently attended to the passengers coming and going from the city's railroad stations. Residents looking for a quick bite or tourists eager for their first taste of New Orleans supplied a ready market. Transportation hubs during times of disaster could prove especially profitable. Ethel Willia Perkins recalled waiting at a depot near Calliope Street to evacuate from the city during the 1878 yellow fever epidemic: "A cistern furnished drinking-water (plus 'wigglers') [mosquito larvae], but except for an occasional Negro mammy with pralines or popcorn-balls, no edibles were to be had." Like the antebellum marchandes, the street vendors provided a lifeline to New Orleanians during times of crisis.[70]

Street sellers regularly crowded around the French Market. In her 1853 account, English traveler Fredrika Bremer marvels, "One feels as if transported at once to a great Paris marché, with this difference, that one here meets with various races of people, hears many different languages spoken, and sees the productions of various zones." Most of the sellers were "black Creoles" who crammed stalls with a stunning range of foods. Bremer "wandered among the stalls, which were piled up with game, and fruit and flowers, bread and confectionary, grain and vegetables, and innumerable good things all nicely arranged, and showing that abundance in the productions of the earth." Even the turmoil of the Civil War and Reconstruction eras could not undermine the splendor of the French Market. Annie Porter, writing for the *Atlantic Monthly* in 1879, describes the French Market as a place populated by "Sicilian, French, Dutch, Creole, and negro craftsmen of every description, butchers, bakers, coffee-vendors, market-gardeners, fishermen, Indian basket-makers, mulatto flower-girls." This marketplace alongside the Mississippi River remained a staple of local shopping into the early twentieth century and continues to draw tourists in the twenty-first century, with several praline shops still catering to sweet tooths.[71]

Sellers crowded outside churches to market to hungry parishioners after services. The African American figure of the "old woman who sold cakes and pralines at the church entrance" was a common sight within New Orleans in the late nineteenth century. This practice lingered. When Millie Ball reported on a musical rehearsal of the Gospel Soul Children Advancement Association at the First Emmanuel Baptist Church in 1982, the predominantly African American congregation encountered in the rear pew a "heavyset woman" with a "grocery bag filled with pralines wrapped in waxed paper." The woman sold them to benefit a sick church member.[72]

All Saints' Day on November 1 was the most lucrative holiday on the praline sellers' calendar. On that day Catholic tradition called on New Orleanians to pay respect to deceased ancestors. This annual pilgrimage remained a widely observed obligation from the mid-nineteenth century until the early twentieth century. The many deaths from the Civil War and from persistent yellow fever outbreaks, the last in 1905, reinforced the tradition.

With cemeteries located far from commercial areas where restaurants, cafes, and stores abounded, street vendors seized the opportunity to cater to the mourners. A reporter in 1887 described a scene common outside the city's cemeteries: "About the gates it will be like a market day—a fair day in some old foreign town. Fat, turbaned negro women, deft men cooks, peddlers of all kinds, are selling their wares. They have put up tables, benches, tents, wooden shanties, and here campfires burn; even a cooking stove or two, with a couple of joints of pipe, has been set up; innumerable charcoal furnaces are at white heat, and on these pots of coffee, gombo, bisque, are boiling." The range of edibles amazed: "Here are displayed for sale pretzels and sausages, greasy doughnuts and poundcake, pralines and chestnuts, peanuts and gingerbread, hard-boiled eggs and sugar cane, cut and split and ready for eating—all mixed in with wreaths, potted plants, candles, and all being bartered for in every tongue that is heard in this cosmopolitan city." African American women jostled with sellers of other races and ethnicities in a competitive frenzy to capture the needs and hunger of those entering the repositories of the dead.[73] An account from the *Daily Picayune* in 1899 described the "cake vendors, the praline sellers, the perambulating refreshment stands, the flower vendors" vying for consumers entering and leaving the cemeteries. The newspaper elaborated, "They erected their booths all around the cemeteries, at the gates and down the streets. All had bargains to offer which would throw the nextdoor [*sic*] neighbor's prices in the shade." Accounts of the cemetery marketplaces always noted the prominence of African American women. Elderly "black marchandes" wearing tignons regularly "sat on low stools, and piled up before them were trays of red and white and brown cocoanut candy, pralines made of pecans and peanuts and almonds, and amid all this delicatesse [*sic*] were the famous 'stage plank' ginger cakes for the people of their own color."[74]

This All Saints' Day tradition (and market) faded after World War I in the face of modern conveniences and improved mortality rates, but New Orleanians remembered with fondness the outings and the excitement of the improvised markets at the cemetery gates. Myldred Masson Costa cherished memories of the annual trip to the cemetery with her family during the early twentieth century. Interviewed in 1984, she remembered, "Of course, tignoned mammies sat at every gate with calas (a type of pastry made from rice) and pralines and coffee, being besieged with people needing food and drink." Costa referenced the emergence of affordable telephones, reducing the need for large familial gatherings. Further, a dirty or forlorn tomb no longer carried social stigma. Mortality rates during the early twentieth century improved with modern drainage systems and mosquito control, eradicating the fear of yellow fever and malaria outbreaks while decreasing the sense of immediacy with death. The advent of automobiles, movie theaters, radio, and other technologies and forms of mass entertainment eroded long-held traditions across the United States.[75]

Mardi Gras similarly stood prominently on the calendar of praline hawkers. Since the 1860s, the press had carried news nationally of the preparations of street vendors and other businesses, eager to capture dollars from Carnival-going tourists. "Great preparations are being made by women of New Orleans to amuse the many northern visitors who will be in their city at the time of the Shrove Tuesday carnival," heralded the *New York World* in 1889. Although most praline sellers worked the crowds passing on the streets, a few gained entry to the city's showcase. During the late nineteenth century, boosters annually constructed a "Cotton Palace" in Lafayette Square, across from New Orleans's City Hall where the municipal leadership toasted the parading Carnival elite. The building "exhibited all the industrial achievements of the southern women." Acadian women sold "their famous blankets . . . spun on the old-fashioned wheels and woven in the primitive hand looms, while the dyes are all made from roots dug on the prairies." Chata and Attakapas Indians offered handwoven baskets. A Creole restaurant also appeared "where fat old negro mammies with their heads tied up in butterfly tignons will prepare the famous Creole dishes in the old-fashioned bake ovens at a huge open-fireplace—'calla tout chaud,' gumbo, crayfish bisque, grillades, Jombolaya, bouille baisse, court bouillon, Creole coffee and potato pone, besides the fried chicken, corn bread and biscuits which are well known pieces de resistance in Southern cookery." The tantalizing list continued: "There are to be sold all the queer, tasty Creole confections too—the drowsy syrups concocted of the fragrant blossoms of orange and the sweet olive tree, pralines of nuts and of every sort of blossom, of which dainty conserves the Creole cooks possess the choicest secrets." Patrons enjoying the food and shopping were regaled with "choruses of negroes, with old plantation songs, and Creole choruses to sing the plaintive melodies patois which George W. Cable has made famous."[76]

A generation of young New Orleanians recalled the praline seller known as Marie Louise, who sold to students at the gates of Newcomb College, a women's school adjacent to Tulane University. Ruth McEnery Stuart, a nationally recognized author from New Orleans, regaled readers of the *Ladies' Home Journal* in 1896 with a tale of this praline hawker: "I do not know the history of the old praline woman but in all probability she is one of the many of her class who have survived the glory of her 'white people,' and is, in consequence, taking her place at doorsteps as a vendor of the confections that she so notably excels in making." According to Stuart, the praline woman at Newcomb imprinted herself on the memories of these collegiate women: "No doubt there are numbers of girls of the Sophie Newcombe [*sic*] College who will be quite unable, when college life becomes only a memory, to recall many of its sweetest and most characteristic pictures without yielding to the old praline woman her humble and patient seat at the outer gate, or even her more ambitious position upon the lower step of the main entrance."

In a society in which young white women led the charge to memorialize the Lost Cause of the Confederacy, praline sellers like Mary Louise at Newcomb sometimes accommodated the saccharine lore so many white southerners craved so they could make a living. Instead of celebrating this entrepreneur's astute positioning near an ample and moneyed clientele, Stuart situates this praline seller as a mammy, a treasured relic of a "regime that has passed away, maybe, a system that is dead." She thus seemingly neutralizes the praline vendor's economic skills. Not only does Stuart thereby honor the antebellum past but she also hints at the preservation of racial customs existing under slavery, a regime of which the mammified praline seller stands as a "true expression of a past, of which she is confessedly proud." A shrewd vendor looking to ensure sales understood the importance of appeasing such worldviews with tongue firmly in cheek.[77]

Indeed, the marketing wisdom and panache of the praline seller at Newcomb College even undermined efforts to provide meals prepared in the campus kitchen. In 1900, alumni launched a Newcomb Creole Kitchen to sell meals to students, with the profits going to endow scholarships. The kitchen was "fitted up in real 'Creole' type, and every day there was a committee of three from the alumnae" who cooked and served hot lunches of "soup, Creole gumbo, hot chocolate, hot tea, dainty home-made bread, hot biscuits, tea cakes," as well as other treats. After six months of operation the alumni association had only earned $75. "The kitchen did not work at all, that is as a financial success," complained the alumni association president. The problem stemmed from the "old colored praline woman" sitting at the school's gate. Each school day she presented a "great basket and her salver spread with a snowy towel, and piles upon piles of pink and white pralines, brown sugar ones, with pecans generously distributed; dainty white paper cases, with the old-fashioned molasses and pecan candy styled by the Creoles 'la colle.'" Faced with competition from the kitchen, the praline hawker "redoubled the size of her pralines, and the girls flocked to purchase them at noon in triple numbers." The clever move worked. The praline woman, interviewed by a newspaper, laughed, "All girl love for eat sugar, and when you take dat sucre and make it in dat Creole praline like my gran muzzer bin show me how for make—mon Dieu!—dat old praline woman gone knock out all dose high school kitchen in de land." The kitchen closed. Subsequent debates over reopening this dining facility centered on its ability to succeed financially, given the popularity of this shrewd off-campus competitor.[78]

Moreover, the praline hawker of Newcomb exploited her connections to female socialites and the popular stereotype of the mammy to gain access to other selling opportunities. In 1904, for instance, she received an invitation to distribute her wares to the women attending the National Wholesale Druggists' Association convention. As their husbands attended a business banquet, some hundred wives from across the country sat in the palm room of the St. Charles Hotel for an evening of bridge, whist, and euchre. In a room decorated with "tall stalks of sugar cane, created with its silver plume," guests gazed in amusement at a bower of plants formed at an end of the room that served as a "stand for 'Marie Louise,' the Newcomb College praline mammy." The *Item* reported, "This famous vendor of the pecan dainty was in her usual costume of gay calico, white kerchief crossed on her bosom and her tignon arranged as only the real old mammies know how." Marie Louise passed among the eight bridge tables and ten euchre tables throughout the evening, replenishing the supply of pralines as the players munched away. She also presented small packages of pralines to each woman as a souvenir of the evening.[79]

Marie Louise of Newcomb fame was not alone in exploiting white nostalgia. Her daughter Azelie took over at the school's gates by the late 1910s, defending the family's profitable turf for another generation by satisfying the sugar cravings and racial expectations of students steeped in Lost Cause mythology. Other African American praline sellers were not beyond co-opting the praline mammy stereotype to capitalize from the tourist trade. At the Jerusalem Temple of Shriners convention in Indianapolis in 1919, the New Orleans members hired a jazz band and three praline hawkers to attend as part of an unsuccessful promotional effort to lure the next national gathering to the Crescent City. The sellers, according to the *States,* were Rose Jones, Henrietta Fargo, and Rosa Patterson, who were assisted by several younger African American women.[80]

These women give a glimpse into who performed the much-in-demand role of praline seller to tourists in the early twentieth century. Such employment became a lifeline for African American women as they aged past 60 years old. Born in Louisiana in 1852, Fargo had headed her household of five children since at least 1900. She operated a laundry from her residence, a property she owned on South Franklin Avenue. By 1920, her household had grown to a total of thirteen, with numerous grandchildren occupying the house. Her daughters ran the laundry. The 1920 census lists no occupation for Fargo, not surprising given that her age made the hard work of laundress difficult. But Fargo's entrepreneurial spirit and the demands of sustaining a large household drew her into performing as a praline-distributing mammy.[81] Given that a Rosa Patterson does not appear in historical records, the reporter likely misidentified Rose Peterson, known to don mammy garb for a local candy firm. Peterson was born around 1850 in Louisiana and had worked as a midwife.[82] Rose Jones appears in census records as a domestic servant and later a laundress born in Louisiana in 1843. Together, these women tempted the Shriners with pralines and coffee prepared over charcoal pots. The press reported that a 76-year-old praline mammy, probably Rose Jones, bowed to those she served while beckoning, "Ah hope you all will come to New Awleans next yeah. You all will be mos' welcome."[83]

Such performances not only served the city's boosters but also promised economic opportunities for the praline sellers who were hoping to be hired for future recitals of the shtick. Mayor Martin Behrman described his disappointment when New Orleans was denied the next Shriner convention, pointing out that the "negro 'mammies' who served the coffee and made the pralines were as much disappointed as any one, and they wept when informed that this city had lost out on the convention."[84] This same tactic of distributing pralines via elderly African Americans in mammy garb proved more successful when repeated at the American Legion convention in Kansas City in 1921. The Legionnaires planned their 1922 convention for New Orleans and, on arriving, encountered French Quarter streets crowded with praline sellers who "cried aloud the values of their wares." Nationally renowned author Meigs O. Frost observed the "fat, black mammy who sells pralines and fat, black mammy dolls with brass earrings." Thus, tourists could purchase not only the confection but also a stereotypical representation of the preparer. The end result was higher profits.[85]

Rose Peterson was a particularly masterful praline seller who was in high demand. In April 1922, the confectionary firm Fuerst & Kraemer was scrambling to prepare for the triennial conclave of the Knights Templar. Seeking an "old negro mammy . . . as she once stood in the kitchen of her plantation cabin in a half hundred years ago," Albert Kraemer soon boasted that he had "obtained her." This "typical mammy" was for the "edification of the visiting Knights Templar." Kraemer converted the chain's 105 Baronne Street location "to conform to those of the old woman." Plantation scenes adorned the walls with a phonograph projecting "plantation melodies." A bale of cotton sat in the middle of the store with "miniature bales of pralines" stacked on top. Rose Peterson, the septuagenarian who wore a red-and-white-checkered tignon and apron, was supposedly the originator of the firm's praline recipe. She stood in the doorway greeting passersby. Peterson knew her trade and performed it well. She confessed to her popularity on the New Orleans tourism circuit, having attended "a hundred conventions where southern atmosphere has been acclaimed."[86]

In the early twentieth century, African American sellers fiercely defended their market share from encroaching white manufacturers. A parade by the New Orleans Lodge of the Benevolent Protective Order of Elks arranged to promote its annual toy fund for Christmas 1918 by featuring a member in mammy garb selling pralines. Although the account of this imitator's confrontation with an African American praline hawker reflected the racist humor of the day, the exchange also captured the frustration of those who survived off their praline sales. An "old negro mammy complete in local color from her plaid head handkerchief to her worn carpet slippers" derided the Elk impersonator: "You ain't no nigger, an' I don't believe you's no woman, yit." For African American women pushed to the social and economic margins, the intrusion of white men across racial and gender lines into one of the few lucrative trades available to Black women stirred resentment and anger. In a short story from the 1930s, Mary Louise Guild captures the shrewd efforts of African American women to undercut the burgeoning number of tourist shops selling manufactured pralines. Guild remarks on the "feud" between a shop operated by a Tante Marie and the "praline woman because she sometimes stationed her basket before the gift shop, claiming much of Tante Marie's trade." The author presents the defiance of this anonymous praline seller: "'Pralines! Pralines! Homemade pralines!' The neat, chocolate-colored mammy took her stand in front of the gift shop."[87]

PRALINE SELLERS REWRITTEN

For most white New Orleanians like Ruth McEnery Stuart and Grace King, acknowledging the independence, skill, and economic prowess of the Black praline-selling entrepreneur undermined Jim Crow myths of African American racial inferiority and contentment with segregation. The first reference in the *Daily Picayune* to a praline seller exemplified the dismissal of Black ingenuity and enterprise. In late September 1876, as Reconstruction waned, the city's leading newspaper carried a tale of street life called "Steal so Gently." It recounted an incident from "a few days ago on one of our up-town avenues" where a "portly but antiquated vendor of cakes and pralines was conversing with one of her sex." Focused on the conversation, "she was unaware of the presence of a little ebony urchin whose wooly head could just be seen above the top of the fence, and whose dilated eyes were feasting on the sweets within his grasp, so neatly clustered in the basket poised upon the venerable head of the old marchande." Reaching down, the boy grabbed as many treats as he could hold before bounding away. The "old negress" remained unaware of the theft as she conversed. This account not only denigrated the business sense of African American women but also attacked their devotion and piety. The conversation that distracted the praline hawker regarded "some of the delinquent 'sisters' of the s'ciety who had failed to liquidate their pro rata of the last 'collation.'" She remained too intent on addressing the "financial problem with her 'Sister of the Cross'" to notice the theft. The *Daily Picayune* thereby managed a backhanded dismissal of Black Catholic piety, a faith particularly prominent among Creoles of color, while deprecating the efforts of Black women to operate their businesses efficiently.[88]

White Americans after the 1870s generally embraced an image of contented African Americans as sectional reconciliation eclipsed racial reform. Economic hopes for African Americans faded as white Americans rejected reconstruction efforts within the former Confederacy, where vigilante violence bulldozed Republican attempts to buoy the Black franchise. Corruption scandals, such as the Credit Mobilier affair involving railroad construction contracts, rocked the Republican Party. A bitter economic depression during the mid-1870s further sowed national distrust of Republican policies. Many white workers who were squeezed by the economic downturn perceived the protection of Blacks' equality as a threat to their employment prospects. The white supremacist aims of self-proclaimed Redeemers in the South who attacked Republican rule thus resonated with struggling whites elsewhere in the nation.[89]

Depicting African Americans as content in their poverty rationalized a rollback of racial reform policies while reinforcing the sense that wealth naturally belonged to whites. Traveling across the American South during the 1870s, Amos Gottschall, a native of Pennsylvania, crafted the image of a seemingly passive and happy Black population that became the norm in white accounts of Black life in the former Confederacy. He wrote, "There are thousands of old colored 'uncles' and 'aunties' all through the South, who, having been the faithful servants and companions of 'massa' and 'missus' for many years, still linger about 'de ole plantation,' and generally being kindly provided for by their former owners, are now passing their declining days in comparative ease." He described younger Black families as similarly carefree despite exploitive agricultural practices such as sharecropping and the biased enforcement of new vagrancy laws and other measures that increasingly restricted African Americans' mobility and belied the narrative of paternalistic whites who supposedly catered to the Black population. Describing African Americans along the river in and around New Orleans, Gottschall wrote, "The colored people are healthy and robust, and are ever happy and cheerful. So long as they have a pound of bacon and a peck of corn-meal in the cabin, they are contented, and strangers to 'dull care.'" Gottschall foreshadowed a voluminous literature that emphasized Black contentment.[90]

Within the Black community, praline sellers remained hard-working mothers, sisters, and daughters. African Americans rightly placed them in the historical context of racial uplift in New Orleans. instead of Lost Cause nostalgia, as most white writers would during the Jim Crow era. For instance, the Epicureans, a Black Carnival organization established in the late 1940s, hosted a ball at the International Longshoremen's Auditorium in 1976 under the theme "Nostalgic Old New Orleans." In this bicentennial year, members marked the progress of African Americans in the push for equality while honoring the institutions that had sustained them. The decorations recalled famed sites associated with Black New Orleanians, including the Roof Garden of the Pythian Temple, the San Jacinto Club, the Sans Souci Hall, and the Bethlehem Temple, along with McDonogh 35 High School, long the only high school open to African Americans in New Orleans. Being honored were famous African Americans, including gospel singer Mahalia Jackson, trumpeter Louis Armstrong, author Alice Dunbar-Nelson, religious leaders Henriette DeLille and Juliette Gaudin, inventor Norbert Rillieux, businessman Thomy Lafon, philanthropist Madame Bernard Couvent, educators Johnson Lockett and Medard Nelson, and fencing master Basile Croquere. These notables spanned the history of New Orleans. Equally noteworthy was the enterprising praline seller: "Adding to the festivities were two women in 'mammy costumes' who distributed pralines and 'calas,' a creole type doughnut, to the female guests."[91]

In contrast to white nostalgia that used praline peddlers to celebrate the antebellum past, African Americans in New Orleans understood the marchandes' entrepreneurial drive. The context at the Longshoremen's Auditorium mattered. No sugarcane stalks decorated the room. No phonograph music of melodies suggestive of plantations as joyous spaces filled the air. Instead, the street hawkers circulated among successful African Americans honoring forebears who had challenged white supremacy by their achievements. What the unnamed reporter, likely white, interpreted as "mammy costumes" were the practical dress of nineteenth-century working-class women plying their trade. As they wandered among the crowd, these two praline distributors told a tale of progress. They were not caricatures but a homage to the economic strivings of Rose Peterson, Marie Albrier, Elizabeth Carter, and all those before them who sustained dockworkers and other laborers, as well as their own families, through sweat and toil.

But of all the edibles carried by African American street merchants, why were pralines so special? Why did this sweet made with brown sugar come to monopolize their basket space in the popular imagination during the late nineteenth and early twentieth centuries?

2

Why Do You Taste So Good?

LOUISIANA SUGAR PLANTATIONS AND THE DECLINE OF AN OLD SOUTH CROP

At the height of his literary career, Mark Twain recognized an opportunity to enhance his reputation and bolster his book sales. The former steamboat pilot turned to recounting changes along the Mississippi River he observed while sailing downstream to the Gulf of Mexico. Twain targeted armchair travelers and the tourists who would flock to New Orleans for the World's Industrial and Cotton Exposition of 1884–1885. His *Life on the Mississippi,* published in 1883, delivered a travelogue that blended, like the exposition itself, the charms of life along the river with accounts of the technologies transforming the waterway. For Twain, sugar production exemplified the industrialization efforts converting seemingly quaint plantations of yore to modern factories of the fields.

Twain described how, from Baton Rouge to New Orleans, the "great sugar plantations border both sides of the river all the way, and stretch their league-wide levels back to the dim forest-walls of bearded cypress in the rear." The cultivated fields carved civilization from the swampy soil. He accepted an invitation to visit the sugar plantation of Henry Clay Warmoth, a postwar carpetbagger and Reconstruction-era Republican governor of Louisiana, located some fifty miles downriver from the Crescent City. Twain expressed awe: "We saw steam-plows at work, here, for the first time." The author detailed how this machine plodded as a "great see-saw . . . rolling and pitching like a ship at sea" across the 650 acres dedicated to sugar production on a plantation of 2,600 acres. "The cane is cultivated after a modern and intricate scientific fashion, too elaborate and complex for me to attempt to describe; but it lost $40,000 last year," continued Twain. The profits from a good crop year typically meant that "last year's loss will not matter." He noted that yields reached two tons an acre, four times the amount from his days as an antebellum river pilot. Refinement procedures had modernized as well. Twain marveled, "The great sugar-house was a wilderness of tubs and tanks and vats and filters, pumps, pipes, and machinery." The Missourian recounted the use of centrifuges to extract the juice, followed by the application of the evaporating pan to extract fibers. The bone filter then removed any alcohol while the clarifying tanks discharged the molasses. A granulating pipe finally condensed the sugar. "To make sugar is really one of the most difficult things in the world," remarked Twain, "And to make it right, is next to impossible."[1]

Twain's book captured major changes to the Louisiana sugar industry that profoundly altered the production and popular perception of the pecan praline and the women of color who labored as street peddlers. Accounts of Black saleswomen in the nineteenth century regularly included mention of calas, coconut confections, and other colorful sweets packed into baskets. Yet, despite the numerous travelers' accounts of antebellum, wartime, and Reconstruction-era New Orleans, pecan pralines went unmentioned. Tales about the praline vendor from the late 1880s onward, however, fixated on the patty of brown sugar populated with pecans, often excluding mention of other items. How could such a supposed staple of Creole New Orleans go largely unnoticed until the 1880s? Why was this sugary flat disk suddenly so much more worthy of attention than all the other delectable treats lugged by African American street sellers during the nineteenth century? And what was changing in Louisiana and New Orleans in the 1880s and 1890s to make the pecan praline so quickly synonymous with the city? Answering why the praline took center stage over other items in the peddlers' baskets from the late 1880s onward requires unpacking the workings of the sugar industry along with the cultural meanings applied to brown sugar.

The estates of antebellum sugar planters had given way after the Civil War to fields and factories owned by new investors like Warmoth. Costly, modern technologies transformed the refinement of sugar, leading to greater centralization. This change reflected a trend common across the U.S. food industry, as businesses vertically and horizontally integrated their production processes. Standardization led companies to branding, as in the case of

Aunt Jemima, to differentiate their mass-market products. For the Louisiana sugar industry, the efficiencies brought by consolidated railroad networks and improved steamships carried both opportunities and threats, especially as the United States joined other imperial nations in controlling far-off sugar-producing territories such as Hawaii, Cuba, and the Philippines.

Although mammy imagery cast the praline as an heirloom of a romanticized Old South, its key ingredient of brown sugar offered consumers a means of celebrating an agrarian past in an imperial present while looking askance at an intensifying industrialism that was revolutionizing American life. Understanding the origins of Louisiana sugar contextualizes the nostalgia evoked by pralines in New Orleans and the confection's role in promoting locally raised sucrose. As anthropologist David Sutton has noted, taste and smell are "interrelated senses" with foods consumed at certain times triggering emotionally charged recollections that can stir decades-old events because these senses "evoke what surrounds them in memory."[2]

The mnemonic cues stirred by pralines remained firmly rooted in Louisiana's plantations. Further, the fixation on plantation-made brown sugar suggested a pursuit of authenticity in a world flooded with industrially refined white sugar. Antebellum Louisianans, as historian J. Carlyle Sitterson noted, favored sugar from certain plantations, with each crop having a different taste, nuances in flavor, and quality of production. For locals, sugar had a terroir. The wartime upheaval and the postwar consolidation of the sugar industry spurred nostalgia among the white population for antebellum days enshrouded in Lost Cause memorialization. New Orleanian Eliza Ripley in her 1912 memoir yearned for the sweet flavors of her childhood and that "luscious 'open kettle' sugar, that dear, fragrant brown sugar no one sees now." The old days of African Americans boiling down cane juice in open cauldrons on each plantation, in Ripley's telling, gratified.[3]

Celebrating the state's plantation sugar eased fears of the threats posed by imports of cane sugar and the growing domestic sugar-beet industry. Moreover, Louisianans celebrated the darker-shaded sugar associated with plantations as a more flavorful sucrose. Brown plantation sugar recalled Louisianans' earliest childhood experiences with their ancestors, even as most Americans preferred white sugar as a seemingly sweeter, purer, and cleaner product. In a sense, the praline reinforced the preservative qualities of sugar by carrying into the present remembrances of the antebellum past while also giving rise to a literary and candy market controlled by whites that skewed those memories to buttress Jim Crow. Whereas Black New Orleanians could enjoy pralines at the Longshoreman's Auditorium in 1976 as a means of communing with enslaved ancestors and marking racial progress out of slavery, white New Orleanians transformed the praline into an ephemeral portal to the big house where the enslaved catered to whites' whims. Louisianans of color saw the praline as a means to a better future. Louisianans committed to white supremacy saw the praline as a sign that the past was still present.[4]

THE SUGAR BOWL

The story of Louisiana sugar dates to the 1790s. A few miles upriver from the colonial settlement of New Orleans, near present-day Audubon Park, Jean Étienne de Boré introduced the new cash crop. Turning away from indigo, Boré planted sugarcane, purchasing the seed cane from a nearby failed planter. He also hired an experienced sugar maker from San Domingue named Antoine Morin to manage the 1795 crop. He built a mill and, in 1796, processed the first granulated sugar produced in the colony. Boiling the cane syrup before witnesses, Boré reportedly cried, "Gentlemen, it grains! It grains!" An antebellum chronicler recounted the excitement of observers: "They rushed in to see the wonder, and when convinced of the fact, scattered in all directions, greeting every body they met, with 'It grains!'" Boré's success made him famous; he became the first mayor of New Orleans under U.S. rule. His achievement spurred fellow planters to invest in sugarcane.[5]

But Louisiana's susceptibility to occasional freezes limited the potential for widespread sugar cultivation. The first experiments with raising sugarcane had begun in 1742. These efforts failed. Technological improvements along with lessons learned through trial and error then allowed Boré and fellow planters to use Creole and Otaheite varieties of cane successfully. These varieties were soft and therefore easy to mill with animal power. However, both types showed a sensitivity to cold weather and an inability to ratoon, or resprout, annually, limiting the production of cane to areas south of New Orleans. Shortly after the War of 1812, as the economy improved, planters ever eager for heartier, more profitable varieties acquired Purple Cheribon and Striped Ribbon cane, plants native to Indonesia that had been carried to the West Indies by Dutch traders. They matured a month earlier than previous cane types and grew larger, thereby producing more sugar. These varieties, due to their harder rind, proved more resistant to frost and less stunted by cold temperatures. The use of purple and ribbon canes expanded the territory open to sugar cultivation to river lands within central Louisiana. Their tougher skin, however, necessitated the development of steam-powered technology capable of efficiently crushing the cane for processing.[6]

From the 1820s onward, the improved speed of steam-powered processing allowed planters more time for the crop to age and sweeten. This technological advancement enhanced the potential of the crop. From fewer than a hundred sugar plantations in 1801, Louisiana contained a peak of 1,536 sugar plantations by 1849. During the 1840s and 1850s, planters improved on the open-kettle boiling of cane by pouring the syrup into a sealed vacuum pan for the final stage of processing, which refined sugar juice quicker while enabling improved quality control of granulation. The vacuum pan, invented by Creole of color Norbert Rillieux of New Orleans, marked "one of the most important contributions ever made to the technical advancement of the sugar industry," according to J. Carlyle Sitterson. Planters also invested in bagasse burners to avoid the increasing problem of wood shortages. Bagasse was the term for the husks left after pressing the juice from sugarcane. The burners allowed planters to rid themselves of the crushed stalks while also providing fuel. Yet sugar production remained the luxury of only the most moneyed planters capable of affording the rich soil, the latest technology, and the high price of human chattel to work the fields and run the mills.[7]

Louisiana's so-called Sugar Bowl contained three regions. The oldest of these stretched along the Mississippi River from its delta upstream to the Mississippi state line. The other regions lay to the south and west of New Orleans in areas historically linked to the Acadians, or Cajuns. One of these extended along Bayou Lafourche in Lafourche and Assumption Parishes. The other section rested along Bayou Teche, Bayou Salé, Bayou Cypremort, and the prairies of St. Martin, Lafayette, St. Mary, and Iberia Parishes. The natural levee of the rivers and bayous gave a gradual slant to the fields, roughly six inches per mile and extending for approximately four or five miles toward a backswamp, facilitating drainage. Occasional floods from the waterways deposited rich nutrients onto the fields while temporarily threatening crops if the inundation arrived at an untimely moment.[8]

Wherever rich bottom lands existed in southern Louisiana, ambitious planters crowded the ground with sugarcane. Many were French, although there were a few Spanish planters who had familial roots in Louisiana since colonial days. These early residents, like Boré, were prepared to seize opportunity and clear land. English speakers, however, could find it daunting to penetrate the Sugar Bowl. An Anglo daughter visiting a sugar plantation near Donaldsonville, Louisiana, in 1847 complained, "I do not like to live up here in this lonesome neighborhood, because there is no body but French and Spanish children. But I know how to speak to the French a little."[9]

This expansionist wave fed Americans' intensifying sweet tooth. Sugar consumption in the United States swelled from 161 million pounds in 1837 to nearly 900 million pounds in 1854. This rising demand partly reflected a dramatic increase in the U.S. population: 9.6 million in 1820, 17 million in 1840, and 31.4 million in 1860. But hunger for sugar increased even more dramatically. The annual per capita consumption of sugar grew from around thirteen pounds in the early 1830s to more than thirty pounds in the late 1850s.[10]

Planters aimed for a twelve- to fifteen-month growing season for sugar cane to reach maturity, with as many days above seventy degrees Fahrenheit as possible to maximize sugar content. This involved planting cane between early October and late March and gambling that no freezes would occur after that. Laying mats on the field protected the seed cane from light frosts. Grinding season typically lasted from October through December before potentially freezing winter temperatures could occur. Letting the cut cane ratoon saved on expenses and labor but led to shoots that contained less sucrose. Thus, wealthier planters tended to replant the crops from seed cane, an equally difficult balancing act because to ensure a good crop in the next harvest, the cane with the highest sugar content would need to be set aside rather than processed. Raising cane was a precarious venture. An ill-timed cold snap could destroy a promising field of cane and leave planters financially buried under debts. Cane production produced not only wealth but also intense pressure to squeeze as much money from the cane as possible, given planters' dependence on creditors to finance, upgrade, and expand their operations, as well as to market their harvest.[11]

No one felt the pressure as much as the enslaved. The number of African Americans forced to plant, nurture, cut, crush, and boil cane steadily rose over the antebellum decades: from roughly 36,000 in 1830, 50,000 in 1840, to

125,000 in 1850. On the eve of the Civil War, more than a hundred enslaved African Americans resided on each Louisiana sugar plantation, up from the fifty-two enslaved typically found on a sugar plantation in 1830. This increase reflected both the expansion of the fields and the consolidation of lands by the wealthiest planters. While riding up the levee to Baton Rouge in April 1860, a reporter for the *New Orleans Crescent* marveled at the sugar plantations with their "long ranks of fifty to a hundred negroes, hoe in hand, working across the fields with almost the precision of military drill." By 1860, roughly five hundred planters controlled more than two-thirds of the enslaved and viable acreage in Louisiana's sugarcane country. As historian Richard Follett notes in his examination of the state's antebellum sugar planters, "Louisiana's sugar order left a brutal and exploitative imprint on those who worked the line and whose days were atomized, routinized, and divided by the ticking clock."[12]

The enslaved experimented with mixing foraged ingredients with sugar. A white northerner hired to teach English to the children of a French-speaking family on a Mississippi River sugar plantation during the 1850s recalled the production of orange flower syrup, a favorite springtime beverage. Enslaved children traversed the plantation's orange groves, using a long thorn to gather fallen orange blossom petals and depositing these in flat baskets. The plantation's "confectioner," an enslaved woman named Toinette, concocted syrups and candies with the sugar produced in the nearby fields. The northern tutor recalled, "A big fire of Copeau (shavings from hogsheads) would be made, and over this would be hung an enormous brass kettle filled with 'syrup naturel,' into which the children would empty their baskets of petals. In this way was made the delicious orange flower syrup, which was the favorite drink in warm weather." This technique enabled flavorful variations. The beverages were the products of African Americans' culinary ingenuity mixed with their foraging skills. For the owner of the enslaved, the drinks conveyed the hospitality of the planter family to their visitors while also displaying the abundance of their agricultural endeavor, both in terms of crops and their enslaved human property. The Yankee teacher noted, "When you call upon a Creole family on a warm summer day . . . you are sure to be served with iced orange flower water; a negro always brings it in on a tray, or the still more delicious violet syrup water, made in the same way with English violets as the orange flower syrup is made."[13]

The enslaved who lived on sugar plantations had ready access to sucrose. Coffee, sugar, and tobacco energized Black bodies for the tough manual labor required on a sugar plantation, especially when cane needed to be cut and processed quickly before a freeze damaged the crop. Pioneering landscapist Frederick Law Olmsted observed sugar harvesting on a visit to Louisiana in the 1850s: "During the grinding season extra rations of flour were served, and hot coffee was kept constantly in the sugar-house, and the hands on duty were allowed to drink it almost *ad libitum.*" Sylvia Handely, born into Louisiana slavery, recalled receiving "plenty of coffee and sugar" to energize her labors. Caffeine fueled the day-and-night, time-sensitive grinding process. Sucrose too powered the workers, providing an energy boost and extra calories to keep bodies at work. Olmsted witnessed, "They were also allowed to drink freely of the hot *sirop,* of which they were extremely fond. A generous allowance of sirop, or molasses, was also given out to them, with their other rations, every week during the winter and early summer." Field hands responsible for cutting the cane and hauling it to the boiling vats of the sugar house snagged cane as well. A New Orleans doctor observed how these enslaved laborers "have the cane stalks, abounding in juice, to eat at will." Yet consumption of the processed sugar and condensed syrup was more closely monitored, with access restricted "except by permission" of the master. Rations of tobacco provided an additional nicotine kick.[14]

Ownership of a human being became a valuable investment measured in the quantity of sugar each enslaved worker could press from the cane, often at brutal human cost. Sugar plantations exhibited a deadly drive to maximize output. As wealthy sugar planters outbid each other for replacement laborers, they pushed slave prices steadily upward during the antebellum period. In March 1853, *DeBow's Review,* a leading business journal based in New Orleans, referred to a particular plantation along the Mississippi River to demonstrate the relationship between product and labor: "Now, the Orange Grove plantation, a little below Donaldsonville, made the last season, with only 106 negroes, old and young, men, women, and children included, 725 hogsheads of first quality sugar, and 175 hogsheads of inferior brown sugar—900 hogsheads in all, of 1,000 lbs. each." Each hogshead was a wooden barrel packed with sugar. To emphasize this achievement, the editors clarified, "Five of the above-mentioned negroes walk on wooden legs."[15]

Sugar production ground human bodies as well as cane. Samuel Blackwell echoed this point. Blackwell, a resident of New Jersey who owned sugar refineries in England and the United States, regularly visited the Louisiana cane fields. He recounted that sugar masters were "*obliged* so to overwork their slaves, during the sugar-making season (from eight to ten weeks), as to *use them up* in seven or eight years." Blackwell continued, "For, they said, after the process is commenced, it must be pushed, without cessation, night and day; and we cannot afford to keep a sufficient number of slaves to do the *extra* work at the time of sugar-making, as we could not profitably employ them the rest of the year." The enslaved were literally worked to death.[16]

With imports of enslaved persons banned by Congress in 1808, potential masters looked for domestic sources of human chattel. A burgeoning internal trade sent enslaved African Americans southwestward from more established states, such as Virginia, Maryland, and Kentucky, that had a surplus of bondspeople. The escaped-slave-turned-abolitionist Frederick Douglass in 1855 described the coffles, a group of slaves chained together and marched from one place to another by slave traders: "You will see one of these human-flesh-jobbers, armed with pistol, whip, and bowie-knife, driving a company of a hundred men, women, and children, from the Potomac to the slave market at New Orleans." Douglass mourned the fate of the enchained: "They are food for the cotton-field and the deadly sugar-mill."[17]

New Orleans emerged as the largest slave market in North America, with sugar planters competing for the healthiest and strongest African Americans on the auction block. When William Waller of Amherst County, Virginia, sought to sell some of his enslaved people in 1847, a friend advised walking the coffle to Natchez, Mississippi, "the great mart of the state & a large proportion of Louisiana & you will come in compition [*sic*] with the sugar purchasers which are giving the highest prices." Increased industrialization and urbanization in northern states spurred the expansion of sugar production in Louisiana. In places like New York, Boston, and Philadelphia, natural population increase, waves of poor European immigrants, and migration off farms into factories heightened demand for cheap calories among the urban poor. The United States was not alone in confronting these nineteenth-century trends. The growth of the British working class due to similar factors pressed the empire's leaders to obtain more sugar and to accept labor conditions in sugar colonies that were similar to slavery in all but name for a century after abolishing the practice in 1833.[18]

The demand for Black bodies to man the sugar fields seemed insatiable. Planters preferred males aged in their late teens or twenties, those most able to bear the harsh demands of sugar production. As a result, the enslaved population in the rural sugar districts of Louisiana was predominantly male. For instance, men accounted for 56 percent of the enslaved in St. James Parish and 57 percent of the enslaved in St. John Parish. The opposite was true for Orleans Parish, home to the Crescent City, where women comprised more than 58 percent of the enslaved.[19]

When twentieth-century white New Orleanians imagined plantation scenes, they romanticized life in the ostentatious homes built by nineteenth-century sugar barons along the Mississippi River. Situated on the alluvial soil deposited by the Big Muddy, owners constructed mansions that heralded their wealth to the passing steamboats. As early as 1833, one traveler remarked on the "often pretty" buildings sprouting from the roughly 400 to 500 acres typical of sugar plantations. He observed, "The negro quarters are sometimes in rows, and painted or whitewashed, and quite neat; and Whitehall, a residence once of Gen. Wade Hampton, has a piazza all around the house, with pillars extending to the second story; and long avenues of trees extend from the river to other planters' houses, and around some you see small groves of orange-trees."[20] Even lesser homes set amid the lush scenery captivated passersby, such as the Bavarian organist Carl Weiss in 1870. He admired the sights as he journeyed upriver to New Orleans: "Orange groves, banana groves, cactus growths spread out between cottages—with their airy balconies, frame walls, and high windows—that lie among the widely spread sugar-cane plantations, mostly surrounded by a series of little, blindingly white houses, the former Negro quarters. Sugar refineries and cotton-gins become visible, and, since the river has many bends, one seems to be in the middle of a large lake, whose banks look picturesque." Such descriptions cast an Edenic light on sugar plantations.[21]

Sugar planters were generally supporters of secession but only tepidly. War threatened to disrupt the sugar trade, cutting off equipment supplies while also severing access to vital export markets. Conflict threatened the institution of slavery too. The wealth and political pull of the sugar masters had ensured the passage of protective tariffs that sheltered the domestic sugar economy from cheaper foreign sugar. The outbreak of fighting buoyed foreign competition as Americans looked for alternative sugar sources. In February 1861, as Louisiana seceded, Senator (and future president) Andrew Johnson of Tennessee rhetorically queried his fellow senators about Louisianans' betrayal of a nation that had protected its sugar investments: "Sir, what are the great wrongs that have been inflicted upon Louisiana?" Johnson sneered, "How much protection has she received upon her sugar? In order to give that protection, the poorest man throughout the United States is taxed for every spoonful that he uses to sweeten his coffee. How many millions, under the operation of a protection upon sugar, have been contributed to the wealth and prosperity of Louisiana?"

Sugar planters thus appreciated the benefits of the Union.[22] The outbreak of civil war disrupted the credit and commodities markets on which sugar growers relied. The arrival of Union troops in New Orleans in April 1862 eventually led to emancipation, eradicating the $100 million invested in human chattel by sugar planters. The number of working sugar plantations declined from roughly 1,200 to 175 during the war. Only a handful of the more than 500 factors responsible for marketing the sugar crop in 1860 remained in operation by 1864. Plantations fell into disrepair. Owners desperately sought to repay debts while negotiating new labor arrangements; some planters simply liquidated their holdings. Such sales during the 1860s and 1870s allowed men with wealth or political connections like Henry Clay Warmoth to elbow into the lucrative if risky sugar-growing business. Planters who held onto their lands diversified or entered sharecropping arrangements.[23]

Edward King, who wrote about his travels through Louisiana in the early 1870s, remarked that the Sugar Bowl had been "languishing because of the disorganization of labor, and because also of the division of large plantations into small farms." He observed that credit-strapped planters "ruined by the war . . . have allowed their sugar-houses to decay, and their splendid machinery to rust in ditches." Whereas Louisiana produced well over 200,000 hogsheads of sugar annually in the late 1850s and a peak of 459,000 hogsheads in 1861, the state produced fewer than 100,000 hogsheads annually in the late 1860s and barely more than 100,000 hogsheads annually during the 1870s.[24]

Although white planters predominated within Louisiana's Sugar Bowl, a small yet significant minority of Black planters squeezed their fortunes from cane fields. Some free persons of color fled San Domingo during the Haitian Revolution, settling in New Orleans and, most notably, along the Cane River in northern Louisiana. After the Civil War, a few free people of color and well-connected former enslaved persons started sugar plantations. The most prominent of these was Theophile Allain, the enslaved son of a wealthy planter in West Baton Rouge Parish born in 1846. His father had used Allain as a personal servant, allowing him to dine at the table and to accompany him to France. Privately educated after the Civil War, Allain entered the grocery trade and eventually assumed ownership of his father's plantation during the 1870s. The presence of such planters, concentrated largely in Iberville, Natchitoches, and Plaquemines Parishes, inspired dreams of economic development as African American merchants and factors emphasized the need to patronize businesses within the Black community to ensure racial uplift.[25]

Under financial strain, planters during the postbellum years asserted mastery over their fields. African American field hands in the sugar districts united to safeguard higher wages, even attracting the assistance of the Knights of Labor. In a particularly bloody clash that ended organized resistance to planters' control over African American life along the sugar-growing waterways, planters and their political allies murdered dozens of striking fieldworkers in the Thibodeaux Massacre of 1887. Nevertheless, as the sugar industry struggled to revive, planters faced a range of new competitors, making nostalgia over the praline's brown sugar all the more powerful.[26]

MODERN SUGAR

A New Orleans woman in 1927 in the *States* newspaper reported on the popularity of the praline in northern states and criticized northern confectioners' attempts to mimic the candy: "Yet the praline, like many of our cherished traditions, is 'suffering a sea-change into something new and strange.' . . . While it was originally made by old colored 'Mammies' by the simple process of cooking the pecans in slowly simmering brown sugar and water, it now has the foreign flavor of 'mapleine,' or an admixture of milk and butter, which compromises the fine flavor of the nut." The application of maple syrup, white sugar, or dairy products modernized the praline that had been made in the nineteenth century out of only water, brown sugar, and pecans. The newspaper warned that "too much adulteration by other ingredients causes the confection to lose all historic connection." The praline, which was synonymous with the brown sugar made on Louisiana plantations, was under threat as the state's Sugar Bowl faced unprecedented competition at home and abroad for access to the American sweet tooth.[27]

Ever since Europeans subjugated Caribbean islands and converted them to sugar production in the seventeenth century, the western desire for sucrose continued to intensify. In his pioneering study of sugar and empire, anthropologist Sidney Mintz showed that as "sugar became cheaper and more plentiful, its potency as a symbol of power declined while its potency as a source of profit gradually increased." Thus, where the grand banquet where du Plessis-Praslin introduced the earliest form of pralines evoked awe of regal might, the pralines of nineteenth- and twentieth-century New Orleans spurred entrepreneurship. Consumption of sugar spread "downward and outward" through the populace, with governments facilitating policies that shoveled ever more sugar to the poor as an act both "patriotic as well as profitable." Mintz observed, "The regular consumption of sugar, particularly of cheap brown sugar or treacle, even in modest quantities, gradually reduced sugar's status as a glamorous luxury." For the working class, sugar provided cheap calories on tight budgets. The simultaneous development of colonial plantations producing tea, coffee, and chocolate increased the demand for sugar while sweetening the palates of consumers. Before 1820, for example, the Exchange Coffee House in New Orleans occasionally served as an auction market for sugar. Supplies of sugar grew so rapidly that after the 1820s auctions usually occurred directly on the levees.[28]

U.S. sugar consumption reached staggering rates over the nineteenth and twentieth centuries. Per capita consumption of sugar in the United States increased from 9.5 pounds in 1822 to 32.6 pounds in 1860. In the early 1880s, Americans consumed 47.6 pounds of sucrose per person each year. Annual per capita consumption rose to 64.9 pounds during the 1890s when tales and recipes about pralines began to circulate. In the first years of the twentieth century, the figure rose to 72.5 pounds. By World War I, as candy companies squeezed independent African American praline sellers out of New Orleans's streets, Americans devoured 86.1 pounds of sugar per capita annually. A nation with such a sweet tooth was ripe for the mass marketing of brown sugar patties.[29]

Much to the consternation of Louisiana planters, however, the greater demand for sugar did not lead to higher prices after the Civil War. Rather, prices declined as beet sugar and foreign cane sugar flooded the U.S. market. Cane sugar brought 18 cents in 1864 and 8.5 cents in 1874, but the price dropped to 6.5 cents in the 1880s and to under 4 cents in the 1890s. Economic concerns led sugar producers to form the Louisiana Planters and Sugar Manufacturers Association in 1877. It coordinated efforts to lobby for protective tariffs, to encourage agricultural research and technological improvements, and to facilitate marketing of the crop through creation of the Louisiana Sugar Exchange. The association informed members and allies of its activities through publication of the weekly *Louisiana Planter and Sugar Manufacturer.* By 1890, the association had established the Sugar Experiment Station in New Orleans's Audubon Park, a facility that became the worldwide leader in sugarcane research for the next decade. Despite these efforts, production of a pound of sugar in Louisiana in 1914 cost more than 3.9 cents compared to roughly 2.8 cents in Puerto Rico, 2.7 cents in Hawaii, and 1.7 cents in Cuba, largely because of cheaper labor costs.[30]

Louisiana planters attempted to maximize profits by adopting more efficient agricultural techniques and new technologies capable of extracting more sugar of greater purity from the cane. They also expanded their acreage. Some growers even extended operations to virgin lands in southern Florida. With railroads reaching Miami by 1896, investors from Louisiana eyed newly accessible wetlands around Lake Okeechobee, with their rich soils and warmer climate better suited to sugarcane cultivation than the Louisiana fields that were prone to occasional freezes. The resulting overproduction of cane sugar drove prices downward, though with a significant but temporary spike upward during World War I, even as demand continued to increase. Financially stretched, the sugar industry consolidated over the late nineteenth and early twentieth centuries. Mill operators came to dominate the sugar trade.[31]

American imperialism presented challenges for Louisiana sugar planters in particular. Eager to join the land grab of European powers, the United States sought colonies of its own. American planters in Hawaii, fearing attempts by the native royalty to reclaim authority over the island chain, staged a successful coup in the 1890s: they immediately petitioned the U.S. government to protect their self-proclaimed Hawaiian republic. Hawaiian sugar thus became American sugar. The Spanish-American War of 1898, fought under the auspices of securing independence for Cuba, instead brought Cuba, Puerto Rico, and the Philippines under the control of the United States. American investors eyed these tropical lands as ideal for sugar production. Though protective tariffs restricted foreign sugar from entering the United States, these semi-colonial possessions enjoyed exemptions and discounts that allowed their sugar into the American market. When Cuba received a preferential tariff in 1903, the island supplied more than half the sugar consumed in the United States for the next several decades.[32]

Louisiana planters also faced competition from an entirely new source of sucrose: beets. Beets accounted for roughly 16 percent of global sugar production on the eve of the Civil War, rising to more than 54 percent by the 1890s. By the twentieth century, beet sugar accounted for 65 percent of all global sugar.[33]

Napoleon had pushed France's leading minds in the early nineteenth century to experiment with sourcing sugar from beets as he struggled to reestablish control over France's cane-sugar colonies. The French Revolution in 1789 had unleashed chaos within the Caribbean colonies, crown jewels of the French Empire because of the wealth produced by sugar plantations. Revolutionaries granted citizenship to wealthy free people of color in 1791. When many white planters refused to recognize this level of racial equality, civil war ensued within the colony of San Domingue, France's most valuable colony and key source of sugar. Enslaved persons there exploited the infighting to launch a rebellion. Resistance by white planters in the colonies grew fiercer when France's government abolished slavery within the empire in 1794. The rise of Napoleon created greater uncertainty. Napoleon reinstituted slavery in France's sugar-producing colonies in 1802. Restoration of France's profitable cane fields served to strengthen Napoleon's hold on France by satisfying the sweet tooth of a French populace ravaged by years of revolution, coups, and international wars. Napoleon similarly sought to placate colonial elites and their allies within France, particularly those from Martinique, the home of his wife Josephine. Restoration of the colonial sugar trade also promised to supplement imperial coffers as France faced costly wars from a range of European monarchies eager to crush the Bonapartists and restore the monarchy. Napoleon's reversal of emancipation strengthened the resolve of enslaved peoples championing the spirit of the French Revolution.[34]

The revolutionary cry of liberty, equality, and fraternity inspired the enslaved, with repercussions that reverberated in Louisiana. Napoleon, in 1802, had ordered his brother-in-law General Charles Leclerc and an army of more than 20,000 soldiers to San Domingue. Yellow fever decimated the troops and killed Leclerc, ending any hope of enforcing France's imperial hold on the colony. After hearing of Leclerc's death, Napoleon exclaimed, "Damn sugar! Damn coffee! Damn colonies!" Without a sizable army in the Americas, Napoleon decided to sell Louisiana to the United States in 1803.[35]

The enslaved defeated the planters in San Domingue in 1804. Their new republic, called Haiti, was the second country to win independence in the Americas after the United States. Thousands of whites and free Black allies from San Domingue, along with their many slaves, fled to nearby Cuba. After several years, Spanish officials governing Cuba expelled them: nine thousand San Domingue exiles then settled in New Orleans in 1809–1811. Others moved to Baltimore and other American cities. To accommodate this influx, the United States exempted the refugees from the ban on slave imports enacted in 1808. The expertise of these planters and their enslaved workers bolstered Louisiana sugar production. Their arrival also rejuvenated the cultural hold of French Creoles over Louisiana society. Many of the white Creoles celebrated by the literati of the late nineteenth century dated to this influx.[36]

Beets offered a solution to the sugar shortage confronted by Napoleon, given the revolt of enslaved persons within the sugar colonies and a British naval blockade that hampered access to France's Caribbean islands. Even with Napoleon dethroned by 1815, French leaders continued to pursue national self-sufficiency regarding sugar. By the 1850s, France's domestic production of sugar from beets surpassed the importation of colonial sugar from cane. As in all the imperial nations of Europe, sugar sustained and satiated the growing masses at a time of widespread calls for labor unity and democratic reform.[37]

Germany too seized on the beet as key to the emerging nation's future. German scientists pioneered methods to maximize the sucrose content of beets in the mid-nineteenth century. As Otto von Bismarck pursued unification of Germanic lands, with successful wars against Denmark (1864), Austria-Hungary (1866), and France (1870–1871), he encouraged the largely landlocked and easily blockaded but expanding nation to develop its own sugar crop to meet the demands of a modern consumer-state facing calls for democratic reforms. German officials eyed the sparsely settled lands of eastern Prussia, in what is today Poland, as ideal for beet cultivation. German politicians and business leaders used the Jim Crow South as an exemplar of efficient agricultural production of a staple crop, even bringing African American scholar W. E. B. Du Bois to study in Berlin so as to hear his perspective on racial conditions and to learn about crop cultivation in Dixie. Graduates from Booker T. Washington's Tuskegee Institute also assisted Germany in its imperial plans. By the early twentieth century, these eastern Prussian fields produced bountiful crops of sugar beets, making Germany a leading power within the sugar market.[38]

The emancipation of enslaved persons throughout the Americas further shifted markets away from the New World's sugarcane fields. As mentioned, Great Britain abolished slavery within its empire in 1833. France permanently abolished slavery in 1848. The Dutch followed in 1863, freeing the enslaved in Suriname and the Dutch Antilles. The Spanish colony of Cuba banned slavery in 1886. The former Portuguese colony of Brazil terminated slavery in 1888. Forced to pay wages (even if meager) and unable (technically under the law) to apply the lash, post-emancipation planters confronted labor resistance that challenged their conviction that force maximized sugar production—all at a time when beet sugar was undercutting prices. As former colonies gained independence and the formerly enslaved competed for governing roles within these new republics, European nations safeguarded their supplies of sugar by cultivating even greater domestic sources.

The statistics on European beet-sugar production chronicle a remarkable agricultural expansion during the nineteenth century. In 1826, France produced a mere 1,500 tons of beet sugar; by 1879, it was cultivating 420,396 tons. More than 30 percent of the sugar consumed by western nations in the 1880s came from beets. In 1889, France ranked third in beet-sugar production, refining 700,000 tons. Austria-Hungary reaped 730,000 tons. Germany produced more than 1.2 million tons of beet sugar, the most sugar of any nation in the world. Germany, Austria-Hungary, and France had become net exporters of sugar by the 1890s.[39]

More disconcerting for Louisiana sugar planters, American farmers too seized the opportunity afforded by sugar beets. Midwestern farmers from Kansas to Indiana successfully experimented with the crop. In 1899, a researcher for the U.S. Department of Agriculture examined the role of sugar in the American diet. She noted that two-thirds of the nation's sugar, like much of that in the rest of the western world at the turn of the century, derived from the sugar beet. She mused, "It would once have seemed incredible that the kitchen garden should furnish a rival for the 'noble plant' that had made the fortunes of Spanish and English colonists, but the cultivation of the beet has in one generation shifted the center of the sugar industry from the tropic to the temperate zone." The engineering and processing of beets emerged as a technological marvel of the industrial age. The government expert concluded, "The manufacture of sugar is now a chemical industry as much as is tanning and dyeing." Sugar was losing its association with the plantation.[40]

Worse, sugarcane planters faced stiff competition not only from foreign cane sugar and domestic beet sugar but also from a growing industry that derived glucose by heavily processing corn. Glucose manufacturing from corn developed as an industry during the 1880s, though with skepticism from American consumers. This changed in the twentieth century as producers heavily marketed their wares to win over the public, signposted by the launch in 1903 of Karo Syrup by the Corn Products Refining Company—headquartered in New York with manufacturing operations outside Chicago. The term *glucose,* long condemned as a food adulterant, soon gave way to the unsullied terms *corn syrup, fructose, dextrose,* and *starch sugar.* But for sugarcane planters the threat remained the same: it was a new consumer product that competed for Americans' sweet tooth.[41]

Technological advances in refining sugar within the United States encouraged the establishment of large processing plants at major railroad hubs with easy access to cheap unskilled labor and to multiple sources of cane or beets. Quantity mattered because corporate profits depended on volume. In the antebellum era, Louisiana's wealthiest planters operated mills on their plantations, offering to process cane from nearby smaller growers and giving their sugar a terroir. After the Civil War, planters banded together to share the costs of establishing larger, centralized mills using the latest technology and taking advantage of new railways. However, improvements to national transportation networks along with the consolidation of the railroad and sugar-refining industries, spurred by the depressions of the 1870s and then the 1890s, facilitated the rise of mills operated by corporations far from the fields where sugar cane or beets were grown.

Louisiana's planters in the late nineteenth century became subject to the demands of the American Sugar Refining Company, otherwise known as the Sugar Trust. Its small number of mills operating from New York and other large Northeast cities dominated the market. With ample lines of credit, the newest equipment, and access to cheap urban labor, the Sugar Trust dictated sugar prices. By 1900, the Trust controlled roughly 80 percent of Louisiana's raw sugar. By 1907, it purchased through various means roughly 98 percent of raw sugar produced within the United States. The trust flooded the market with cheap refined sugar to drive out competition and set the price for refining nationwide. Independent mills servicing local or even regional markets could not compete. Louisiana's sugar planters were largely at the mercy of large refinery corporations working to ensure a monopoly on price.[42]

Congressional hearings on the Sugar Trust in 1911 allowed Louisiana planters to air their grievances but to no avail. Although white southerners generally applauded the election of fellow southerner and Democrat Woodrow Wilson to the presidency, he pushed for the Underwood-Simmons Tariff Act in 1913, which annually reduced the tariff on sugar until its complete removal in 1916: this legislation decimated Louisiana planters as sugar flooded the United States. Wartime demand temporarily bolstered prices. As peace came to Europe, however, depression conditions spread across Louisiana's Sugar Bowl as commodity prices plummeted.[43]

A variety of problems struck planters who persisted in raising cane into the 1920s. Poor weather conditions, mosaic disease, and the Mississippi River flood of 1927 ravaged Louisiana fields. Land on which Louisiana's southernmost plantations depended also suffered from severe subsidence. The artificial levees meant to protect the fields from floods halted soil deposits from overflowing waterways. The marshy backlands of plantations witnessed a slow encroachment of brackish water by the early twentieth century. This necessitated more levees, more canals, and more pumps, thereby raising the costs of maintenance.

Subsidence worsened with development of the diesel engine during the 1890s. Diesel engines revolutionized barge traffic and spurred construction of navigable canals. Congress passed the Rivers and Harbors Act of 1909, launching development of the Intracoastal Waterway from Boston to Brownsville, Texas, which was completed in 1949. As early as the late 1920s, a channel connected New Orleans to eastern Texas and westward to the Florida Panhandle as the oil industry expanded. New channels off the waterway were dug, worsening the potential for saltwater encroachment, subsidence, and pollution within the Sugar Bowl. Oil wildcatters joined trappers and loggers in cutting paths through the marsh. These incursions turned the soil of some plantations into a briny wasteland. One planter explained to popular author Harnett Kane the pain of seeing crystallized salt form in his fields: "When I saw that, I decided to leave. . . . I could deal with everything else—enemies in business, brokers, labor. But not the Gulf of Mexico." At a time when New Orleanians celebrated the praline made of plantation sugar, sugar growers in Louisiana faced near-collapse.[44]

BROWN SUGAR, WHY DO YOU TASTE SO GOOD?

Lafcadio Hearn capitalized on American interest in the New Orleans exposition of 1884–1885 by publishing *La Cuisine Creole: A Collection of Culinary Recipes,* a foundational text documenting New Orleans cuisine. Recipes for gumbo and jambalaya appear, as do concoctions called Louisiana Orange-Flower Macaroons and Louisiana Hard-Times Cake. Hearn, noting that the book "partakes of the nature of its birthplace—New Orleans—which is cosmopolitan," also includes such items as Boston Caramels, Wisconsin Fruit Cake, Irish Stew, German Ladies' Fingers, and Sicilian Biscuits. Yet Hearn ignores pralines. This was no oversight. After all, Hearn's introduction to the cookbook claims to aid the "young housekeeper to learn the art of cooking" by presenting to "her a number of recipes all thoroughly tested by experience, and embracing the entire field of the 'Cuisine.'"[45]

Like Hearn, the women of the Christian Woman's Exchange of New Orleans excluded pralines from the recipes gathered for *The Creole Cookery Book,* the other pioneering cookbook published in 1885 shortly after Hearn's compilation. The women preface their publication by noting that the recipes were published so that these "should cease to be the hereditary lore of our negro mammies, and should be allowed its proper place in the gastronomical world." Nevertheless, the praline, so synonymous with African American street peddlers and venerated as a treat enjoyed by Creole elites, is not included. Like Hearn, the women were unaware of the praline, even as the cookbook preserved "what is best in the Creole and American cuisine."[46]

These absences reflected the still-marginal status of pralines; they were not yet a staple of Creole households in New Orleans. The confection had yet to reach beyond the African American community that had fled Louisiana's sugar plantations. Possibly, Hearn and the members of the Christian Women's Exchange decided that white female consumers visiting New Orleans for the exposition would cringe at a recipe associated with working-class Black women. But Hearn's multicultural background and acceptance of African Americans, both in his personal and literary life, indicate that he had more likely excluded a praline recipe because the treat remained obscure beyond a few African Americans with the know-how to perfect the brittle patty of foraged pecans and plantation sugar. After all, none of the numerous travel accounts of New Orleans, despite their detailed attention to the city's foodways and its marchandes, mentioned the confection until the 1880s.

The New Orleans exposition was a turning point for the praline: northern tourists pursued local flavors, Hearn and the Christian Woman's Exchange looked to profit by filling bookshelves with Creole recipes from New Orleans, and Black street vendors likely responded to the influx of thousands of travelers by crowding the streets and popularizing a confection born on the plantations. The praline of brown sugar and pecans suddenly entered New Orleans lore.

The sudden popularity of the praline among whites from the late 1880s onward rested partly on intensifying Lost Cause nostalgia for the Old South after the collapse of Reconstruction. By the 1890s, sectional reconciliation celebrated a shared national interest in white supremacy as the country pursued overseas colonies. To understand the stereotyping of the praline peddler as a mammy requires grappling with the equally important cultural meaning given to brown sugar in the late nineteenth and early twentieth centuries.[47]

The two paintings decorating the Louisiana Pavilion at the Jamestown Exposition hosted by Virginia in 1907 highlight the link between plantation sugar, African American laborers, and the New Orleans praline as imagined by white Louisianans. These artworks were the creation of John Pemberton, a New Orleanian born in 1873 and affiliated for much of his life with the local art scene. H. Chapman Williams, reporting for the *Item,* cheered that the painter had "reached the heights of Louisiana realism when he produced 'The Cane Cart' and the "Praline Woman,' subjects to inspire emotions in the heart of the wandering Louisianian." Nearby a display celebrated the state's productivity in a "miniature cane field showing the darkies at work."[48]

The highly refined and consistent purity of industrialized sugar increased consumers' focus on the whiteness of modern sugar after the Civil War. Even in Louisiana, some marketers celebrated white sugar as a symbol of purity at a time of concern over food adulteration. The purity of the sugar marked a selling point within a crowded market for sweets. The Nutqueet Company in 1919 emphasized that the firm's pralines consisted of healthful, pure cane sugar: "IT'S GOOD, WHOLESOME AND INEXPENSIVE." The business stressed that the candy was "ABSOLUTELY PURE" and "CLEAN," as well as "SCIENTIFICALLY MADE UNDER MODERN CONDITIONS." Such emphasis on purity was code for white. Louise Cook's, a candy shop at 114 University Place, made this connection clear, linking whiteness with cleanliness and well-being. "The doctor will tell you the praline made of pure white sugar and wholesome pecans is a nourishing confection for your growing children," chimed a promotional blurb from 1929. To hammer the point, the proprietor emphasized that the pralines "are as pure as they are delicious." But such celebrations of white sugar were rare in regard to pralines.[49]

Brown sugar symbolized a Louisiana agricultural product resistant to the homogeneity of industrialized refinement represented by white sugar, even if many of those same planters invested in mills and marketed cane to corporations to produce the seemingly purest, whitest sugar. Sugar producers for much of the nineteenth century relied on the Dutch Color Standard. The Standard used a series of sealed, clear glass jars containing a range of sugars of different hues produced by brokers in Amsterdam with the sanction of the Dutch government. These jars measured the supposed quality of sugar based on color, from least valuable (dark brown) to most valuable (white). Congress applied the Standard to grade sugars under a tariff passed in 1861. Yet color was no sure measure of sucrose content, and importers began darkening sugar shipments to avoid high tariffs. Soon the U.S. government added the chemical analysis of sugar through polariscopes and saccharimeters to their assessment methods, though it did not abandon the Standard until 1909. Thus, the popular perception that the color of sugar represented the degree of sweetness and quality remained strong and still lingers, with white sugar perceived as the purest and sweetest. Celebrating brown sugar evened the playing field for Louisiana planters competing over price in a consumer market increasingly dominated by the Sugar Trust.[50]

The brown color of the less refined plantation sugar typically used for pralines reinforced its agrarian and racial connotations. Brown sugar recalled a social system of racial hierarchy rooted in plantation fields. Promoters of beet sugar presented their crop as a more civilized sugar grown by hard-working white farmers in temperate zones, in contrast to sugar cane that was rooted in tropical zones populated by peoples of color associated with indolence, decay, and racial decline. In *The Aryans and Mongrelized America,* published under the pseudonym Junius Aryan in Philadelphia in 1912, the author argues that "beet sugar is better for the Aryan stomach and other digestive organs than the cane sugars of the tropics, and the getting and using of cane sugars from the tropics for an Aryan people's stomach and digestive organs is unnatural, as the acids of the tropical cane sugars are more detrimental to Aryan stomachs and other digestive organs than the acids of beet sugars indigenous to the Aryan country." Race and place were thus inseparable. For this reason, the writer makes a slight concession by claiming that the "cane sugar of Louisiana and Texas, being grown in the extreme northern part of the cane sugar zone, is very much better for the Aryan digestive organs, than the cane sugar farther south and in the tropics." Nevertheless, the racial politics of the cane versus beet sugar debate cast doubt on the quality of sugars raised by Black hands, even though the sugars were scientifically identical.[51]

Indeed, the color of many edibles carried racial and class implications. Within folk religious practices, white and brown items were believed to have power over the two races. A woman who performed conjuring in New Orleans during the early twentieth century emphasized the importance of applying "brown sugar for colored people—for white people . . . white sugar." Similar prescriptions involved using pepper or salt, brown or white eggs, and other racialized pairings.[52] Food scholar Jennifer Wallach notes that in the Jim Crow South even a common, brown-tinged white sauce "might have had some potentially subversive connotations or may have functioned as a culinary commentary about American racism." Such racialized references to food could be both highly political and seemingly mundane and commercialized. The New Orleans bakery chain McKenzie's in the 1950s, for instance, marketed a Congo Pie described as two devil's food cake layers with vanilla cream trapped in the middle, referencing an intensifying decolonization movement in the Belgian Congo at a time when the U.S. civil rights struggle was also gaining momentum.[53]

Food references that allowed white consumers to devour figurative Black bodies, as implied by darkly hued foods, affirmed white supremacy even while recognizing the dependence of white society on the sustenance provided by Blacks' labor. Florence King, a white southerner growing up in the 1940s, recalled a popular licorice candy shaped as Black children sold by the Woolworth chain: "Everybody privately called them 'nigger babies.'" For many white southerners, Brazil nuts were called "nigger toes" into the late twentieth century. Even some companies adopted such lingo. A firm with operations in Baltimore and Biloxi marketed the "Nigger Head" brand of canned oysters, produced from the 1890s into the 1950s.[54] "Nigger Head" and other racialized brands from the late nineteenth and early twentieth centuries bore labels produced by the lithography firm Walle and Company of New Orleans. According to one historian, the business "virtually cornered the market as producers of lithographed labels for all types of canned products" across the United States.[55]

The link between brown sugar and Black bodies is particularly strong. American opponents of slavery long condemned the labor system as a "form of social cannibalism," as literary scholar Vincent Woodward states. As the consumption of sugar increased, Americans devoured more and more of the sugarcane raised by plantations powered by forced labor. Antebellum consumers of sugar pushed Black bodies to their breaking point, intertwining sugar and Blackness. Kyla Wazana Tompkins, another scholar of American culture, notes the "common troping of the black body as sweet." Whites' fear of Blackness, most manifest in the paranoia over slave revolts, clashed with their desire for Blackness, in terms of owning both the bodies of the enslaved and the goods produced by Black bodies. The solution, according to Tompkins, was for white popular culture "to actually internalize and obliterate blackness." Emancipation heightened this cultural cannibalism among white Americans as freed persons then claimed social and political equality. Representations in literature, advertising, art, and other media during the Jim Crow era worked to keep Blackness consumable and thus controllable. Doing so, however, raised contradictions given Blacks' humanity and, Tompkins argues, caused whites "indigestion" as African Americans resisted, as evident by the defiance of Mary Louise, the praline seller at Newcomb College.[56]

Few have captured the historical connections linking sugar, consumerism, labor, and race as powerfully as African American artist Kara Walker. Her celebrated sculpture "A Subtlety, or the Marvelous Sugar Baby" from 2014 appeared in the cavernous warehouse of the defunct Domino Sugar refinery in Brooklyn, New York. Built in the 1880s, the building was the largest sugar refinery in the world. It was owned by the American Sugar Refining Company, a corporation considered such a bellwether for the U.S. economy that it became one of the twelve original members of the Dow Jones Industrial Average. In the vernacular of the time, the company was *the* Sugar Trust. The artwork's title references a European culinary practice during the Middle Ages of creating ornate figures crafted from sugar. It was an era when sugar—whether eaten or shaped into a subtlety, a sculpture formed from foods—suggested imperial might and luxury, as Marshal du Plessis-Praslin demonstrated while awing rebels in Bordeaux with sugar-coated nuts in 1649.[57]

Walker's sculpture mimics the massive size of the sugar refining industry built on Black labor and racial imagery. A journalist visiting the installation, formed from forty tons of white sugar standing thirty-five feet tall and seventy-five feet long, marveled at the "Sphinx creature with the kerchiefed head of a mammy figure, her breasts naked, her vulva prominent . . . a chimera of unvarnished American desires, protected by an infantry of black-boy figurines carrying agricultural bounty." The Sphinx not only references ancient Africa but also the riddle of racial meanings buried within sugar. Walker offers no captions or fliers explaining the work but lets observers interpret the object for themselves. The design makes visible the laborers of color who grew the sugarcane that fed Americans' unsatiable hunger for sucrose during the nineteenth and twentieth centuries. The location in a sugar refinery, the site where brown sugar turned white, references cultural cannibalism. To emphasize this point, the childlike workers around the white sphinx are coated in dark molasses. These figures display numerous deformities, reflecting the physical harms inflected on sugarcane workers by planters like those in Louisiana. Walker further undermines racial stereotypes by exhibiting the mammy's long-denied sexuality. The subtle meanings conveyed by sugar were on display in a public exhibition that challenged viewers to ponder the historical meanings of food, where it came from, how it is processed, and who suffers and who benefits. Walker's work exposes the "terrors of sentimentalist history," a history on which the sugar growers of Louisiana and tourism boosters of New Orleans heavily relied during Jim Crow.[58]

The crises confronting Louisiana sugar planters in the late nineteenth and early twentieth centuries made the New Orleans praline symbolic of a traditional way of life that was fading in the face of urbanization and mechanization, consolidation and competition within the expanding American empire. By the 1890s, white Louisianans generally yearned for the sugar produced by area plantations. Brown sugar was traditional, the type of sugar that was widely available before heavy industrialization made white sugar ubiquitous and cheap. S. W. Clark and Sons, in 1899, advertised that their two stores in New Orleans offered sugar "received by us direct from the plantation." Such emphasis became standard marketing in the early twentieth century.[59]

The use of cane sugar from Louisiana plantations accentuated the authenticity of the praline. Thomas H. Handy and Company on Royal Street promoted their "Original Sazerac Creole Pralines" by stressing that they were made "of choice pecans and pure Louisiana sugar."[60] The Grunewald Hotel in 1918 offered via its grocery department "our famous Grunewald Creole Pralines, made of the finest Louisiana Cane Sugar and Pecans." A promotion a year later beckoned, "Our pralines are 'made,' not manufactured by machines. Scrupulous care is maintained throughout in producing this famous candy. That's why Original Creole Pralines (Grunewald), made only of Louisiana cane sugar and Louisiana (whole half) pecan meats, are regarded everywhere as the highest quality Creole Pralines made." Not that production was on a small scale. The Grunewald reassured customers that pralines could be made in quantities sufficient for large conventions: "The daily output of Original Creole Pralines (Grunewald) is forty thousand (maximum)." Tours of the "Candy Kitchen" celebrated the production line.[61] Yorkman Candy Company noted that its Creole pralines were "real" because of "pure Louisiana sugar and the finest pecans, following the original recipe handed down from earliest days." Solari's in 1928 harped on its Creole pralines formed from "pure sugar from Louisiana plantations and paper-shelled pecans."[62] Elmer and Company promised that its "Dixie delicacies," including pecan pralines, were "all made of sugar from our own plantations." In 1930, the firm emphasized the use of "Louisiana Open Kettle Sugar and selected Louisiana pecans." The praline had become the ultimate embodiment of the Louisiana sugar plantation.[63]

Given the association of brown sugar with plantations populated by people of color—a people believed by whites to be less sexually inhibited than them—it is not surprising that white flappers of the 1920s adopted the hue labeled "praline." It emerged as a fashionable color popular with the New Woman who was elbowing her way into political, social, and economic spheres of American life. American women adopted the trendy styles of Paris to display their sophistication, fashion sense, sexuality, and independence. And Parisians—long familiar with New Orleans and captivated by Josephine Baker, jazz, and so-called primitivism—turned praline into a trendy hue that linked the supposed looser sexual mores of people of color with the supposed natural sweetness and innocence of white women. For example, the early and mid-twentieth century marked a time when tanning suggested racial play. Whites browned themselves and adopted, briefly, stereotypical traits associated with people of color by indulging in food, sex, or rest. Scholars term this attitude toward tanning "brown-face." The growing cosmetics industry assisted with such racial play.[64] The transformation provided by donning praline-colored makeup and clothes permitted white women to transgress, temporarily, boundaries of propriety. As Corinne Lowe informed readers of the *Item* in November 1925, "Do you know that pink which often appears in the ensemble costume of a chocolate bonbon? Well, this tone, known by the French as praline, has made its appearance for the winter." Holland, a clothier for women located on Canal Street, echoed the celebration of the color praline in 1928 by announcing it as the "new beige." The color remained all the rage in Parisian fashion circles: "Paris calls the newest and most delectable of colors. . . Praline . . . a sugary brown Praline . . . just like the Old New Orleans candy of that name." The use of the color in a stylish outfit created a result "simply delicious and newly feminine." Another clothier in New Orleans offered hosiery for women in "Praline Beige," which was all the more important to don because "of the trend of shorter skirts."[65]

The transformation of the praline from a confection to a color opened even more opportunities to market Louisiana and New Orleans, especially as tourism skyrocketed during the interwar years. In 1926, the *Times-Picayune* advocated that women don clothing in colors that promoted their community: "If you want to advertise Louisiana and the Gulf coast to your friends at a distance, the way is easy. Have your dress made of Creole and wear it with a sugar cane scarf embroidered in plantation." The newspaper explained that "Creole is about the color of newly-made pralines, and sugar cane is a pinkish buff, while plantation is a dark ruddy brown." Marjorie Roehl, advising readers of the *Item* about fashion in 1941, boasted that women across the United States wore "'Louisiana' styles." She reported on designer-photographer Truman Bailey who came to the state to create a new line of dresses. He promoted colors named "plantation yellow, bayou blue, swamp green, and Creole red." Bailey offered women a hat modeled on the praline seller seen at Jackson Square. Roehl explained, "It's a variation of the tignon, or bandanna, as the ancient Negro women have worn them for generations, and it's far more becoming than the present bandanna. The bow can be placed rakishly in back or demurely in front, where the two stick-up ends give an angelic effect." This was not all. The fashion conscious could add an accessory: "A tiny mammy head gives promise of being A No 1 costume jewelry."[66]

By donning clothes or cosmetics shaded praline, white women presented themselves as sweet and alluring—a candy to be devoured or savored in the pursuit of what cultural observers at the time labeled "sex appeal." White women donning praline-colored cosmetics or clothes during the flapper era and afterward thus announced their sexuality—a tempting sweetness to be enjoyed. In 1952, for example, the milliner popularly known as Mr. John, who designed hats for Vivien Leigh in *Gone with the Wind,* revealed his southern-themed designs, with New Orleans receiving top billing. Confederate flags decorated his New York City showroom as pralines, mammy dolls, and head kerchiefs were distributed to patrons. Colors were described as praline brown, camellia pink, honeysuckle white, and Dixie red. Any white woman could be a southern belle, a temptress akin to Scarlett O'Hara.[67]

By the late nineteenth century, sugar had become culturally associated with women. Whereas alcohol and tobacco were viewed as male pleasures, sugar, especially in the form of candies and desserts, was an indulgence best enjoyed by females. Michel De Lucas's business in the suburban Carrollton neighborhood in the 1890s captured well the gendered divide in stimulants. He invited streetcar riders to his Ladies' Refreshment Saloon, where he offered cakes, candies, ice cream, and soda water. In smaller print at the bottom of his advertisement, he eased the concerns of any male company: "Also a Fine Assortment of Havana Cigars, Cigarettes, Tobacco, Etc." This association of sugar with femininity permeated twentieth-century American culture. When Vice President Gerald Ford and his wife visited New Orleans in May 1974, he received a basket with "doubloons, stereo jazz albums featuring Ronnie Kole, Al Hirt, Pete Fountain, and the Olympia Brass Band." Betty Ford, in contrast, received a "Creole cookbook and a box of creamy pralines."[68]

Louisiana sugar plantations by the twentieth century stood apart from the male world of modern, industrial growth in the popular imagination. The mechanized fields that made Mark Twain stand in wonder during the 1880s were now reimagined as quaint, romantic attractions meant more for the enjoyment of women. When the Southern Industrial Convention convened in New Orleans in 1900, organizers arranged a tour for the wives, described in a brochure with a flyleaf featuring a "typical etching of a 'praline woman,' with all her dainty wares ranged before her, and the great palmetto fan with which she is keeping cool and fresh her beautiful pink and white pralines." As men discussed industrial development, the women trekked to a plantation. Visiting and observing the source of sweetness were appropriate for the ladies while their husbands talked business. The last page of the "pretty leaflet tells of the programme arranged for the plantation trip, when the day will be spent in visiting the plantations and sugar-houses, where sugar any [*sic*] syrup-making will be seen in every stage." The Louisiana display at the Purchase Centennial Exposition at St. Louis in 1904, in another example, presented a "field of cane made of wax with negroes cutting the same, and from this field there is a train of cars carrying cane to the sugar-house." A functioning mill demonstrated the crushing and processing of sugarcane. But the centerpiece, a statue of Louisiana gendered as a woman, equated femininity and sweetness. Visitors gazed on "commercial samples of plantation and refined sugars, and a life-size model of 'Miss Louisiana' made of sugar."[69]

Such gendering of sugar carried profound implications. Commenting on the rise of the U.S. candy industry during the late nineteenth century, historian Wendy Woloson notes, "Not only did sugar's feminization objectify women, but it also made them saccharine—nonessential, decorative, sweet, ethereal, and generally lacking in substance." Not until the late 1910s, as a substitute for alcohol and as a ration for soldiers fighting in World War I, would candy consumption by men gain acceptance. Yet the link between sweets and femininity remained strong, as a visit to shops on Valentine's Day confirms. This gendering of sugar influenced popular perceptions of African American praline peddlers. Brown sugar and brown skin became synonymous. The Black saleswoman's stronger association with the praline than with the variety of other homemade goods she peddled hurt her efforts to attain economic equality, at least within the white imagination of Jim Crow New

Orleans. Instead, as Woloson alludes, she became decorative, a hollow foil to the vital role that the marchandes served within the city.[70]

PLANTATION SUGAR REBORN

The story of the praline is inseparable from the history of Louisiana plantations and the popular perceptions of those plantations' most-prized product—brown sugar. Journalist John Lester noted in 1945 that within New Orleans some considered pralines to be "sugar envelopes with pecans enclosed." As envelopes, the praline carried messages about New Orleans and Louisiana that reflected local whites' longing for the plantation days of yore and a noble French past. Although whites generally applied their own meanings to plantations and brown sugar, the African American praline sellers had seized on the crop to chase the American dream of freedom and prosperity. Their entrepreneurship was repeatedly thwarted, but their ingenuity laid the foundation for the praline industry so central to New Orleans tourism.[71]

The 1920s marked the nadir of the Louisiana sugar industry. The state's sugar plantations had long depended on a single variety of plant, with growers wary of switching from a time-tested variety. From the late 1700s through the 1820s, Creole cane dominated the fields. Black Cheribon, also called Louisiana Purple, served as the standard variety of sugarcane used within the state from the 1830s through the 1890s. G. B. Sartoris, a pathologist specializing in sugarcane in the early twentieth century, noted that the "sugar cane industry of the United States was founded upon it [Black Cheribon]." In 1898, D-74, a cane variety developed in British Guiana, became the planters' preference. The scientific name—a mere letter and number—reflected the advent of modern research into the creation of hybrids best suited to specific areas of the United States; this trend was evident throughout the agricultural sector as corporations, governments, and universities honed their programs in the late nineteenth century. Each new variety upped the production of sugar and its heartiness for Louisiana's environment. The drawback came in greater susceptibility to new diseases because growers tended to plant and stick to the same variety. The onset of mosaic disease crippled Louisiana's planters during the 1920s, plunging production from 324,000 tons of sugar in 1921 to 47,000 tons of sugar in 1926. Desperate planters quickly turned to a range of varieties, some thirty-four being introduced between 1926 and 1978, in contrast to only ten varieties developed between 1742 and 1940. The introduction of cane varieties resistant to mosaic, along with better land management through crop rotation and application of the latest scientific research, led to a rapid revival in sugar production and increased acreage devoted to cane during the 1930s.[72] The resurrection of the Louisiana sugar industry after the 1920s also depended on mechanizing the fields. The introduction of the mechanical harvester during the 1930s and 1940s increased the speed and efficiency of harvests while reducing a dependence on manual labor.[73]

Improved tractors and other equipment further increased efficiency. The Great Migration of African Americans to nearby New Orleans and especially to northern and western cities— mainly Chicago, Detroit, and Los Angeles—spurred planters to "do something about labor," in the words of David Pipes, president of the American Cane Sugar Cane League in 1927.[74] The coming of New Deal regulations along with the continued out-migration of Black workers reinforced calls for mechanization. Cost increases from mechanization spurred consolidation, reducing the number of sugarcane farms from more than 10,000 in 1937 to only 2,686 by 1959, with the average acreage per farm increasing from 28 to 101 acres. The number of sugar mills dropped from 92 in 1937 to 47 in 1959, with grinding capacity increasing from 57,000 to 116,000 tons per mill. The completion of the Intracoastal Waterway in 1949 cut through Louisiana's Sugar Bowl, decreasing the costs of shipping sugar by barge to area refineries.[75]

Congressmen and senators from Louisiana labored tirelessly to shelter the remaining planters by advocating for federal subsidies and tariffs on sugar imports. In 1968, Louisiana led all states in the production of sugar cane and pecans, but fewer planters reaped the wealth from white gold. Louisiana contained only 202 sugar plantations with 44 processing factories. In 1993, the state claimed only eighty-two sugar plantations with twenty factories. Sugar planting, whether for owners or workers, white or Black, was no longer a way of life for many Louisianans.[76]

Yet the racial connotations of brown sugar remained largely intact throughout the twentieth century. The Rolling Stones, for example, scored a massive hit with the rock song "Brown Sugar," recorded in Muscle Shoals, Alabama, in 1969. After asking why brown sugar tastes so good, the lyrics describe the Middle Passage of an enslaved African woman sold in the markets in New Orleans, where she is whipped and forced to provide sexual labor. The cravings for this brown sugar—Black female sexuality—prove as insatiable as the desire for the crystalline commodity. The vocal trio Labelle echoed the message with "Lady Marmalade" in 1974, a hit about a Creole of color in New Orleans. Recorded in the Crescent City and featuring local musicians, the song describes her calling in French to passersby as she attempts to sell her sexual services. The lyrics reference the sweetness not only of marmalade but also of skin shaded like café au lait. This lady of the evening is explicitly linked to mocha and chocolate. As with the lingering popularity of "Brown Sugar" into the twenty-first century, "Lady Marmalade" persists on the airwaves and received new life when Mya, Christina Aguilera, and Lil' Kim scored their own hit with the song in 2001.

Although the praline seller was desexualized within white New Orleanians' imagination, her body and her pralines nevertheless served as a vessel to satisfy fantasies of a romanticized Old South and a tranquil New South. That seeming tranquility under Jim Crow partly depended on the literati emphasizing the advanced age and portliness of these Black peddlers while highlighting maternal traits over sexual allure. As scholars have long noted, the stereotype of the mammy as elderly and overweight not only conveyed that Blacks had seemingly enjoyed good health as well as benevolent care from whites under slavery and Jim Crow but also countered any sexual appeal or sexual availability. This emphasis was particularly important given the prominence of women of color sold as sex slaves in antebellum New Orleans and working the city's notorious red-light district Storyville from the 1890s through the 1910s. National awareness of sexually available Black women within the city ran deep, as the rock classics "Brown Sugar" and "Lady Marmalade" show.[77]

How had the marchandes and postwar praline peddlers become such stock figures within New Orleans culture? What stories were told about these street sellers within popular culture, which reduced these proud entrepreneurs to caricatures by the twentieth century?

3

What Shall We Do?

THE PRALINE MAMMY, MEMORY, AND OLD NEW ORLEANS

Readers relished finding another story about New Orleans when they opened the November 1890 issue of *Harper's New Monthly Magazine.* Inside was Grace King's "Madrilène; or, the Festival of the Dead." Recounting local customs at the "oldest, most aristocratic" cemetery in the city, King told of the loving care New Orleanians gave to the famed above-ground tombs on All Saints' Day and how African Americans gathered at the entrance to hawk wares to the families honoring their deceased. Most prominent were the praline sellers. King wrote, "And wherever one could edge herself in, sat old negro women in *tignons,* before waiters of *pralines,* molasses and cocoa-nut candy, or pans of *pain patate,* or skillets of doughnuts frying over lighted furnaces; keeping the flies and the gamins off with long whisks of split palmetto, while they nodded their heavy sleepy heads." The saleswomen's voices related the diverse histories of the local population. King elaborated, "All the vendors crying their wares at once, in the deteriorated traditions or personal perversions of half a score of dialects, with a vociferousness and persistence that proclaimed the transient nature of the opportunity." Although the mammy was emerging as a stock figure in southern literature, King anticipated how she and her pralines would serve as a trope within Louisiana.[1]

King's 1890 short story recast the entrepreneurial peddler as a praline-selling mammy who represented "deteriorated traditions" and "personal perversions" linked to the decline of slavery and to racial mixing, as suggested by the blended dialects. The stereotype of the praline mammy provided a means through which King, along with myriad other New Orleans writers, crafted a myth of racial purity separating whites from persons of color. The one-drop rule—that any African ancestry in the bloodline made a person colored—defined race for King. She packaged her native New Orleans as a land of white Creoles. Although unacknowledged miscegenation might occur, racial passing by light-skinned African Americans did not happen, at least according to King's fiction. Tellingly, the praline seller happily served Creole visitors outside the cemetery but did not herself enter the hallowed ground. In this story King was following in the footsteps of historian Charles Gayarré, her mentor. Gayarré, who pioneered the writing of Louisiana history during a life spanning the nineteenth century, depicted Louisiana's Creoles as patriotic Americans with a proud Francophone heritage that was often linked to European aristocracy. King took to paper and pen to defend this fabricated heritage.

Grace King particularly chafed at the depiction of the city's Creoles as families with muddled bloodlines who included—and, worse, sometimes accepted—relatives of African descent: this reality was captured by fellow white New Orleanian George Washington Cable in his best-selling novel *The Grandissimes: A Story of Creole Life* (1880). Cable, much to King's horror, also admitted the cruelty of slavery. The teenage Cable had witnessed the fall of the city to Union troops in April 1862. Afterward, he enlisted in the Confederate cavalry, largely serving in Mississippi. The destruction and death he witnessed disillusioned Cable about the Confederate cause and the racism targeting African Americans.

Returning home after the war, Cable vented his disgust with Lost Cause mythologizing through his historical fiction. Cable fondly recalled hearing the marchandes "every morning" during his childhood and respected their drive. The women earned his admiration for their work ethic and independence. In *The Grandissimes,* Cable introduces an elderly *marchande des calas* named Clemence to give voice to his sharp criticism of slavery and racism, attacking romantic delusions about bondage popular among white Louisianans like King and Gayarré. When confronted with whites' views of the enslaved as among the "happiest people under the sun," Clemence pointedly "made bold to deny this with argumentative indignation." Slavery produced unmentionable horrors in the marchande's telling. Clemence's outspokenness and public prominence eventually are punished by a mob that seizes her. She is taken to where the city meets the swamp and, after pleading not to be hanged, is told to run. The vigilantes then shoot her in the back. Cable's novel, though initially well received in Anglo circles given the book's focus on French Creoles, stirred outrage within Francophone New Orleans. Gayarré, who had befriended Cable, turned on the author, who by then was nationally celebrated, for seemingly slandering French Creoles' whiteness and racial paternalism. He also chafed at Cable's popularity and financial success gained by chronicling a culture that Gayarré deemed his own preserve. Cable's continued criticism of racial segregation, peonage, and disfranchisement in the years after release of *The Grandissimes* turned more and more white southerners against him. Public furor within New Orleans drove Cable from his lifelong residency in the Crescent City to a new home in Massachusetts in 1885, but his works regularly became bestsellers and lingered in Americans' minds.[2]

King's outrage about Cable's writings motivated her to counter the suggestion of racial mixing among Louisiana's Creoles and of whites' mistreatment of the enslaved. Expressing a widely shared though hyperbolic view, King fumes in her memoirs "that Cable proclaimed his preference for colored people over white and assumed the inevitable superiority—according to his theories—of the quadroons over the Creoles." She continues, "He was a native of New Orleans and had been well treated by its people, and yet he stabbed the city in the back, as we felt, in a dastardly way to please the Northern press." Her and other Louisianans' reconciliation with Cable would wait until 1915.[3]

After Cable used the fictional marchande Clemence to condemn racial injustice, King and other local writers responded with contrasting accounts of African American vendors that reinforced the myths of benevolent masters, happy slaves, and contented free persons. In these tales, the sellers are transformed into mammies. The post–Civil War image of the praline-carrying mammy that saturated New Orleans culture into the late twentieth century belied the sweat and strivings of Black free women who converted plantation sugar, foraged pecans, and the labor they owned for themselves into New Orleans's most famous confection. Yet, whether in literature or on the streets of the Crescent City, white residents and tourists viewed praline sellers as former slaves devoted to preserving white supremacy. Their supposed loyalty reinforced efforts to present slavery as a benign labor system in which masters and their human chattel shared a mutual affection. The diversity of New Orleans's Black heritage, the economic strivings of Black workers, and any rumblings of Black dissatisfaction with the racial hierarchy were boiled down to the literary image of the Black praline seller eager to serve white New Orleanians a taste of the antebellum past for just a few pennies.

THE LOUISIANA MAMMY

Tales about the praline mammy were a New Orleans riff on a regional chord. Understanding praline mammy lore requires understanding her place within the wider southern context and her appeal to white Americans in general. When white southerners in their memoirs or novels crafted a romanticized Old South that sugarcoated slavery, they most frequently pointed to the mammy as the pivotal figure on the plantations and within urban homes. By bridging the Civil War, the mammy figure suggested that emancipation changed little about southern life, given that African Americans had been and continued, supposedly, to be well supported, joyful, and loyal to their white caretakers. Erasing the horrors of slavery cleansed the Lost Cause of any shame in the fight to preserve human bondage. Such a salve was particularly needed in New Orleans where Confederate sympathizers dealt with the dual shames of having housed the United States' largest slave market and of surrendering the city without a fight to federal forces so early in the Confederacy's struggle for independence.[4]

Nothing affirmed the moonlight and magnolias mythos of the Old South and the respectability of the Lost Cause as much as the Black mammy who devotedly cared for her master's children as if her own. Historian Micki McElya, in her assessment of racial stereotypes during the Jim Crow era, explains, "The mammy figure in particular was an essential site for grappling with the meaning and burden of slavery for American capitalist democracy." This rotund Black figure carried a heavy burden for a white society that maintained rigid racial barriers for a century after the Civil War. "Loving, hating, pitying, or pining for mammy in the twentieth century became a way for Americans to define the character of the nation, the meaning of freedom, and the racial and gender boundaries of the citizenry," stresses McElya. The devoted Black female laborer of the popular imagination perpetuated whites' faith in the racial status quo.[5]

The mammy archetype shared several features. The "regulation mammy," according to one account of plantation life from 1916, possessed "fat sides, rolling gait, Black shining features, and a kindly smile."[6] She was a maternal figure, rather than a sexualized one that might suggest the widespread miscegenation (and rape) committed under slavery. Her ample size implied that masters catered well to their slaves' needs, maybe even too well. Her sizable weight also highlighted her cooking skills. Her smile suggested a contentment with white supremacy. Descriptions of the mammy presented her as a woman of late middle age or older. She was thus past her childbearing years. Instead, she cleaned, prepared meals, and anticipated the needs of whites, no matter their age, as if they were her children. Her clothes suggested an eagerness to work. Depictions of the mammy showed clean teeth and unsoiled clothes, hinting at some degree of good hygiene. This was a sharp contrast to representations of Black men within white popular culture under Jim Crow: they often appeared as slovenly with broken teeth, thereby undermining their claims to political and social equality with whites.

Equally important, the mammy's features desexualized Black women. This desexualization of Black women through the mammy stereotype was especially important in New Orleans, where sex across the color line first captivated white Americans during the antebellum era. The slave market and, later, the prominence of brothels in New Orleans's Storyville red-light district turned Black women into purchasable sexual objects. The evidence of such relationships—very light-skinned women known as quadroons and octoroons, who had only one-fourth and one-eighth of their bloodlines, respectively, from an African ancestor—particularly fascinated white Americans and informed views on Louisiana's Creoles. The octoroon became a stock figure in American literature. To counter this, the mammy was often very dark skinned, belying the possibility of miscegenation.[7]

Overall, as interdisciplinary scholar Psyche Forson-Williams argues, the mammy possessed little "sense of self" because she lived to satisfy whites. Rarely did tales of the mammy present her personal concerns or those of her family other than caring for whites. Her face exhibited "no element of femininity or softness," while her body suggested a "masculine tower of strength." Only her cooking skills hinted at her femininity, even as some could read into her image "credence to the tradition of competition" among African American women cooks. The more ensconced the mammy image became within popular culture, the more whites "mammified" actual Black women, expecting them to live up to the artificial ideal celebrated by white society.[8]

The mammy became a key part of branding New Orleans and its pralines as the city tapped a nascent tourism trade dependent on northern vacationers who had been influenced by popular literature. An ambassador of southern culture, the mammy was uniquely situated as both a living relic ideal for piquing tourists' curiosity and an ideal servant eager to please travelers as if they were her former masters.

The fictionalized mammy faithfully preserved white southerners' history and customs, including their culinary culture. As white advocates of a postbellum New South pursued industrialization and fostered a growing, urbanized middle class, the loyal mammy served as a comforting reminder that old times were not forgotten. Born on an Alabama plantation in 1860, Martha Gielow fondly recalled the Black maternal figures who safeguarded her family's heritage: "Those who have never known a Mammy can have but little conception of the love that existed between that dear, Black foster-parent and 'dem chillum what she's done raised.' Nor can they realize the charm of listening to the tales of the past related by those dear old chroniclers of the Old South." Another white southerner in 1914 recounted tales told "on an old sugar plantation in Louisiana within fifty miles of New Orleans." This author noted how the white children "were much attached to their old 'Black Mammy,' their faithful nurse and devoted attendant since the days of their earliest infancy, whom they regarded as a member of the family." The "venerable negro woman" had cared for "three generations" of the white family, and "once having been owned as a slave, she had owned, ruled, served and loved" her wards. In this reimagined world, the bonds of slavery were tied with unshatterable affection, not breakable chains.[9]

Similarly, white northerners experiencing rapid technological, economic, and demographic changes during the late nineteenth and early twentieth centuries fondly read local-color tales about an old-fashioned, agrarian Dixie or viewed how the new medium of film depicted the storied past of the region. The mammy helped make modernization palatable to white Americans, whether they were immigrants or of native stock, especially as growing numbers of urbanites incorporated phonographs, telephones, electric lights, automobiles, and, lastly, radio into their lives. The mammy provided a quaint reminder of a supposedly simpler past. She also reassured whites of their continued supremacy, despite the social changes unleashed by these disruptive technologies.[10]

Understanding the praline mammy requires confronting her fictional sister Aunt Jemima, the most influential mammy within American popular culture. Marketers packaged Aunt Jemima as a Louisianan. The name, derived from a popular minstrel song, branded a pancake mix introduced to grocery shelves in 1889, part of a flood of new, easy-to-prepare foods marketed nationally in the late nineteenth and early twentieth centuries. The mix did not gain widespread appeal until 1893, when the R. T. Davis Mill Company, which owned the brand, hired Nancy Green to play Aunt Jemima at the World's Columbian Exposition in Chicago. Green was born a slave in Kentucky in 1834, so she was of a background and age old enough to satisfy white spectators' expectations of a devoted Black matriarchal figure. At the exposition, Green cooked pancakes and regaled audiences with tales of plantation life. To make the character more believable, company directors compiled a backstory for Aunt Jemima that identified her as a former slave on a Louisiana plantation; this tale was subsequently published as *The Life of Aunt Jemima: The Most Famous Colored Woman in the World* (1895). By the next decade, advertising campaigns offered customers coupons redeemable for dolls depicting Aunt Jemima and her family so that everyone could own miniatures of these formerly enslaved persons. An ad from 1915 offered "Aunt Jemima herself, funny old Uncle Mose, the little rascal, Wade Davis, and the cute little pickaninny Diana in her red and yellow pinafore."[11]

A national ad campaign in 1919 elaborated on Aunt Jemima's ties to Louisiana. She rose to fame when "all the guests at Colonel Higbee's plantation in Louisiana, where Aunt Jemima was cook, said they had never tasted such cakes before. They came from miles around to get them!" Her fame, according to this account, increased following emancipation: "After the war had freed her, Aunt Jemima lived for years in her little cabin close to the Mississippi." Here, she served customers from the "famous old river steamer, the 'Robert E. Lee.'" The steamboat brought famished northerners to Aunt Jemima's door. The ad recounted that she had sold her recipe, after considerable negotiations, for a gold payment, which she insisted on "after several unfortunate experiences with paper money during the war." The company that marketed Aunt Jemima's recipe reassured buyers that when they purchased a box of pancake mix they were re-creating the antebellum fare and flair described by the ad. By possessing the mix, Americans "too, can serve the tender, delicious cakes that were praised so highly by all the guests on that old Louisiana plantation!" Thus, a modern consumer product linked to the industrialization of food within the United States was packaged in the sentimental imagery of romantic southern agrarianism.[12]

Although the account of Aunt Jemima as a faithful servant with impeccable cooking skills dominated the mammy image and continues to garner considerable attention from scholars, Aunt Jemima's association with Louisiana remains underappreciated. Literary scholar Doris Witt notes that Aunt Jemima and her link with Louisiana appeared at a time when the "Creole had again emerged in popular fiction and entertainment as a site of anxiety over the threat of miscegenation." The "racially ambiguous" Creole had first entered American popular culture during the antebellum era in debates over the immorality of slavery. In the late nineteenth century, emancipation and imperialism rekindled white Americans' fears of racial mixing. Aunt Jemima by her happy servitude eased those concerns. Yet the focus on Louisiana also culturally contrasted Aunt Jemima to the enslaved in *Uncle Tom's Cabin* and linked her to the state's culinary renown. All these connections explain the emphasis on the praline-selling mammy in New Orleans—a marketing approach that intensified when the city's white confectioners adopted praline mammy imagery for their own products during much of the twentieth century.[13]

When marketers placed the famed Aunt Jemima on a Louisiana plantation, she, like her praline-peddler-turned-mammy kin, directly countered the notorious account of slavery in New Orleans and at the Red River plantation in Harriet Beecher Stowe's best-selling, abolitionist novel *Uncle Tom's Cabin* (1852). The mental footprint of the Crescent City's slave market and enslaver Simon Legree's brutal plantation near Alexandria, Louisiana, as told by Stowe, loomed over any promotion of a romanticized antebellum past.[14]

Stowe exposed the cold business aims of Louisiana's enslavers. In the slave pens of New Orleans, readers could "find an abundance of husbands, wives, brothers, sisters, fathers, mothers, and young children, to be 'sold separately, or in lots to suit the convenience of the purchaser'; and . . . can be sold, leased, mortgaged, exchanged for groceries or dry goods, to suit the phases of trade, or the fancy of the purchaser." The enslaved were commodities akin to hogsheads of sugar or bales of cotton. Slave trading, according to Stowe, was "systematically directed towards making him [the enslaved] callous, unthinking, and brutal." Business calculations ripped apart Black families despite white southerners' claims of being sympathetic owners.[15]

Uncle Tom, sold by his Kentucky enslaver to a New Orleans family, is then sold to Simon Legree, a vicious cotton planter in rural central Louisiana. Stowe describes Tom sitting on a "small, mean boat," moving up the Red River with "chains on his wrists, chains on his feet, and a weight heavier than chains" burdening his emotions. On arrival, Legree instructs his new property, "Well, I tell ye this yer fist has got as hard as iron knocking down niggers. I never see the nigger, yet, I couldn't bring down with one crack." Far from the paternal owner celebrated by white southerners as typical, Legree epitomized the cruel realities of human bondage—and Stowe presented enslavers of New Orleans and Louisiana as the worst offenders.[16]

Uncle Tom's Cabin haunted white southerners into the twentieth century as they affirmed the Lost Cause. Hunter McGuire, the former surgeon-in-chief to Confederate general Stonewall Jackson, penned the introduction to a fellow southerner's romanticized study of slavery, titled *The Old Plantation* (1901), that denounced Stowe's "sensational and overwrought story." McGuire condemns the "ignorant aspersions of 'Uncle Tom's Cabin' and kindred exhalations from a distempered brain." N. B. De Saussure echoes these sentiments in her memoirs from 1909. De Saussure addresses her book to her granddaughter: "Grandmother is growing to be an old lady, and as you are still too young to remember all she has told you of her own and your mother's people, she is going to write down her recollections that you may thus gain a true knowledge of the old plantation days, now forever gone, from one whose life was spent amid those scenes." Again, countering Stowe's narrative motivated De Saussure to document her perspective: "'Uncle Tom's Cabin' has set the standard in the North, and it seems useless for those who owned and loved the negroes to say there was any other method used in their management than that of strictest severity." John Clinkscales, a white southerner born before the Civil War, similarly explained the compulsion to publish his 1916 memoirs: "Too many of our young people know of the institution of slavery only what they've learned from 'Uncle Tom's Cabin.' Knowing only the negro who has grown up since the Civil War . . . they cannot have a correct idea of 'a civilization that is gone.'" The myth of the mammy was a counter to the nightmare told by Stowe.[17]

In addition, Aunt Jemima's connection to Louisiana explicitly linked her to the southern state with the most celebrated culinary culture, a tie that highlights why the praline mammy also became such a prominent marketing ploy.

Louisiana's cuisine differed considerably—and favorably—from that found elsewhere in the former Confederacy. Isabelle Post, in an infamous article titled "The Truth about Southern Cooking" published by the *American Mercury* in 1939, captured a widespread sentiment as northern tourists increasingly flooded southward during the twentieth century. She wrote, "Meager and unsatisfactory as are the ingredients of Southern food, the preparation renders them even worse. True, tradition has exalted the fat mammy of the ante-bellum kitchens—and who am I to cast aspersions on one so securely enshrined?—but it is remarkable that, Mendel's law to the contrary notwithstanding, no whit of Mammy's talents was passed down to her descendants." Post then spat, "Evidently those celebrated secret recipes have been so successfully concealed that not even the South can find them." Travelers venturing through Dixie confronted a culinary desert. The harsh regional fare reflected the severe poverty suffered by millions within a region ravaged by decades of cotton overproduction and racial animosity. Simple fare of cornmeal and hog meat predominated. Post declared, "But if the Southerner himself must subsist on such rations, consider the plight of the visitor in search of an adequate restaurant. He can travel from Richmond to El Paso, from Memphis to Miami, without finding a café or hotel dining-room sufficiently good to make him want to go back for another meal." The only exception was the Crescent City: "New Orleans, of course, has several good French restaurants, but then New Orleans is more old-world than Southern," concluded Post.[18]

The praline mammy, like Aunt Jemima, challenged popular perceptions of poor-quality and bad-tasting southern fare by pushing Louisiana to the fore. The uniqueness of the praline mammy rested on the uniqueness of New Orleans within the United States. Some southerners, including Ellen Foley, editor of the women's page of the *Times-Picayune,* raged against Post's harsh critique of the regional cuisine. But most respondents in a subsequent flurry of letters to the *American Mercury* noted the kernel of truth identified by Post, especially regarding rural areas mired in poverty and the staples of pork, cornmeal, and molasses. A traveling "Damyankee" salesman commented, "To get even fair food in the South one has to go to the larger cities and find the restaurant patronized by tourists, but when you find such a place you will probably discover that it's run by a party from the North."[19]

In New Orleans, however, a polygot assortment of chefs and cooks catered to diners. The celebration of New Orleans's cuisine began in the mid-nineteenth century. As the former French and Spanish colonial outpost ballooned into a major American metropolis during the antebellum era, New Orleans became a nexus for different food cultures. African slaves retained their culinary traditions. Native Americans ventured to the city to trade, sharing their food customs. Immigrants such as the Germans and Irish also influenced the city's foodways. The burgeoning commercial trade along the Mississippi River and from across the oceans brought diverse edibles to the docks. This abundance of consumables and peoples flowing through the port turned New Orleans's restaurants into national landmarks and the city's food products into treasures. For advertisers, the Louisiana mammy highlighted New Orleans as a culinary oasis within the South.[20]

FROM MARCHANDE TO MAMMY

Within the American imagination, New Orleans was a distinct place that reflected the strong foreign influence of its French and Spanish colonial past. "The visitor finds the city very unlike northern towns with which he has been familiar," remarked Willard Glazier in his account of American cities in 1883. He elaborated, "To the Creole quarter [French Quarter] especially there is a foreign look, which is intensified by the frequent sound of foreign speech. It is as if one had stepped into some old-world town, and left America, with its newness and its harshness of speech, far behind." The city offered not only a foreign space but also a place that seemingly stood apart from the flow of time: "New Orleans of the nineteenth century jostles New Orleans of the eighteenth on every hand," observed Glazier. In the popular literary imagination, American capitalism as a driving force of modernization had largely overlooked New Orleans, where the architectural influences of France and Spain along with remnants of a Francophone populace seemingly resisted change. Complacency among the merchant class after the Civil War certainly hindered the modernization brought elsewhere by railroads and industrialization. Despite aggressive modernization efforts by the early twentieth century, including constructing water systems, paving roads, and adopting Progressive Era reforms, the image of New Orleans as out of step with time remained. The result was a city described as awash in time-tested Creole recipes preserved by formerly enslaved cooks.[21]

For local authors during the 1880s and 1890s, Blacks' sweat in the present fed whites' nostalgia for the past. The tignon represented this tension. The Spanish government in 1786 ordered women of African descent in New Orleans, whether free or enslaved, to wear headscarves as a sign of racial submission. Although this law was rarely enforced and fell by the wayside under U.S. rule, its effect on local culture was profound. Women of African descent donned colorful tignons in defiance of the law. This headwear worn by working-class Black women also had practical applications. The cloth absorbed perspiration and kept hair from falling into their wares. For marchandes, brightly colored headscarves caught the attention of potential customers. For people of color, the tignon therefore symbolized both racial defiance and ingenuity, and praline sellers rarely appeared without this head covering. In contrast, many white writers saw the tignon as conveying Blacks' submission to white authority. Such literary depictions, as in King's "Madrilène," ran off the presses in droves in the late nineteenth and early twentieth centuries, given white southerners' general fixation on preserving local history, safeguarding white supremacy, and cultivating nostalgia for the slave regime.[22]

Mollie Evelyn Moore emerged as one of the earliest and more prominent writers in this vein. Born in Alabama in 1844, Moore married the editor of the *Daily Picayune* and settled in a French Quarter residence in 1874. The author closely studied Creole society and observed street life in her new neighborhood. By the 1880s, she had launched a popular short-story series called "Keren-Happuch and I" in her husband's newspaper. The series featured two recurring female characters who share adventures around New Orleans.[23]

In a tale from 1885, the pair run away from the residence of the "Voodoo Queen," the Creole of color Marie Laveau. The "wrathful" air surrounding the home of the priestess only dissipates on encountering a Black figure selling pralines along Rampart Street, a thoroughfare bounding one edge of the French Quarter. Moore writes, "But there was something peaceful and reassuring in the very sight of a great fat, turbaned old mammy who sat against the wall on the banquette there, flanked by the two small low tables loaded with cocoanut cake and gingerbread, and blinking in the sunshine." One of two black cats "dozed on a table among the pralines." The mammy, named Lizette, spoke in a "soft, slurring tone peculiar to the French negro," yet with traces of an English accent that recalled her origins as a child born on a tobacco plantation along the James River in Virginia. When asked how long she had traded in pralines, the mammy, trailing off in French, did not recall. Moore contrasts the threatening Creole of color Marie Laveau—infamous for her spiritual powers, societal connections, and mixed-race ancestry that included a white veteran of the Battle of New Orleans who passed as Black to marry her mother in the 1820s—with the passive, praline-selling mammy who fondly recalls life in "Ole Virginny." Lizette also remembers dancing in New Orleans's Congo Square in the 1830s. For Moore, the peddler's fond recollection of Congo Square as a site for carefree frolicking neutralized a location notorious within white popular culture for enslaved persons' voodoo rituals. The praline mammy thus counteracted the historic power of voodoo with its interracial pull within New Orleans. Moore also links the praline mammy's racial contentment to the wider Black population of the South by tracing her lineage to Virginia. The praline mammy thereby became a local manifestation of contented Black freed persons who preserved memories of a happy life under slavery.[24]

White writers typically downplayed the independence and entrepreneurship of Black praline sellers by presenting them as contented preservers of Creole culture who often marketed their creations to sustain the white households they still loyally served. An 1887 short story from the *Daily Picayune* recounts a prominent white tenor cared for by his "short, very fat and very old" mammy. Her white hair was tucked beneath a "big, fantastical-arranged head-handkerchief." Yet she was recognized as a skilled preparer of pralines, some of which she made for her "master" and others that she sold at a local market. When asked to demonstrate her skills, she "went to business immediately . . . deep in the mysteries of praline-making." This included grating coconut to mix into the confection. She remained a repository of recipes from the fading French population, including her expertise on "how to make gombo Creole fashion and jambolaya."[25]

In the imagination of white New Orleans writers of the 1880s and 1890s, pralines became a marker of Creole identity by becoming a delicacy that white French descendants consumed aplenty, though rarely prepared with their own hands. In a tale published by *Harper's New Monthly Magazine* in November 1894, Grace King recounts the activities of a white Creole named Tante Liane. Her fortunes in decline, Tante Liane forages for books tossed into the trash and stops at the famed French Market where she purchases an abundance of pralines. The treat was a constant presence around her. Tante

Liane was "always munching them, had a passion, an insatiable passion, for them." She so enjoyed the candy that her residence was littered with the "unfinished munchings of pralines." Pralines thus symbolized a leisurely past in which Black labor eased the travails of white Creoles. As part of a fading white Creole culture, Tante Liane ravenously consumes the markers of refinement: books and pralines. Pralines offered her escape and reminders of former glory.[26]

The attempt to rewrite the history of race within antebellum New Orleans appears clearest in Louise Livingston Hunt's biography of Louise Livingston in 1886. Louise Livingston spent her youth on a large plantation in San Domingue surrounded by some eight hundred enslaved persons. She and her family fled to New Orleans during the Haitian Revolution. She married Edward Livingston, the politically connected jurist largely responsible for drafting Louisiana's Civil Code of 1825. Brother to Robert Livingston, negotiator of the Louisiana Purchase, Edmund Livingston subsequently served as a congressman and senator from Louisiana. Louise, age 19 in 1805 when she married the 41-year-old lawyer, was widely recognized as a shrewd adviser to her husband. Louise Livingston Hunt sought to honor her great aunt and namesake, who died in 1860, by drafting a biography packaged as a memoir. She promises readers, "The letters and other materials from which it has been derived have found their way altogether, in the natural order of things, into the author's hands, as a relation bound to Mrs. Livingston by the most endearing ties, and often living with her." In other words, a few documents and family tales masked some literary flourishes.[27]

Louise Livingston Hunt was born in New Orleans in 1834 and, through her great aunt, understood Creoles' sensitivity to suggestions of miscegenation and the evils of slavery. She describes Louise and her ancestors as "'des negrophiles'; they were kindness itself to their slaves." The enslaved responded with devotion. "Some sold 'calas,' a breakfast cake to eat with coffee, much liked in Louisiana; their cry was 'Belles calas tout chauds!' Others sold preserves freshly made, and cried out, 'Confitures figues!' 'Confitures coco!' or 'Pralines pistache! pralines pacanes!' which were sugar-cakes filled with nuts." In this manner, the marchandes "took a great deal of money, which, as they were slaves, was carried home to their owners regularly in the evening and the day's sales accounted for."[28]

Hunt summons fabricated memories of Zabette Philosophe, a praline seller in early nineteenth-century New Orleans, to emphasize the amicable race relations fostered by slavery. Although Zabette was a "free and independent marchande," her surname was "given her" by Louise Livingston's older brother. Philosophe was a hardworking saleswoman who freely dispensed her personal wisdom to passersby, thus earning herself the unique last name. She had received her freedom from the widow of an officer under Bienville, who had founded New Orleans. Hunt describes her as "very black, with teeth of dazzling whiteness." Each morning, New Orleanians could find Philosophe "stationed with her basket in the shade of the old cathedral, where she sold pralines (cakes made of nuts and sugar), and also shelled pecan-nuts." In the afternoon, she moves to the adjoining courthouse on Jackson Square, selling wares to lawyers, judges, and those tending to legal matters. In the evening, she moves to the entrance gate of the square. Locals admire her as a person "shrewd, witty, sarcastic, and original in her opinions." Philosophe died at the age of a hundred. "Everybody knew Zabette Philosphe, and she knew everybody," writes Hunt.[29]

Dead for decades before Hunt's birth, Zabette Philosophe is a fictional elaboration on the marchandes of antebellum New Orleans, reimagined for the Jim Crow era. The name is far-fetched. The description provided by Hunt conforms to racial imagery common in southern literature emerging after Reconstruction. For a saleswoman supposedly prominent in the memory of New Orleanians, no other mention of Zabette Philosophe appears in the historical record. Yet by packaging this marchande for readers, Hunt not only enlivens her text but also depicts a free Black woman—a French-speaking Creole of color—as purely black, not a brown product of miscegenation. Her description also uses the marchande to herald the mutual fondness between whites and Blacks within colonial and antebellum New Orleans. The tale of Zabette Philosophe lingered within the city, even serving as the centerpiece in a historical pageant hosted by the public school system to celebrate, belatedly by two years because of World War I, New Orleans's bicentennial in 1920.[30]

Accounts of the praline-selling mammy grew more elaborate during the 1890s, a trend highlighted by the evolving work of Marie Louise Points. Her publications also reflect racial trends in a decade when segregation, disfranchisement, and violence against African Americans all gained legal sanction. Points's family had resided in the South since colonial times. Her father was a Virginian who claimed a personal friendship with Robert E. Lee. He taught his children "to love and revere that greatest of generals." Her mother's family was said to be of "blue-blooded ancestry" traced from French Creole landowners in New Orleans and Mobile. Points, born after the Civil War, grew up with four brothers and six sisters all steeped in the lore of the Lost Cause.[31]

Points's writings about praline mammies were a direct literary assault on the entrepreneurship displayed by women of color in New Orleans. In 1891, she recounted the efforts of an unnamed "old negro woman dressed in dark blue calico and wearing a picturesque bandana 'tignon' on her head." This woman carried a basket laden with "cakes made of rice and flour, fried in grease to a crisp brown and sprinkled with white sugar." These cakes were said to be a favorite treat among "Creole children, and even their elders." Points heralds, "There is something in the old woman's face which tells its own tale of suffering, heroism and unswerving fidelity." This street seller could supposedly be found in the evening at Jackson Square, "fanning with a huge palmetto the flies from her basket of pink and white pralines." Catering to residents and tourists at this popular site, the praline mammy does not hoard her profits. Points boasts, with a fictional flourish given the acknowledged refusal of the seller to be interviewed, that the praline hawker labors out of pious devotion to her former enslaver; "The old woman counts her money with a smile of satisfaction and hobbles off, not, however, without stopping before the altar of the Madonna in the cathedral to say an 'Ave Maria' for her decrepit 'old missus' at home, who never knows, in the altered state of her fortune, where the money comes from with which the comforts of the olden days are bought, to soothe her declining years."[32]

When not serving whites with a fealty that suggested longings for antebellum Louisiana, praline mammies, according to white writers like Points, worked to raise money to care for their white families. African Americans were portrayed as caregivers, sacrificing their freedom to sustain their former enslavers who are languishing in worsening poverty due to the war and the economic upheaval caused by emancipation. This depiction turned the financial drive of Black women on its head.

Points's 1894 reiteration of her earlier tale marks a pivotal moment in the history of pralines and the creation of the praline seller mythos within New Orleans. Points now names the seller "Toto" and places her on Canal Street, giving her a more detailed biography. Toto had been enslaved on a Louisiana plantation. Her owner subsequently sold her at the infamous auctions of human chattel held in the rotunda of the St. Louis Hotel. Eventually Toto found herself in loyal service to her mistress, who in this telling had died a decade before. The Civil War, according to Points, had not disrupted the romanticized bonds between enslaver and enslaved.

The wares hawked by Points's praline mammy of 1894 receive more consideration too. Toto's basket of treats contains "savory ones made of 'syrop,' with 'pecans' stuck here and there by way of ornamentation and still more delightful eating." These were "molasses pralines fixed so neatly and compactly in tiny molds of white cut paper," in contrast to the other "'Creole pralines,' made of ground cocoanut and white sugar delightfully assimilated together and formed into round pink and white cakes." This is the earliest detailed description of the famed, flat praline formed from boiled sugar and populated with pecans. The story also includes the first illustration of a praline vendor to appear in the local press.[33]

The literary conjurers of praline mammies understood them to be the antithesis of modernity. The praline mammy represented a person and culture displaced by progress. Molly Moore Davis captures this symbolism in a poem within the "Keren-Happuch and I" series in March 1907. The rhymes relate to the demolition of a block of the French Quarter designated for the new Louisiana State Supreme Court. This displacement threatened to reduce to poverty the white residents who might out of necessity have joined the street vendors to survive. She writes,

Dear Neighbor mine, what shall be [*sic*] do,
        We Two.
When brick by brick they tear apart
(With stern iconoclastic spade,
And pick, and hammer fast arrayed)
The walls so precious to the heart?
When, with a smile, mayhap a shout,
They turn us out!
        What shall we do?
Sit on the banquette, shall we? I
To sell pralines with streaming eye?
A hurdy-gurdy you to play
For dimes and nickels day by day?

Oh, tell me true?
What-shall-we-do?[34]

The sentiment captures the anxiety evoked by the modernization of New Orleans and the fear that poverty could lead whites across the color line and into work previously reserved for African Americans and recently arrived immigrants. Such angst made the legendary fealty and self-sacrifice of the praline mammy more reassuring to whites, even as she seemed destined to disappear into history.

Although romanticized images of African American life in the South initially emerged in the antebellum period to counter abolitionist depictions of slavery, white southerners placed renewed emphasis on these portrayals in the late nineteenth century. White women authors marched in the vanguard of those who absolved former Confederates of the shame of defeat and reinforced the mythos of the Old South as a noble civilization. Their publications served as paper monuments to a fallen civilization akin to the monuments erected to Confederate generals and common soldiers by the United Daughters of the Confederacy. Former enslavers were reimagined well into the twentieth century as paternalistic benefactors of their appreciative Black "servants." These servants displayed self-sacrificing loyalty to white families, as portrayed by King, Points, Stuart, and others. Born during Reconstruction, a white southern woman in 1908 recounts her return to the cotton plantation along the Mississippi River where she was raised: "Not the least pleasure of travel is the joy of home coming, and I am never happier than when here, among the old-time, faithful darkies who have watched me grow from infancy to womanhood, for they seem so happy as they gather around me when I visit their humble, but neatly-kept cabins." The same held true for urban goers as they ignored slum conditions in Black neighborhoods while waxing fondly of street scenes in historic neighborhoods and shopping districts populated with mammified praline vendors.[35]

A PRALINE MAMMY

With mammies symbolizing Black fealty to whites, advocates for the Lost Cause and Jim Crow easily trotted out the praline mammy for their own uses.

Kate and Jean Gordon, the well-known Louisiana suffragists and avowed white supremacists, for instance, embraced pralines as a symbol of their state. In November 1900, Jean Gordon operated the Louisiana booth at a "suffrage bazar" in New York. "All manner of typical things will be sent from Louisiana," announced members of the pro-suffrage Era Club in New Orleans. In addition to literary works of Mollie Moore Davis and others, the booth presented "miniature praline women, Acadian stuffs and all manner of interesting work of the women of Louisiana." Kate Gordon and other club members prepared a "basket of pralines" that was express mailed to New York for her sister to sell. Similarly, in 1916, the New Orleans chapter of the United Daughters of the Confederacy contributed a booth to the organization's bazaar in Washington, DC, that featured gumbo filé, pralines, café noir, and books and color sketches by New Orleans-based authors and artists. Bessie Harrison, spokeswoman for the chapter, explained, "You know the native Washingtonians have heard so much of New Orleans 'specialties,' but have never had the real thing." Reality became branded with the praline mammy: her confections were seen as representing an authentic New Orleans. Miniature praline mammy dolls and the pralines popularized by African American women fell into the hands of white women, such as the Gordons, who controlled the historical narrative and co-opted the entrepreneurship of Black women while refusing those same Black women a political voice.[36]

By the early twentieth century, a visit to New Orleans was incomplete without an encounter with a praline mammy. She became a staple of social gatherings and business conventions. In 1902, for instance, the National Hardware Association convened at the St. Charles Hotel for its annual meeting. The *Daily Picayune* described the local organizers' efforts: "The gentlemen wished in every way to make this reception typically Louisianian, and the refreshments would be peculiarly to this clime. A feature would be the presence of six or eight old negro mammies, who would pass pralines in brown wrapping paper around in baskets." The planning committee had ordered "700 beautiful little square boxes . . . ornamented on the outside with the picture of a praline woman" containing inside "three kinds of pralines made here—the white, the pink and the pecan or brown." These favors were distributed on an evening labeled "A Night in Dixie Land" that featured "sweet old plantation melodies sung by real darkies." The Black women dispersing pralines gripped the attention of the northern conventioneers, many of whom had likely eaten Aunt Jemima pancake mix, read local-color tales set in the South, or perused stock travel narratives about New Orleans. These African American women "seemed, indeed, relics of the good old days before the war every one of them; for their quaint old-time courtesy, so different from the rude manners of the day, their neat old-time blue gingham dresses, with white kerchief and quaint bandana tignon, made up a typical picture that can nowhere be seen but in this dear old Crescent City."[37]

Any economic strivings by these African American women were buried beneath white nostalgia. The performance of racial supplication erased African Americans' opposition to Jim Crow. When the praline "mammies" performed their street cries, one announced "in her broken English how she was a good cook in a fine old family before the war, but now she 'got ole; no money, no more ole mistress. She got for ter make livin,' and so she go roun' dem street for sell dose nice praline.'" When she then burst forth with a tune in French, the guests "went fairly wild; they applauded and applauded." Never mind that the local hardware merchants had arranged this racial performance to satisfy the expectations of their guests from around the nation. And never mind that the African American woman explicitly voiced that her performance stemmed from financial need, not devotion to the white population. The act resonated.[38]

The popularity of praline mammies convinced local white boosters to make their presence a staple of the promotional repertoire. When the Annual Convention of the American Association of General Passenger and Ticket Agents came to New Orleans in 1903, the reception featured the "serving of pralines by four old negro mammies." Northern educators visiting Newcomb College in 1908 similarly received pralines from mammified Black women. Attendees of the Southern Conference of the Unitarian Churches convention held in New Orleans in 1909 enjoyed a particularly revealing performance by a praline peddler famed for selling to young socialites attending Newcomb College, discussed in chapter 1. At one session, an organizer announced a surprise for the guests, and "drawing aside an American flag which hung like a curtain over an alcove, [it] disclosed to view Marie Louise, the Old Praline Woman, gay in bright calico, bandana and apron." The symbolism of hiding Marie Louise behind an American flag defined her as a national treasure. The conventioneers "clapped their hands in pleasure" as the vendor distributed pralines from her wicker basket. The guests attending the Associated Advertising Clubs of the World convention in 1919 were likewise treated to a "plantation band, a pickin'nny [*sic*] to swing the old-fashioned 'punkah,' or ceiling fan, and negro mammies to serve pralines from baskets."[39]

The praline mammy provided a living centerpiece that granted supposed authenticity to venues attempting to distill the essence of the South. The mammy took center stage at a display for a New York fair planned by the Business Men's League in 1910. These boosters erected a "booth typical of New Orleans at the fair and stock[ed] it with products of the Pelican State." Visitors to the booth, which was decorated with palmetto and moss, received "coffee and other Creole beverages" while viewing "all kinds of sauces and seasonings typical of Louisiana, coffee, canned shrimp, Indian baskets and souvenirs, such as spoons, steins and miniature cotton bales." The businessmen also brought "two old negro mammies . . . in order to add a touch of real South by having pralines and other strictly Creole dainties on sale." Those attending the American Institute of Architects convention in 1913 visited a plantation house furnished in the "magnificently solid style of the famous days of old." White university students from Tulane University and Newcomb College performed the "old-time dances" while African Americans sang "old-time songs." Such a scene was not complete without the appearance of mammies distributing pralines to the guests, thus adding a "further touch of realism" to the occasion.[40]

The citywide bicentennial event in April 1920 exposed the extent of whites' devotion to the praline mammy. Schools across New Orleans staged a major pageant recalling the history of the city. The two-day affair involved five thousand children. One hundred white boys and girls were, according to the *States*, "costumed exactly as were the negroes of those days" to re-create the "Bamboula Congo Slave Dance." The dance was the "most interesting as well as most carefully prepared of all the features of the pageant, so as to have it absolutely correct." Others dressed as mammies carrying babies or as Confederate soldiers. A few represented benefactors famed within New Orleans, such as Paul Tulane, John McDonogh, Margaret Haughery, Sophie Newcomb, and Judah Touro. Yet most attention focused on Reina Dunn, selected to play the role of fictional and slightly renamed Zabetta Philosof, created by Louise Livingston Hunt in 1886 and described by the *Item* as "the celebrated old vendor of pralines and dispenser of a laconic sort of wisdom in New Orleans back in 1812 and 1815." Of all the children who performed, Dunn received top billing, even getting her photograph on the front page of the *States*. More than thirty thousand tickets were sold for this pageant.[41]

The presence of the praline mammy remained important because, as a living relic, she temporarily resurrected the Old South—making it "real," according to observers—at galas and receptions. The St. Charles Hotel "converted" its main reception room for a New Year's Eve gala in 1920 "into an old-time Louisiana plantation—cotton bales on the levee, waving sugar cane, steamboat coming down the river, and all that." An African American choir performed "old plantation songs" while "mammies of the past generation" disbursed pralines. The *Item* proclaimed, "It will be the real thing." Plans to give a tour of the French Quarter, organized by Helen Schertz for attendees of the Investment Bankers' Association of America in October 1921, called for the streets "to be planted with mammies selling pralines and calas, figures carefully reproduced from old records."[42] Schertz's use of the word "planted" hinted at the mental link between sugarcane and Black labor. A reception for these bankers at the Patio Royal returned guests to the antebellum time of Paul Morphy, the famed chess master. The festivities again gained credibility as historic re-creations by incorporating "real mammies" carrying pralines. In 1928, the Krewe of Aglaia, a Carnival organization, held an 1850s-themed ball. Despite the extravagant decor and costumes, it was the "presence of old negro mammies and pickaninnies, distributing pralines to those favored with call-outs" who "lent a realistic feature to the ball."[43]

The role of the praline mammy in conjuring forth a seemingly authentic, historic New Orleans became most evident in her appearance at the annual Spring Fiesta. To satisfy public curiosity about the French Quarter, preservationists in 1937 created the festival, mimicking the successful efforts of the Natchez Pilgrimage in Mississippi. The Spring Fiesta encouraged residents to open their homes for tours of the beloved colonial and antebellum structures. A featured aspect of the program during the 1930s and 1940s was a "Night in Old New Orleans." The organizers turned back the clock a century to "give Fiesta visitors a more graphic picture of what this old Quarter was when it was at its height."[44] Hoop-skirted socialites sang from the iron-laced balconies. A parade featured "typical old characters; the clothespole man, the chimney sweeps, the moss man, the blackberry women, the calas tout chaud women, the praline vendors, all advertising their wares with their curious street cries."[45] The procession displayed sanitized history in a consumable form for tourists to ogle and photograph.

As elderly Black women linked to the antebellum past died off, homages to the disappearing praline sellers abounded in the 1910s and 1920s. The *Item* in 1912 mourned, "The praline woman is hard to find." Like many street characters such as the chimney sweep, bottle collector, and wood sawyer, she was "crushed beneath the iron heel of ruthless progress." The newspaper noted that a few examples of the "praline woman, the old, fat mammy, who watched beside her gold brown wares and sold them to you as conferring a favor," still patrolled the city. However, the "vast majority have gone to join the old black 'mammies' of the ancient past," leaving only a scattered, aging few who are "now seldom or never seen." By 1922, local historian Thomas Ewing Dabney wrote of the 1890s as a time "when real 'mammies' went about the streets selling pralines," recognizing that those seen in the 1920s were often novelty acts hired by whites.[46]

With the passing of praline vendors, whites themselves occasionally performed the praline mammy role by donning blackface. A fundraiser held on prestigious St. Charles Avenue in 1919 featured "two girls in negro mammy costume."[47] The socialites Sadie Griffin and Alice Jumonville proved the "hit of the evening" for the "coal black countenance" disguising their "true colors."[48] One of the most elaborate displays of whites' mimicry of Black peddlers occurred in 1923. "Pralines sold quickly when offered by white-skinned 'mammies,' members of the Business and Professional Women's Club, who raised several hundred dollars from the candy sale," reported the *Times-Picayune.* The club's eight downtown booths catered to Mardi Gras celebrants.[49] Four automobiles served as mobile booths along the St. Charles Avenue parade route. About fifty members wore mammy garb, some of whom even donned blackface or black masks with black gloves. The club member who sold the most pralines received a $100 prize, with the rest of the profits set aside to defray travel costs to the next national convention.[50] As late as 1960, the Orleans Club greeted Fiesta visitors with one local socialite and her two daughters in black-face and mammy garb singing plantation songs while distributing pralines.

The praline mammy stereotype remained a staple of New Orleans conventions, social soirees, and fundraisers into the late 1960s, right through the civil rights struggle. Attendees at the Knights Templar in New Orleans in 1952 were given four thousand pralines and three thousand small mammy dolls as mementos. The Krewe of Mid-City in 1955 included a float titled "Pralines" shaped as "one huge basket," with a "grotesque figure of the customary Mammy selling pralines" visible from each side. At a Carnival celebration for patients at Charity Hospital in 1959, children "danced joyously, maskers frolicked, and pralines were distributed by red-kerchiefed mammies."[51] The Carnival ball hosted by the Krewe of Moslem in 1961, with the theme "Gay Old Days Panorama" referencing the 1890s, included a scene of a couple pausing to "buy pralines from an aged Negro Mammy." Guests of the New Orleans Dental Conference in 1963 enjoyed a "taste of old New Orleans' history and menus" at a luncheon celebrating imagined plantation grandeur featuring "'Negro mammies' . . . handing out pralines from their baskets." Arrivals to the international convention of Epsilon Sigma Phi held in New Orleans in 1968 were greeted with decorations celebrating New Orleans's 250th anniversary, which included typical local fare such as "Mammies in costume" distributing pralines.[52] Sunny Schiro, the wife of New Orleans's mayor, commented on a similar gimmick undertaken at the national gathering of the General Federation of Women's Clubs during the mid-1960s: "There was almost a stampede when we gave out pralines. There's big excitement all over the world about coming to New Orleans."[53]

THE GREAT GOD JUNK

White popular culture within New Orleans refused to allow alterations to the image of the praline mammy crafted in the late nineteenth century. Yet, the stagnancy of the praline mammy image was already apparent by July 1925 when Joseph Gogarty contacted the *Times-Picayune* to note an unusual sight: "There has appeared recently in the main entrance of the new courthouse building, a surviving member of the 'Old Praline Woman,' seated on her chair—offering 'homemade pralines' from her lap basket." The presence of this living embodiment of the antebellum past stopped him in his tracks. Gogarty explained, "On stopping to admire and gaze again on this quaint sight (disappearing from the streets), I was surprised finding her wearing modern horned-rimmed colored goggles." This "'vivid' contrast to her other 'oldtime settings'" presented a jarring "new version of an old mammy." Modern stylishness undermined the mammy image and the racial order that imagination reinforced by suggesting the possibility of change.[54]

By the interwar years, as mass tourism emerged as a vital economic sector within New Orleans, the mammy with her basket of pralines appeared so often in so many places as a representation of "real" New Orleans that she became more and more exposed as a gimmick. Readers of *Scribner's Magazine* in January 1928, for instance, encountered a mammy figure that harkened to a shabby rather than romantic past. Recounting a stroll through the French Quarter, travel writer George Wright discovered a "charming little courtyard." But rather than a quaint spot to enjoy, Wright noted that the "Great God Junk has his lair here, and if anything of value to the antiquarians is there, I missed it." Nearby was a "colored lady of form and fashion, but of no particular consequence, and the old praline-woman, who spends a good part of the day in front of the Patio Royal." The mammy, although still wildly popular, had become outdated junk, a symbol of a white New Orleans trapped in its past in an effort to uphold the Lost Cause with one hand while picking the pockets of tourists with the other.[55]

The local white literati had transformed the praline vendor into a caricature divorced from the reality of hardscrabble entrepreneurship by Black women. An aging white population of former enslavers promoted rosy memories of antebellum slavery to address criticisms of the peculiar institution before they left life's stage. Their children too wanted to honor their Confederate mothers and fathers. Ironically, the passing of Black women who could have believably been antebellum slaves led to the proliferation of mammy imagery that was further divorced from historical and contemporary reality within southern society, as displayed again and again at conventions and local soirees. This proliferation and abstraction of the praline-hawking mammy partly reflected whites' angst over the passing of the enslaved generations. Elderly praline vendors became enshrouded in an inescapable lore in their own lifetimes. The resilience of the praline mammy stereotype also reflected the growing importance of the tourism industry within New Orleans. The praline-peddling mammy was an exotic ambassador of local culture. She proved ideal in capturing tourist dollars from the predominantly white trade. In her hands, pralines could make a fortune for a business.

Yet why did tales about praline sellers fixate on the pecan pralines over her coconut pralines and other morsels? What made this nut so special that it complemented plantation brown sugar and nostalgia for the Old South?

In the late 1890s, George François Mugnier, a Swiss-born photographer residing in New Orleans since 1868, snapped the first photograph of a praline seller. Mugnier labeled the image "Plarine Seller." Here and in another photograph of this seller taken at the time, African American laborers stand at the fringes. The seller is situated next to a steamboat's gangplank, an ideal location for selling to dockworkers and passengers. Note the umbrella for shade, the colorful tignon to absorb sweat and attract attention, and the light-colored apron and basket lining to convey cleanliness. (Courtesy of the Louisiana State Museum, Museum Purchase, 09813.0022)

Postcard of a praline vendor sketched by Selina Bres at Newcomb College in 1895. This is the first postcard of a New Orleans scene and one of the earliest postcards produced in the world. This example, mailed on Mardi Gras 1899 from New Orleans to St. Galen, Switzerland, highlights the global reach of the mythologized praline peddler during the 1890s. (Anthony J. Stanonis Collection, Special Collections and Archives, Loyola University New Orleans)

This postcard shows the transformation of the praline vendor into the mammified praline seller. Based on two photographs by George François Mugnier, the postcard removes the African American laborers to her left and right, as well as the steamboat gangplank. The drayage operator over her shoulder is replaced with a white family approaching to make a purchase. The firm of John Scordill on Canal Street published this version of the image during the 1910s. (Anthony J. Stanonis Collection, Special Collections and Archives, Loyola University New Orleans)

The Creole Praline Department of Fuerst & Kraemer incorporated the sanitary mass-production facilities heralded by new candy companies in New Orleans. Young white women were often hired as candymakers, as seen here. (Courtesy of the Louisiana State Museum, Gift of the New Orleans Association of Commerce, 09028.1.043.1)

One of the few remaining independent praline street vendors, photographed by Arnold Genthe in the early 1920s. As in the 1890s photograph by Mugnier, note the umbrella for shade, the colorful tignon to absorb sweat and catch the attention of passersby, and the light-colored clothing and basket cloth to convey cleanliness. Another photograph snapped by Genthe shows her near a white workman standing next to a stack of lumber at the neighboring property, likely a construction site that attracted this vendor. (Arnold Genthe Photograph Collection, Library of Congress Prints and Photographs Division)

The 1930s marked an era when highly competitive tourist shops used trademarks and patents to safeguard their brands and products. Pierre Bagur of Aunt Sally's Original Creole Pralines patented his cotton bale boxes used to package pralines. Léda Plauché of the Green Orchid patented mammy dolls with brown skin. This business card of Louise Cook's Pecan Pralines trademarked this image of a praline mammy as part of her brand. (Anthony J. Stanonis Collection, Special Collections and Archives, Loyola University New Orleans)

Stella Harris was employed by Louise Glynn of Old Town Pralines to sell pralines and mammy dolls at Jackson Square. Harris donned the mammy outfit and accentuated it with a pipe to differentiate herself from competitors. ("The Old Town Pralines Mammy," New Orleans, 1937. Photograph by John Gutmann. Collection Center for Creative Photography. © Center for Creative Photography, Arizona Board of Regents.)

Postcard of Aunt Sally's Candy Shop and the carriage ride service in the French Quarter in the 1940s. Pierre Bagur, founder of the company, introduced carriage rides with African American drivers in the French Quarter during the 1940s to complement the sale of pralines. (Anthony J. Stanonis Collection, Special Collections and Archives, Loyola University New Orleans)

The interior of Kate Latter Candy Shop, seen here in 1958, combined pralines and other sweets to the left with a variety of souvenirs available to the right, including a selection of mammy dolls along the back wall. (Charles L. Franck and Franck-Bertacci Photographers Collection, The Historic New Orleans Collection, 1994.94.2.964)

Mannequins of the praline mammy abounded in the French Quarter from the 1920s through the 1980s. This photograph from September 1967 shows a tourist posing next to a mammified mannequin holding a box of pralines on Chartres Street near Jackson Square. (Anthony J. Stanonis Collection, Special Collections and Archives, Loyola University New Orleans)

4

Why Pecans?

LOUISIANA PECANS AND THE BIRTH OF A NEW SOUTH INDUSTRY

"When the wild Indian had this country all to himself and roamed through these vast forests, the Pecan tree furnished him a very reliable source from which to lay up a store of most excellent food," boasted a promotional pamphlet from the Stuart Pecan Company of Ocean Springs, Mississippi, in 1893. The newly established nursery dispersed the botanical work of Colonel W. R. Stuart, whose grafting of pecan trees popularized the nut native to the Mississippi River Valley. Stuart's nursery had promoted his self-named variety of pecan tree at the Columbian Exposition in Chicago. The sale of pecan trees birthed a new agricultural industry in the American South. "The white man has never paid much attention to the nut until within the last few years, and now they are proving themselves more worthy of cultivation each succeeding year on account of their superior excellence," heralded the pamphlet.[1]

The account of the pecan provided by the Stuart Nursery Company was only partially accurate. The pamphlet included excerpts of an immodest speech made by Stuart to the Mississippi State Horticultural Society in 1891: "Some writers have been pleased to call me 'The Father of Pecan Culture.' If my humble efforts have been instrumental in giving this branch of horticulture the prominence it has attained, surely those years were well spent." Although Stuart significantly contributed to the proliferation of pecan trees across the American South and even beyond, he was not the father of pecan horticulture. Even though there was increased interest in pecan production in the late nineteenth century, planters and, most importantly, enslaved persons along the waterways of the Mississippi River Valley had pioneered pecan cultivation and integrated the nut into their diets during the antebellum era.[2]

The growing popularity of the praline from the late nineteenth century onward depended on the entrepreneurship of African American women, the yearning for an agrarian past of romanticized plantations represented by Louisiana's production of brown sugar, and the literary celebration of the fictionalized praline-peddling mammy who loyally preserved Creole recipes. Yet it was the focus on the pecan praline, of all the vendors' wares, that linked nostalgia for the Old South with the desire for a resurrected New South. The pecan was a New South success story symbolizing the diversification of southern farming via the scientific management of agriculture. Though reassuringly contained by plantation sugar, the pecans threatened to burst from the crumbly patty. The farmed nut increasingly trumped the foraged nut, the ingredient so vital to Black praline producers' bottom line in the late nineteenth century. The availability of grafted varieties of pecan, like the Stuart tree, improved quality and consistency, raising consumers' expectations. Foraged pecans lacked the uniform attractiveness, flavor, and size of cultivated nuts. As cultivated pecan orchards matured during the early twentieth century, shelling firms were established to process the nuts, flooding the market with ready-to-use kernels. African Americans dependent on pecans gathered freely from wild trees could not afford the added expense of purchasing pecans given tight household budgets. This provided white candy manufacturers, which had the necessary financial resources to purchase improved shelled pecans, an opportunity to seize the praline market by the interwar years: they drove out the independent, entrepreneurial African American producers dependent on foraged nuts and replaced them with Black employees who performed the praline mammy on the streets for those engaged in a highly competitive tourist trade.

A NATIVE NUT

Early explorers of the Mississippi River Valley marveled at the pecan. Journeying downriver from Pennsylvania in 1816, Davis Thomas appreciated the majestic tree: "The pecan is only found on the first flats, and appears to be confined within the limits of common floods. It is a stately tree." With travel by boat the surest way to traverse the thickets of the antebellum era, venturers could hardly miss the pecan trees. "Pecans are the most numerous trees, and their fine foliage keeps the water, for the most part, in shadow," remarked a wayfarer in 1855. The wide canopy made the pecan the "loftiest and most beautiful tree" in the lowlands.[3]

Settlers arriving in the river bottoms adopted a Native American name for these trees lining the alluvial ridges. The word "pecan" derived from the Native American word "pakan." The word meant "nut requiring a stone to crack," thus applying to pecans, hickories, and walnuts. Variously pronounced, this word was used widely, with European explorers in the 1700s recording the term among the Algonquins in Quebec and the Natchez along the Mississippi River. Native American nations found hard-shelled nuts ideal for transport over long distances. The hard shell also offered northern nations such as the Algonquins an easily stored, nutrient-rich food source essential for surviving the frozen winters. Scientists contend that Native Americans some 8,000–10,000 years ago facilitated the spread of pecan trees through the Mississippi River Valley as they planted nuts near their campsites. They also spread the tree southward into what is now Mexico. A hundred grams of wild pecans, the equivalent of two handfuls, supply on average 718 calories, 9.7 grams of protein, 2.4 grams of fiber, and 74 grams of fat. The nuts also include trace amounts of nutrients such as iron, magnesium, potassium, beta-carotene, niacin, thiamine, riboflavin, and ascorbic acid. Rich in antioxidants, pecans were a superfood for native peoples dependent on hunting and gathering.[4]

As settlers established farmsteads along the waterways of the Mississippi River Valley, they often preserved the pecan trees bunched on the banks, enjoying their beauty, shade, and nuts. A farmer from Bluffton, Missouri, commended settlers' foresight: "In clearing the bottom lands along the Missouri river many farmers had the wisdom to leave pecan trees standing and have sometimes more than the wheat crop of the same ground." The same was true for plantations in Louisiana. The secretary to Revolutionary War hero Marquis de Lafayette marveled at the scenery along the Mississippi River during a tour of the United States in 1825. Journeying by steamboat between New Orleans and Baton Rouge, he observed plantations "embellished with orange groves, in the center of which are located the snow white mansions of the planters. There are avenues of oaks, cedars, and magnolias, numerous bearing pecan trees, and hedges of osage orange and Cherokee rose." Flatboatmen transporting goods found pecans a vital and accessible addition to their diet as they drifted downriver with the end-of-year harvests. Even as late as the 1940s, a visitor to New Orleans noted the importance of the nut to those working the river. Clark Firestone remarked on a sign offering goods for sale near the waterfront: he noted that it "recites, 'Furs, Alligator Skins and Pecans,' and that is old-time American."[5]

As sugar plantations took root, the pecan tree nourished enslaved people. With their land devoted to maximizing sugar production, planters relied heavily on purchases of pork and cornmeal from the midwestern states to feed their captive laborers. A physician in 1849 warned sugar planters: "The diet of negroes on most plantations being salt pork, corn bread and molasses—rarely eating fresh meat and vegetables—a condition of the system is thus produced, closely allied to *scurvy.*"[6] The enslaved scoured the countryside to supplement their rations. Enslavers encouraged such efforts. Planters often permitted the enslaved to maintain a garden patch near their quarters to grow vegetables, thereby reducing the owners' food costs, giving the enslaved a sense of ownership, and ensuring a more nutritious diet. The gardens were tended at night after the daily field work or on Sundays, a common day off. Some enslavers allowed their human property to raise their own pigs, chickens, turkeys, and ducks. Trusted slaves might even be permitted to hunt for game while others fished the nearby waterways. The enslaved also foraged for wild produce. Pecans provided a crucial form of sustenance. Gathering pecans required familiarity with the landscape and the memory of which trees produced the best nuts, given the inconsistent quality of wild pecan trees. Mississippi novelist James Peacocke in 1856 described enslaved children who "brought a lot of pecans 'to keep . . . from bein' hungry on de road.'"[7] One scholar in his study of the pecan singled out the nut as a particularly "excellent forage crop . . . passively cultivated" by the enslaved.[8]

Given African Americans' familiarity with pecans, it should not be surprising that an enslaved gardener at the Oak Alley sugar plantation on the Mississippi River discovered the importance of grafting pecan trees. Pecans are notoriously unpredictable when grown from seed, although many farmers into the late nineteenth century continued to plant the nut of a productive pecan tree in hopes of replicating the parent. The pecan tree's female flower forms a nut after pollination and fertilization from the pollen of a male flower, resulting in considerable variation in trees grown from seed, even from a tree known for excellent quality and production. Worse, a planted pecan seed took at least a decade to begin masting. The solution to replicating consistency and quality lay in grafting. In the winter of 1846–1847, the enslaver Jacques Télésphore Roman accepted scions from a friend named Dr. A. E. Colomb, who had repeatedly failed in attempts to graft pecan trees from a fruitful tree on the Anita Plantation situated on the opposite bank of the Mississippi River. Colomb contacted Roman because of the reputation within St. James Parish of his talented, enslaved horticulturalist Antoine, who was around 38 years old and had a wealth of experience. Antoine successfully grafted sixteen pecan trees. When these bore well, Roman instructed Antoine to graft 110 additional trees to populate a pasture along the river. Over the next two decades, Antoine's 126 pecan trees grew into an impressive orchard.[9]

Antoine's genius with horticulture was a sharply honed survival skill. His father Zephyr was an African, born around 1782. Captured and sold into slavery, Zephyr learned the intricacies of sugar processing so well that Jacques Télésphore Roman placed him in charge of sugar refinement at Oak Alley. Facing the deadly conditions of enslavement, Zephyr made himself indispensable. Antoine's knowledge of plants thus came from his father. While Zephyr managed the cane fields, Roman charged Antoine with care of the ostentatious garden around the main house and the extensive garden of a relative on a nearby plantation. The experience familiarized Antoine with a stunning variety of local and foreign plant life as Roman sought to impress fellow planters with exotic flora.[10]

The disruptions caused by the Civil War carried Antoine's discovery from local lore to national attention, although Antoine himself never profited or gained recognition for his achievement until the twenty-first century. He died sometime in the 1870s, spending his entire life in the vicinity of Oak Alley. His son had enlisted in the Union Army in 1863 and saw combat the next year during the Red River Campaign. He mustered out and returned home in 1866. By the early 1880s, Antoine's grandson moved to Algiers, across the river from New Orleans, where he worked as a truck farmer and laborer. In appreciation for how Antoine's skills built a reputation at Oak Alley that safeguarded his family, relatives adopted "Antoine" as their surname after emancipation.[11]

Jacques Télésphore Roman died of tuberculosis in 1848, leaving the plantation to his wife. She sold Oak Alley plantation in 1866 to cover its debts. The new owner cleared the pasture of Antoine's 110 trees, just as they reached the age of prime production, to maximize sugarcane acreage. Only the sixteen original trees survived. In the early 1870s, Oak Alley plantation was sold again. Hubert Bonzano, a German immigrant who arrived in Louisiana in 1845 and won election to various minor positions, purchased the property. Bonzano intended to profit from sugarcane, but he noted the impressive output and quality of Antoine's pecan trees. Bonzano arranged a display of the nuts at the Centennial Exposition in Philadelphia in 1876. The nuts received awards, and the trees gained an official name, the Centennial variety. Richard Frotscher of New Orleans and his partner William Nelson in 1882 were the first to offer grafted pecan trees for sale from their nursery. They cataloged the Centennial name in 1885, just as many tourists flocked to the Crescent City for its own international exposition. Antoine's grafts thus paved the way for the commercialization of a wild tree used for forage.[12]

The upheaval of war and Reconstruction made pecans even more vital to survival. Foraging allowed freed persons, poor whites, army deserters, and even wealthy white refugees fleeing the front to sustain themselves. In her 1872 novel about plantation life along the Mississippi River where she lived, Jeannette Walworth describes characters who "ramble after wild grapes, muscadines, or pecans." Walworth dedicated the novel to the people of Tensas Parish, Louisiana, who struggled with the hardship of war and its aftermath. Gathering blackberries and other edibles from the wild sustained families and generated income to cover other family necessities such as clothing. The dire condition of southerners after the war, whether African Americans who had long been denied education and were confronted with racist violence or whites often bearing the twin wounds of defeat and disability—all in a land ravaged by warfare—made foraging essential to survival.[13]

Archaeologists examining African American homes of the nineteenth century note the extent of hunting, fishing, and gathering that occurred to supplement household finances, even among relatively prosperous Blacks. Skills honed by pursuing game and searching for wild produce during slavery proved very useful after the Civil War. Hunting and gathering provided not only food but also resources to sell, with the proceeds used to purchase other necessities. Foraging became a lifeline for freed people earning meager wages or working as sharecroppers. Such skills also transferred to urban environments, where Black women scavenged markets for discarded produce, ventured into emerging suburbs to scout for wild edibles, or eyed neighborhoods for trees producing nuts and fruits.[14]

From the 1880s, foraging for the pecan declined. Local historian Flo Field recalled how "forest floors of this state were covered in the Teche and northern regions with a wasting wealth of wild nuts. Folks just didn't gather them." Wild nuts, including pecans, were generally poor in quality and instead were used to feed hogs. Crude techniques used to gather nuts during the 1860s and 1870s, such as sawing off nut-laden limbs or cutting down entire trees, had decimated some of the better wild pecan trees. A horticulturist witnessed the practices of some poor southerners during the late nineteenth century: "In Texas and Louisiana and along the Mississippi River bottoms, the trees are cut down or the nuts beaten off by negroes or the poor whites, and the nuts are collected in that way." The wild pecan trees with the best nuts ironically faced the most risk.[15]

Thus, the rise of the pecan as a southern culinary staple depended not on foraging but on agricultural modernization. Postwar advocates for a New South called for diversifying crops, loosening the stranglehold of staples like cotton and sugar on the regional economy. Cotton had proven a pretender to the throne, rather than a king. Regional boosters, led by *Atlanta Constitution* editor Henry Grady, advocated development of a range of crops to protect farm incomes while bolstering the South's economic security. Southerners turned their interest to the pecan to obtain a steady income and sustain their food supply. In the *Southern Cultivator* in 1868, S. B. Buckley of Austin called on fellow farmers across the defeated Confederacy to plant pecan trees, noting that they had "much neglected" the promising nut. Agricultural scientists at Louisiana State University in the 1890s boasted that a pecan orchard "would be a source of great pleasure and considerable profit when established near the farm or plantation home." Editors for the *Irrigation Age* in 1894 remarked, "Considerable attention is being given to the establishment of pecan groves in various parts of the country." The boon brought by pecan trees within their native grounds enticed an increasing number of farmers. "The natural groves of Texas and Louisiana, by the good profits they have given in recent years, have stimulated the culture of this valuable tree."[16]

Such rhetoric grew more intense in the early twentieth century as cotton monoculture across the South exhausted fields and drove many farmers deep into debt. The New Orleans Pecan Nursery Company, with headquarters in the city and fields north of Lake Pontchartrain, in 1917 self-servingly labeled the pecan the most valuable tree for southern farmers: "If the owners of cotton fields and cut-over pine lands had been able to procure grafted paper-shell pecan trees twenty years ago of the approved varieties we are offering to-day, thousands of them would have planted and would be independent to-day." The nursery operators elaborated, "It has been proven that five acres of pecan grove of full bearing size will make a living for a small family, while a ten-acre grove will yield a princely income." With overproduction leading to low prices for the inedible crop of cotton, the pecan beckoned to farmers as a backstop against destitution and starvation. The New Orleans-based nursery thus christened the South's cotton belt as the region's future pecan belt.[17]

Pecan trees were celebrated not only as a shade tree, a food source, and a producer of a marketable nut that could supplement income but also as a showcase of regional pride. The Jennings Nursery of Jennings, Louisiana, boasted of its stock with an intense southern pride at a time when nostalgia about the Lost Cause crested. The proprietors urged, "Plant them in the barn yard, in the corners where you can't plant anything else; care for and fertilize well, and in a very few years you will be doubly rewarded with Shade and The Best of all Nuts." Most importantly, the trees were from Dixie. Nursery officials boasted, "Our Trees are grown in the South, for the South; we handle no Northern grown stock."[18]

The rapid popularity of the pecan tree as a shade, food, and monetary source in the late nineteenth and early twentieth centuries led to a flood of scammers profiting from the craze. The faculty at Louisiana State University warned prospective pecan farmers in 1898: "The heavy demand for desirable varieties of pecans, has led many unscrupulous persons to enter the pecan nursery business in name only, and these people send out anything that even looks like a young pecan tree, give it either the name of a well-established variety or a new one, and sell it at a high price." Con artists exploited overeager cultivators. The faculty cautioned, "A number of these persons have been reported from various parts of the State, during the last season, as they have been scouring the swamps and open woods, selecting not only the young pecans, but the pignuts and other hickories as well, and have sold these to unsuspecting purchasers." The push to diversify farm production with pecan trees led to some seedy practices.[19]

Professional nurseries proliferated across the former Confederacy to meet the increased demand for pecan trees. These businesses slowly standardized the trade in trees and earned reputations that drove out the swindlers. They also stood in the vanguard of the diversification movement, encouraging farmers to experiment with various new fruit and nut trees. Rapid urban and suburban development further spurred demand for trees and shrubbery, both for food and decoration. Symbolic of this trend was the popularity of planting satsuma trees along the Gulf Coast—promoted as the Satsuma Belt by real estate brokers—from the 1880s through the 1920s. Freezes and disease have since largely erased this belt, but satsumas remain common in the yards of New Orleanians and even in commercial groves south of the city. Along the Gulf Coast, farmers also explored planting tung trees for their oil, an industry that thrived from the early to mid-twentieth century. Homeowners often selected tung trees for their springtime floral displays. Pecans joined the frenzy.[20]

Central Louisiana presented particularly fertile ground for the budding nursery industry, not because of the richness of the soil but for its usefulness in handling saplings, including pecan trees. Samuel Stokes, born in Mississippi in 1866, pioneered the industry in Louisiana. His parents moved near the central Louisiana village of Forest Hill in 1869. The family purchased a cheap fifty-acre farmstead, but the soil of sand and clay produced a hardscrabble life. Stokes as a youth taught himself grafting. When neighbors clamored for his plants, he opened a nursery in 1901. Though the soil proved barren for crops, the porous soil provided good drainage and enabled the easy removal of young plants. The surrounding piney woods offered young plants shelter from wind and cold. When ready for market, the trees were dug up and the roots dipped in a mud hole mixed with red clay to trap moisture. The roots were then surrounded by straw before being placed in a sack, typically made from burlap. Stokes used the railroad network built after the Civil War to reach customers in nearby Alexandria and those roughly two hundred miles away in New Orleans. The nursery Stokes founded remains active in the twenty-first century, run by his descendants, though with competition from some 220 other nurseries in and around Forest Hill; today, this town has a population of under a thousand residents and is home to the annual Louisiana Nursery Festival. The village proudly proclaims itself the "Nursery Capital of Louisiana," challenging boosters in McMinnville, Tennessee, who, building on the first such business opened in 1902, proclaim their town the "Nursery Capital of the World."[21]

The pivotal moment for commercial pecan cultivation occurred in the mid-1870s in Ocean Springs, Mississippi, a popular vacation spot on the Gulf Coast frequented by New Orleanians escaping the diseases and heat plaguing the city during the summer months. One such vacationer who settled in the town was William R. Stuart, born in Kentucky in 1820. He moved to Louisiana in the 1840s to launch a career in sugar and cotton trading. In 1871, he left politically tumultuous New Orleans for a retirement focused on raising livestock and pecan trees in Ocean Springs. Along the way, he gained the honorary title "colonel," which regularly prefaced his name. As described earlier, Stuart experimented with systemic grafting after gathering a hundred seedlings from Mobile and New Orleans. His work led to the creation of several cultivars still widely planted today. The high yield, large nut size, and considerable resistance to disease of one variety that Stuart developed brought increased fame, especially when he named this most promising cultivar after himself after bringing it to market in 1892. Roughly one-quarter of pecan orchards in the early twenty-first century still consist of the Stuart variety.[22]

Although Stuart died in 1894, his legacy remained strong, as did that of Ocean Springs and the surrounding county as a center for pecan tree development into the early twentieth century. Horticulturalist Lenny Wells, in tracing the history of pecans, argues, "If Oak Alley Plantation was the birthplace of commercial pecan production, then Jackson County, Mississippi, was its cradle of infancy." Though just outside the native range of the pecan tree, Jackson County sat between Mobile and New Orleans, allowing residents to market their wares easily by railway while also acquiring ample seedlings and scions to experiment with in creating new varieties. The soil also allowed for easy removal of plants, much like in the Forest Hill area of central Louisiana. Further, as a county populated both by wealthy retirees like Stuart and a significant number of transplants on the make, money and entrepreneurial spirit drove the development of the nursery center.

Nurseries abounded around the one established by Stuart. The German-born Charles Pabst launched one in 1883. In the 1890s, Pabst invested heavily in the pecan tree trade after bringing the Pabst variety to market. Pabst was far from alone in tapping this new agricultural industry. The arrival of 36-year-old, Illinois-born Theodore Bechtel in 1899, who sold off his fruit tree nursery in his home state to launch a new nursery on the Gulf Coast, eventually led to the creation of the cleverly named Success variety in 1903.

Bechtel marketed the Candy variety a decade later. This pecan tree produced smaller but consistently full, attractive kernels that are ideal for confectioners. The Candy variety became and remains especially popular within Louisiana. Bechtel's firm competed with thirty-two other pecan nurseries in Jackson County by the 1920s. When Bechtel died in 1931, his nursery alone contained more than 13,000 young pecan trees.[23]

The growing knowledge about pecan trees inspired horticulturists and entrepreneurs across the South to identify and market promising varieties. Emil Bourgeois, a native of St. James Parish, not far from where Antoine pioneered successful grafting techniques for the pecan, propagated young trees from what locals called the Duminie Mire pecan. Mire had been a sugar planter who experimented with raising pecan trees from seed in 1836. One of these trees became widely recognized as exceptional. In 1877, Bourgeois, a sugar planter operating Rapidan Plantation in St. James Parish, began grafting from the Duminie Mire pecan tree, selling to neighbors along the Mississippi River. William Stuart renamed the variety "Van Deman" after U.S. Department of Agriculture professor H. E. Van Deman. Extensively advertised in the 1890s, the Van Deman pecan spread across the South. In more arid Texas, Edmond E. Risien, an English cabinetmaker arriving in Galveston in 1872, soon played a key role in the spread of cultivated pecans in the Lone Star State. He settled in San Saba, Texas, and quickly developed an interest in pecan cultivation. His experiments led to the creation of numerous pecan varieties, most famously the Western Schley, still the most popular variety grown in the western United States and Mexico. Risien launched the West Texas Pecan Nursery in 1888. A shrewd marketer, he sold pecans to Queen Victoria, President William McKinley, and poet Alfred Lord Tennyson, among others. From a salvage crop meant for home consumption through the 1870s, the pecan emerged in the New South as a highly marketable orchard crop of a new agricultural industry.[24]

Pecan groves sprouted across the southern landscape in the early twentieth century. The crops produced by high-yielding, grafted pecan trees planted in the 1880s and 1890s convinced reluctant farmers of the value of diversifying into nut cultivation over coming decades. Given the long wait for a pecan tree to reach full production, the reluctance of farmers to devote acreage to an orchard was understandable, especially with the professional nursery industry still in its infancy. The Centennial variety, for instance, took as much as fifteen years from the time of grafting until it grew mature enough to bear nuts. Even today, a pecan tree needs three to four years to bear nuts and six to eight years to reach viability for commercial harvesting. Furthermore, pecans only fruit every two to four years after they reach maturity. This cycle likely evolved to ward off predatory insect infestations and to enable rest between mastings. Only the passage of time answered farmers' questions about the wisdom of planting pecan trees. The development of insecticides to protect pecan trees made investing in orchards an easier decision. The arrival of the boll weevil and its decimation of cotton fields in the early twentieth century convinced many cotton farmers to plant pecan orchards.[25]

The number of cultivated trees increased at a staggering rate between 1900 and 1925, an era when pecan production evolved into a consolidated industry with a reach extending far beyond Louisiana. In Alabama, the number of trees in orchards rose from roughly 25,000 to 170,000. Mississippi increased its orchards from 40,000 to 710,000 trees. Florida's orchards expanded from 39,000 to 524,000 trees, and South Carolina's orchards grew from 10,000 to 200,000 trees. Yet the two largest pecan-producing states dwarfed these figures. Georgia's pecan industry rose from 30,000 to 2,368,000 trees, and Texas's pecan industry leapt from 359,000 to 2,419,000 trees. Farmers clearly heeded the call of nurserymen like J. B. Miller of Baconton, Georgia, who published a brochure in 1917 with a forthright title: "Plant Pecans and Prosper." The reach of pecan trees now stretched far beyond the river bottoms.[26]

The 1910s were a pivotal decade, with the number of trees recorded in the South rising by 70 percent. The tree had become so prominent that Edwin Jackson Kyle, dean of the School of Agriculture at Texas A & M University, launched the first academic course on pecan culture in 1911. The first serious text on pecan culture, cowritten by Kyle and University of Georgia Agricultural Experiment Station director Henry Perkins Stuckey, appeared in 1925 under the title *Pecan Growing*. By the 1920s, with so many trees maturing and farmers investing their well-being in the nut, pecans finally gained recognition as a stand-alone cash crop.[27]

AN INDUSTRIAL NUT

Boosterism about the pecan's benefits intensified public cravings for the nut. But given the length of time required for a pecan orchard to reach peak productivity, the supply of pecans remained heavily dependent on foraged nuts until the 1920s. In 1899, for instance, the total production of pecans in the United States amounted to barely over 3.2 million pounds. Managers of a nursery based in Chicago commented, "Practically all of these were of the small, wild, uncultivated varieties, not to be compared with the improved paper shell pecan now being grown, either in taste, size or flavor." Praline-selling African Americans, who had generational knowledge of the location of the best pecan trees to forage, enjoyed a considerable economic advantage that prevented white candymakers from seizing market share for the increasingly popular treat. This, however, changed as pecan orchards matured, and shelling became an industrial process that flooded the market with affordable, quality pecans.[28]

Early marketers of pecans employed tricks to beautify subpar nuts, and buyers could not be confident that they were buying quality nuts. Marketers manipulated the shells to disguise poor-quality pecans, passing off inconsistent foraged nuts and nuts from low-quality orchards. The *Daily Picayune* in 1907 advised consumers to understand the seasonality of the pecan: "Pecan pralines are always favored for holiday candies. It is only in the winter the rich pecan nut is wholesome, and when once [*sic*] can procure the present-year product, about the finest nut that grows." The article warned New Orleanians, "But, as there are tricks in all trades, one often pays a big price for nuts that are literally Dead Sea fruit, inasmuch as they have no kernel whatever, the outside being polished, even varnished, to look so fine and good. The best pecans are a dull grayish-brown without polish, the shell thin and the meat rich and oily." Only these nuts were ideal to "make flat cakes" of pralines.[29]

From the early twentieth century onward, professional shelling operators opened as pecan orchards matured, saturating the market with quality nuts. The pecan trees supplied by celebrated cultivators like Stuart, Pabst, Bechtel, and Risien, among others, not only improved consistency of the nut but, equally important, created thinner shells to reduce the labor involved in accessing the fruit. Across the United States employment in shelling companies increased as the country moved to industrial food production in the late nineteenth and early twentieth centuries. Exposing the fruit ensured that only high-quality pecans could be sold. The exposed nut also encouraged consumers to eat and cook pecans, particularly housewives who might struggle breaking the notoriously hard pecan shell. Furthermore, the rise of pecan shelling businesses, initially concentrated in San Antonio, St. Louis, and New

Orleans, encouraged farmers to raise more pecans because the wider availability of the kernel prompted confectioners and candymakers to incorporate the nut into their products, further spurring demand.[30]

Processing became key to the modern market. Whereas nuts before the twentieth century, according to professor of nutrition M. E. Jaffa at the University of California in 1908, were often "to be had in country regions for the gathering and were of no commercial importance," the proliferation of orchards and rise of industrial food production dramatically altered attitudes. Jaffa noted a significant shift in the consumer market: "Within the last few years the trade in shelled nuts has very markedly increased, and shelled walnuts, hickory nuts, almonds, English walnuts, pecans, etc., are now very commonly found in shops."[31] The 1910s witnessed a revolution within the nut sector as these various shelled nuts surpassed unshelled nuts in retail sales. The public grew accustomed to the convenience of nuts freed from their husks. Pecans were still largely sold whole to consumers through the interwar period, although a growing proportion went to shellers as more orchards matured. Wild pecans, known on the market as seedling pecans, were shelled before distributed by wholesalers to ensure uniformity and satisfaction.[32]

The nut shelling industry increased the presence of nuts in the American diet. Cashews, for instance, were barely present in the U.S. marketplace before World War I. Imports of cashews increased from 100,000 pounds in 1923 to 14.9 million pounds in 1934 and 26.2 million pounds in 1938. Other nuts also grew in popularity. Americans imported 12.4 million pounds of Brazil nuts, with domestic production adding an additional 6.4 million pounds during the late 1930s. Consumers ate one-tenth of a pound per capita. Walnuts proved the chief competitor to pecans for the American palate. Total walnut production in the United States amounted to 116.6 million pounds in 1938, with an additional 4.8 million pounds imported, compared to the pecan harvest of 76.9 million pounds. Americans consumed 0.38 pounds of walnuts per capita annually in the late 1930s, compared to 0.22 pounds of pecans per capita. The only other rival to pecans were almonds, with the country producing 40 million pounds and importing an additional 2.9 million pounds in 1938.[33]

By the interwar period, pecans were mainstream and provided a valuable source of nutrition and income to hard-hit farmers during the Great Depression. Farmers across the United States produced 2.2 million pounds of improved pecans in 1920, 12.3 million in 1925, 13.2 million in 1930, and 20.5 million in 1935. During this same period, seedling pecans sent to market typically hovered steadily between 30 million and 50 million pounds. R. C. Wright, writing for the U.S. Department of Agriculture in 1940, described the production and marking of nuts in the United States as "an industry of considerable importance and magnitude." The twelve top-producing states harvested a pecan crop worth some $5,736,200. Further, the nut market thrived year-round rather than largely during the winter. "A large part of this output is consumed during the winter months, especially during the Christmas holidays; but with the increasing use of nuts by bakers, confectioners, and ice-cream manufacturers, the marketing season has been spread throughout the year." Easily stored and shipped, pecans proved a bounty.[34]

Small-scale shelling operations, like the one described in E. V. Jameson's novel *Little Jane* in the 1890s, faded in the face of competition from large-scale shelling plants that flooded the market with cheap shelled pecans. The processors of San Antonio, St. Louis, and New Orleans easily accessed the wild stands and improved groves reaching maturity in the early twentieth century.[35]

San Antonio's advantages quickly turned the city into the primary hub for the pecan shelling industry. Railroads were essential for concentrating the South's pecan crop in San Antonio and then dispersing the shelled product nationwide to food manufacturers and consumers. Labor costs in San Antonio were low. Indeed, they were so low that mechanical innovations to the shelling process were minimal until the late 1930s. Hands were cheaper to hire and fire than machines to buy and maintain. These shelling companies, entirely owned by white investors, depended on Mexican laborers who worked long hours for poverty-level pay. Some of these workers were long-time San Antonians of Mexican descent. Many, however, had crossed into the United States as refugees, escaping the chaotic Mexican Revolution that raged from 1910 to 1920. Some 20,000 Mexicans fled annually to the United States in the 1910s. This figure jumped to between 50,000 and 100,000 per year in the 1920s as immigration laws in the United States restricted foreign arrivals for all but the Western Hemisphere, encouraging labor recruitment among Mexicans who continued to flee unrest in their home country. The racial violence encountered across rural Texas and the worsening drought associated with the Dust Bowl made the urban center of San Antonio a safer harbor.[36]

Each year during the 1930s, more than half of all shelled pecans entering the U.S. market came from San Antonio. These shellers processed 30 million pounds of pecans annually during the interwar period. On the eve of World War II, about 62 percent of the pecan meats from San Antonio shellers derived from improved nuts. Whereas mechanization continued among shellers outside Texas, the abundance of Mexican workers willing to earn from a dollar to three dollars a week sorting and cracking pecans by hand proved cheaper than purchasing and maintaining machines designed for that purpose. Julius Seligmann and Joe Freeman recognized the opportunities in exploiting the supersaturated labor market in central Texas. They opened the Southern Pecan Shelling Company in 1926, a firm that soon shelled more than one-quarter of the pecans passing through San Antonio. The company sold contractors whole pecans and then bought back the shelled nuts, thereby controlling the sale and purchase prices of an essentially monopolized commodity. Some 400 variously sized shelling operations copied this contracting system, employing between 10,000 and 20,000 workers depending on the size of the annual crop. Federal investigators in 1938 considered San Antonio's pecan shellers "one of the lowest-paid groups of industrial workers in the United States." Average annual family income amounted to $251 dollars for a family of 4.6 persons, with each member working roughly fifty-one hours per week. Some made ends meet in the highly seasonal pecan shelling business by picking cotton or traveling to northern sugar-beet fields. Pecan shellers tended to range in age from their twenties through forties. The difficulty of cracking even thin-shelled pecans over long periods precluded youths and the elderly from such work. The high frequency of finger maiming meant few could continue into their fifties.[37]

Worsening economic conditions during the Great Depression and intensive efforts to organize labor, safeguarded under the New Deal, sparked a strike among San Antonio shellers in 1938 that revolutionized pecan production within the United States. After several failed efforts at unionization during the mid-1930s, the Congress of Industrial Organizations finally succeeded in making inroads among the pecan-shelling workforce. A spontaneous walkout in January 1938, after contractors announced a wage cut, spread rapidly across San Antonio, dragging the union into the fight. Police Chief Owen Kilday guided the city's policemen and firemen in heavy-handed attacks on the strikers; they regularly fired teargas and arrested more than a thousand picketers. Kilday stated, "You call it a strike; I call it a disturbance out of Washington, DC." Despite the brutality, more than half of the approximately 12,000 shellers then in San Antonio remained on strike through mid-February. Union membership rose dramatically, with roughly three thousand members paying dues even while out on picket lines. The harsh tactics of Kilday and the resilience of the pecan shellers garnered the attention of Governor James Allred, who ordered Texas's Industrial Commission to investigate. With the battlelines hardened, Allred finally convinced Seligmann to negotiate with the union. Where the Southern Pecan Shelling Company led, the rest of San Antonio's shellers followed. In early March, a deal ended the strike. Workers agreed to a smaller pay raise than initially demanded, pending a review by an arbitration board. The board soon confirmed a compromise on wages, ensuring workers a slightly higher income.[38]

An even bigger problem soon confronted the shelling operators. Passage of the Fair Labor Standards Act in October 1938 would require wages to be raised from five cents to twenty-five cents an hour and working conditions to be improved for the pecan shellers. Company owners resisted, closing their businesses rather than meet the provisions of the act. Some eight thousand workers were thrown out of work. The prospect of this legislation and the earlier strike led employers to mechanize the shelling process, thereby decreasing their reliance on manual laborers and minimizing government interference. The firms kept their doors locked until shelling equipment could be installed. Shelling operators by June 1939 rehired roughly 1,600 laborers. In doing so, San Antonio finally copied the actions of pecan shelling businesses elsewhere that opted for mechanization during the Depression to cut labor costs. The R. E. Funsten Company in St. Louis, for example, mechanized its factory after a successful strike by its 1,600 employees in 1933. Nearly 90 percent of this workforce were Black women; the rest were Polish women. After introducing shelling machines, the company only employed 230 young women, mostly the Polish immigrants, at the higher wages dictated by New Deal legislation.[39]

AND PRALINES TOO

"What a glorious tree it was!" proclaimed Mrs. W. M. Murphy of Tallulah, Louisiana, in 1934. Her reminiscence of a childhood spent on a plantation, published in the normally staid *Louisiana Historical Quarterly,* centered on her nostalgic admiration of a large pecan tree. The family plantation was a place "the very best I have known," and the "old Pecan Tree, so straight and strong, with wide protecting arms, was the greatest tree that ever grew." She recalled marking her growing height in the bark and stretching her arms around the "wondrous bulk." Animals and insects found homes in the branches. Friends and family enjoyed the shade. Children feigned imaginary cockfights, tea parties, and other games under the tree. Murphy's foundational years unfolded beneath the "shielding arms of the old Pecan Tree." The tree was an "ancient protector of many generations of young life."

Murphy also related the fading plantation culture of Louisiana via the life of the pecan tree. The tree, seemingly so sturdy and timeless, proved vulnerable after all. The river, "in the stillness of the night, with no one to witness the tragedy, bore away on his swirling current the dear, old Pecan Tree with its wealth of knowledge, of sacred confidences and loving memories!" The flow of time eroded Louisiana's plantation economy and lifestyle as industrialized production, the ongoing out-migration of African Americans, the focus on labor protections, and concern over civil rights altered the cultural landscape during the twentieth century. The wild pecan tree of the Old South and its fruit were erased by scientific agriculture and mechanized processes in the New South.[40]

Advertisements in New Orleans heralded the pecan as more farmers invested in the crop during the early twentieth century, with the mythologized praline well situated as a vehicle to deliver the nut to consumers. S. W. Clark and Sons in New Orleans offered cans of "Creole pralines" and two-pound packages of "Louisiana Pecans" ready for shipment as Christmas gifts by 1901. Solari's too sold "Louisiana pecans" by 1904 among other local goods, such as "Creole Pecan Pralines."[41] An ad for Solari's in 1908 declared, "STRANGERS VISITING THE CITY will find us headquarters for Louisiana Pecans, all sizes." The local Katz and Besthoff retail chain offered pralines "chuck-full of Louisiana pecans" in 1918. D. H. Holmes Department Store harped on the quality of the 1919 Louisiana pecan crop, offering customers some of the five hundred pounds purchased by the firm. An ad boasted, "These are splendid nuts, full of rich fat meat and they break so that the meats fall out practically whole. They make wonderful pralines."[42]

The industrialization of American foodways and fears over food purity that spurred the Pure Food and Drug Act of 1906 encouraged an emphasis on the health benefits of pecans. Yorkman Candy Company in 1919 went so far as to credit its Creole pralines as an excellent health preservative. The company bragged, "Get the habit of eating one or more every day. They're full of nuts—the most digestible of all foods, and nourishing."[43] Another ad claimed, "Original Creole Pralines Are Good for You and Good to You." The company further asserted, "Chuck full of large pecans, which contain most of the elements that build both frame and body tissues." Such rhetoric presented the pecan as a superfood. In 1948, the year Louisiana marketed fifteen million pounds of pecans, Maida Tabor, Orleans Parish home demonstration agent, instructed local housewives that the pecan was the "king of nuts." "The pecan can't be beat in the culinary field," she declared.[44]

Politicians, journalists, assorted businessmen, and cultural commentators celebrated the pecan as representative of a bountiful Louisiana. U.S. senator Joseph E. Ransdell of Lake Providence, Louisiana, became known for distributing pecans from his estate to fellow members of the Senate Rivers and Harbors Committee. When a fellow politician queried whether they could expect a gift of pecans after the 1917 harvest, Ransdell boasted, "Yes, and pralines, too." Helen Robbins in 1922 encouraged readers of the *Times-Picayune* to shop locally for unique Christmas gifts that advertised Louisiana: "Pralines or pecans, distinctive of New Orleans and the South, would carry thorough enjoyment to Northern or Western friends."[45] By the 1920s, the term "pralines" had become synonymous in the United States with the use of pecans. The *Times-Picayune* in 1931 noted that pleasurable "crunching of the Creole pecan praline" had provided pecan growers with a "confection supreme which has helped carry the fame of Southern pecans far and wide."[46]

Hospitality packages and educational lectures in the interwar period spread word about the Louisiana pecan and the candy it enhanced. On the recommendation of Mayor Martin Behrman, schoolchildren were incorporated into a "Sell New Orleans" campaign in 1925 featuring pecans and pralines. One school packed pecans "away into every available corner of a box of Louisiana products," along with a recipe for pralines for shipment to schools in Vermont. Organizers targeted press coverage and thus publicity for the city to bolster tourism and the sales of locally produced goods. Included in the shipment was a miniature Mardi Gras float depicting the harvesting of pecans.[47] The students also sent a wax figure of a praline vendor accompanied by booklets titled "Tante Clementine" and "The Evolution of the Praline." Similar packages reached schools in New Hampshire in 1926.[48] The superintendent of schools in Buenos Aires also received a parcel featuring pralines, pecans, and other "dainties peculiar to New Orleans" along with promotional literature in 1926.[49]

Pecans became ever more ubiquitous in the American diet. The defeat of the Mexican shellers in San Antonio in 1938, along with the continued maturation of pecan orchards across the southern and western United States, enabled larger mechanized shelling firms to undercut the prices of smaller operators, much as the Sugar Trust had consolidated refining sugarcane and beets a generation earlier. Mechanized plants in Pittsburgh, St. Louis, and Chicago soon predominated, flooding the market with cheap, shelled pecans. World War II spurred the federal government to encourage greater consumption of pecans and other nuts as a substitute for meat. Bumper crops during the 1940s and 1950s further galvanized efforts by growers and sellers to increase Americans' consumption of pecans. Historian James McWilliams identified the mid-twentieth century as an era of "relentless pecan surplus" that led to advocates calling for pecans "to be stuffed into all manner of food" ranging from rice dishes to bread.[50]

Although pecans were mixed into a range of recipes, desserts served as the primary avenue for shoveling pecans into consumers' stomachs. Bakeries across the United States experimented with new cookies and cakes that would need the widely available and cheap pecan. The trend intensified over the mid- to late twentieth century. In 1954, for example, Mack's Bakery in New Orleans hawked pecan praline cakes as the business's signature creation. Keith Courrégée, writing for the Cane River Pecan Company in Nachitoches, Louisiana, in 1984, prefaced his cookbook by noting the range of recipes for pecans: "Pecans have long been used in cakes, candies, pies, cookies, and desserts but imaginative cooks are now using them successfully with fish, meat, poultry, salads, vegetables, dressings, and soups." Although advocates of pecans had long heralded the benefits of the nut, Courrégée went a step further, capturing with a healthy dose of hyperbole the fervency of pecan boosters and the intense competition for consumers. He warned, "Other kinds of nuts are NEVER substituted for pecans. To do so would certainly incur the wrath of the Gods and bring down disgrace and destruction upon the head of such a renegade and heretic!!!" Promoters most successfully popularized the pecan pie, which first appeared in Texas in the 1880s and strengthened national interest in New Orleans's praline.[51]

Yet no product pushed the pecan and the praline into national consciousness like the advent of pralines-and-cream ice cream. With the United States awash in milk, sugar, and pecans after World War II due to farm subsidies born of the New Deal, continued orchard maturation, and Cold War–era concerns over national fitness, ice cream emerged as a mass treat to provide youths the fat and calcium needed to develop after the lean years of the Great Depression. A national grid of affordable electricity, bolstered by the New Deal development of the Tennessee Valley Authority and other hydroelectric projects, and the mass production of refrigerators equipped with freezers for homes in the burgeoning suburbs made ice cream a popular household treat. In 1947, the *Times-Picayune* and *States,* recognizing the national trend, carried the earliest local recipes for "Praline Ice-Cream."[52] The flavor allowed Americans to take an ephemeral journey to New Orleans a bowl at a time while offsetting the nation's agricultural surpluses. Local historian Pie Dufour in 1950 laughed that a traveler could buy praline ice cream at the Waldorf Astoria in New York City but could barely find the concoction in New Orleans.[53]

A national campaign during the 1950s by the Borden Company, a dairy and food conglomerate, brought pralines-and-cream flavored ice cream into the mainstream. Borden rolled out a brand named "Lady Borden Ice Cream" to appeal to the housewives raising the children of the postwar baby boom. The brand frequently rotated flavors to entice consumers, with one of the featured flavors tapping Americans' fascination with New Orleans by blending pralines into ice cream. A full-page ad published in *Life* magazine in November 1951 suggested consumers could adventure to the Crescent City while spooning away at the creamy concoction: "Ever tasted pralines . . . those big beautiful nut-filled candies from New Orleans?" Readers were quickly reassured that Lady Borden Praline Pecan Ice Cream "tastes like pralines . . . only better!" The ad depicted an ice cream parlor advertising pecans, pralines, and bon-bons. A mother and her young daughter, dressed as if from the 1890s, leave the premises with a brown grocery bag of sweets. Above, on the second floor, a southern belle in a hoop skirt stands behind an iron-lace balcony. The scene recalled the French Quarter.[54]

The flavor proved so popular that Borden reissued the ice cream in 1953. An ad published in *Life* magazine promised, "A return engagement from New Orleans!" The praline-studded product again brought the fun of the city home to consumers across the United States: "Here's a gay and festive ice cream, rich with buttered pecans and the flavor of pralines, those wonderful sugar-nut candies from New Orleans." Rather than a French Quarter scene, this bowl of Lady Borden was accompanied by an image of a home decorated with iron lace and surrounded by a large yard populated by live oaks draped in Spanish moss, with this domestic space protected by an iron picket fence. The carton of Lady Borden Praline Pecan bursts through the gates toward the reader. To reinforce the message that the ice cream brought home the flavors of elsewhere, the bottom of the full-page ad featured a train with the tagline, "All aboard! All a-Borden's! Get Lady Borden."[55] National ad campaigns for the popular flavor continued into the 1960s. Whether from its cartons or from the company's chain of ice cream shops, the last of which still survives as a culinary landmark in Lafayette, Louisiana, the Borden Company brought the taste of pralines into American homes everywhere during the mid-twentieth century.[56]

Praline ice cream grew in such popularity nationwide by the 1970s that a corporate showdown over the profitable flavor became a textbook legal case of trademark enforcement, giving pralines of all forms even more publicity. Baskin-Robbins, the nationally prominent ice cream chain, began distribution of its own version trademarked as "Pralines 'N Cream" in September 1979.[57] "Pralines 'N Cream" became the best-selling ice cream for the company's franchisees during the 1980s, so much so that numerous other brands copied the flavor. Soon, competitor Häagen-Dazs was scooping its own version branded "Pralines & Cream" at its parlors. Baskin-Robbins sued for trademark infringement. The company lost the lawsuit in 1985 when the court ruled that Baskin-Robbins had already allowed too many competitors to market versions of pralines-and-cream ice cream before acting against Häagen-Dazs for its trademark breach. Pralines-and-cream had entered a very public domain.[58]

Other companies, even those national corporations far from the dairy and pecan trades, noted the success of those hawking praline-flavored ice cream. Car manufacturers in the 1970s offered models painted with the color "Pralines and Cream."[59] New Orleans mayor Dutch Morial joined executives of the alcohol producer Hiram Walker to launch praline liqueur at a New Orleans press conference in 1979. Consumers were enticed to drink the liqueur straight or to pour it over ice cream. According to spokesperson Sandy Weisenauer, Hiram Walker preserved the beverage's New Orleans connotations even to the point of having the liqueur bottled in the city. Weisenauer emphasized that, when "taken straight, it tastes exactly like a praline." The product sold roughly 25,000 cases a year nationwide by 1983.[60] National sales struggled, however, because of the sweetness and oddity of alcoholic pralines in liquid form. Not surprisingly, Louisiana became one of the largest markets for the product, accounting for approximately 12 percent of consumption.[61]

A GAUNTLET OF PECAN STANDS

Small dealers in and around New Orleans continued to supplement farm income through pecan sales during the mid- to late twentieth century. Hermann Deutsch, reporting for the *Item* in November 1951, observed that pecan vendors lined the highways into New Orleans. He remarked on a recent journey along the Gulf Coast between Mobile and New Orleans: "Of course, you'll have to run a gantlet of pecan stands wherever you go along the Coast these days. Harvest time for pecans is here. In every orchard or grove you will see pickers with long bamboo canes 'thrash' the laden trees and then gather the newly fallen brown nuts from the grass." Brian Martinez of Donaldsonville, Louisiana, regularly took a leave of absence from his U.S. Department of Agriculture job as a computer programmer to sell pecans from a pickup truck during the 1980s. The nuts came from a family-run farm of twenty-five acres populated with pecan trees. Beginning in October each year, Martinez and most of his eight siblings began gathering nuts on his father's farm. Some were sold to various grocery stores in the area. Martinez manned the roadside pickup truck loaded with 300 pounds of pecans on the main shopping thoroughfare in Metairie from November through January. "People buy pecans now to make candy and pralines for the holidays," he explained. He sold about a hundred pounds a day at ninety-nine cents a pound.[62]

By the mid-twentieth century, pecan trees and their fruit became ubiquitous within the national diet but grew ever less associated with the Mississippi River Valley. A growing multi-billion-dollar pecan industry flourished. In 1950, Georgia became the leading producer of pecans in the United States. The state remains so, typically marketing some 95 million pounds of the nut annually from 140,000 acres. Today, the United States produces 80 percent of the world's pecans, with Mexico harvesting the other 20 percent. Although states such as Louisiana, Mississippi, Georgia, and Texas remain prominent players in the growing of pecan orchards, stands in New Mexico and Arizona have now muscled into the lucrative market. Doña Ana County in New Mexico produced more pecans than any other county in the United States during the 2010s. The popularity of pecans internationally, especially in China, which purchased upward of 25 percent of the crop in the 2010s, has raised prices, spurring farmers to plant more pecan orchards.[63]

Along the way, the pecan praline has lost some of its panache. With few Louisianans living on sugar plantations with their pecan trees, and tourists increasingly aware of the troubled history of these sites as forced labor camps for the enslaved, nostalgia for the Old South has faded. So too has the urgency of creating an agriculturally diverse New South. Largely gone is the hand labor of harvesting and cracking pecans: machines in northern cities now process the nuts gathered from scientifically managed fields that often stretch far beyond the Mississippi River Valley. Industrial processes and mass manufacturing produce and refine the pecan, countering the popular image of New Orleans as a leisurely city out of step with modernity. The pastoral pecan of the plantation, like those produced by the tree described by Mrs. W. M. Murphy in 1934, has been washed away by the tides of time.

The birth of the commercial pecan orchard during the twentieth century contributed to the marginalization of the African American praline seller working the New Orleans streets with a product made of foraged nuts. Quality shelled pecans and processed sugar, even though they were cheap, proved an unaffordable luxury to working-class Black women operating on shoestring budgets. Some with the best recipes or most gumption still sold their wares in the streets. But a growing number of white male confectioners and several white female socialites elbowed into the trade by the 1920s, making the praline mammy an exhausted gimmick and largely erasing independent Black praline sellers from their choice haunts, even if they remained active within Black neighborhoods. Although their founders have long passed, some of these white-owned businesses established before World War II still dominate the praline market.

How did the pecan-filled praline change from a nineteenth-century street food, powering Black workers and empowering Black peddlers, into a twentieth-century souvenir, enriching white businesspersons and enchanting white tourists? Why did these white entrepreneurs emerge as supposedly authentic arbiters of New Orleans's Creole culture? And how did they rewrite the history of the praline and New Orleans to affirm their hold over the confection?

5

Like a Disneyland of Pralines?

MARKETING PRALINES AND MODERN TOURISM

It must have been a proud moment in 1912 for the Sicilian parents who had recently moved to New Orleans from Chicago. An *Item* reporter snapped a photo of their son and daughter costumed for Mardi Gras. The sister, carrying a white doll, appeared in mammy garb complete with tignon and blackface. Curiously, her seven-year-old brother, wearing a tignon and blackface, also dressed as a mammy. He carried a basket of pralines as an accessory. Such racial- and gender-crossing performances of the Black praline seller were common. At a New Year's Eve masquerade in 1913, a socialite attended "as an old praline woman, with blackened face, tignon of every color tied about her head, full blue old-fashioned Guinea blue calico, snowy apron and neck kerchief, and carrying a large basket of pralines." In 1915, H. E. Ulm, a barbers union leader, volunteered to "represent an old Creole Mammy" at a fundraiser for public schools held in Heinemann Park. The black-faced, feminized Ulm sold pralines "so identified with Old New Orleans."[1]

The praline mammy costumes worn by the siblings Bettina and Victor Hugo Schiro that Carnival Day in 1912 certainly reflected their generation's views on race in New Orleans. Victor worked a variety of jobs in his teens and twenties, even serving briefly as a Hollywood cameraman for Frank Capra during the mid-1920s. He then pursued a career selling insurance in New Orleans and, after World War II, established his own insurance agency. Victor also dabbled in local politics. He joined the ticket of reformer mayoral candidate Chep Morrison in 1950, winning a seat on the city's commission council as commissioner of public buildings and parks. In July 1961, he became interim mayor of New Orleans when Morrison resigned to accept an ambassadorship. Schiro subsequently won two full mayoral terms by casting himself as a segregationist tempered by pragmatism. A businessman and politician well aware of the importance of tourism to New Orleans's economy and municipal budget, Schiro shepherded the city through the turbulent 1960s by personally negotiating with civil rights leaders and their opponents. When he left office in May 1970, New Orleans had integrated while largely avoiding the bloody racial clashes that plagued other southern cities like Memphis and Birmingham, as well as tourist centers like Natchez in Mississippi and St. Augustine in Florida. Schiro's life framed an era when tourism emerged as New Orleans's economic centerpiece, with the praline serving as the most symbolic souvenir within its hospitality industry.[2]

Professional confectioners and socialites seized on the praline to rake in profits. To compete, they converted the praline seller into a caricature. They flooded the streets with Black women dressed in mammy outfits and splashed images of the praline mammy on packaging and signs. And, on occasion, these white latecomers to the praline trade donned blackface and stereotypical garb themselves to hawk the confection. Although a few of the formerly enslaved survived into the 1930s and 1940s, the oldest were barely teenagers during the last days of slavery. The passing of former enslaved cooks disembodied the praline mammy at the same time as professional white confectioners were using plantation sugar and farmed pecans to appeal to a growing tourism industry hungry for local items that served as representative souvenirs of New Orleans. Whites ever more easily co-opted the role as the decades of the twentieth century passed, occasionally hiring African Americans of the post–Civil War generation to impersonate the mythologized praline mammy of yore. Equally important, by preserving the myth of the praline as a core tradition of antebellum Creole life in New Orleans, these shopkeepers became the guardians of supposedly authentic Creole history, retold one praline box after another.

COOKING UP HISTORY

Whereas white women writers of the late nineteenth century reimagined the entrepreneurial drive of Black women through fiction that packaged them as mammies eager to aid whites and heed Jim Crow, one Louisiana author in the 1890s focused attention on the praline itself. Through his writings, Henry Castellanos ensured that everyone understood that the praline had arrived in New Orleans via a nobleman fleeing the French Revolution, not from working-class Blacks who had fled Louisiana's sugar plantations during the Civil War. This local writer invented an origin story for the Creole praline that cast the confection's creator and its initial consumers as male, further distancing Black women from the candy.

In 1895, lawyer and journalist Henry Castellanos published the influential *New Orleans as It Was.* Castellanos, born in 1828 and a lifelong resident, promoted his book as a reservoir of New Orleans's nearly forgotten history. In a chapter on odd characters and celebrities, he recounted the tale of an unnamed "chevalier" exiled from revolutionary France in 1795. This aristocrat landed in New Orleans, opening a shop supposedly on "Condé street, near Dumaine, which he pompously dubbed a 'confectionery.'" The store was said to have operated until his return to France in 1814. Castellanos gave pralines a lineage by writing of the chevalier and his sweets: "Pralines, the necessary adjunct of ginger cakes, 'estomacs mulâtres,' and spruce beer, once so common upon the little stands kept by colored women, were, as he claimed, his exclusive invention, and, be the case or not as it may, he became by this new industry the most popular man in the little community in his 'quartier,' particularly among boys." The chevalier thus introduced the praline, "by which we must understand the kernels of pecans, ground nuts or peach stones, inclosed [*sic*] in an envelope of burnt sugar." At a time when white southerners strove to maintain segregation and prevent miscegenation by passing ever stricter laws in the 1890s, Castellanos made sure that everyone understood that pralines were created by an aristocratic French man.[3]

For white New Orleanians, Castellanos racially liberated the praline by giving it a clear French genealogy. The author did for the Creole praline what Grace King did for Creole families. Both authors argued for the pure French whiteness of New Orleans goods and founders. Such whitewashing of southern foodways through fabricated histories was commonplace in the late nineteenth and early twentieth centuries, despite efforts by Black southerners to publish their own cookbooks noting their achievements and seeking, according to literary scholar Rafia Zafar, "gastronomic deténte."[4]

The narrative offered by Castellanos denied Black Louisianans' creative power. In his telling, African American cooks merely preserved this tradition through mimicry—a mimicry so perfect that it signified their admiration of and loyalty to white Creole society. Although the praline peddler, as a mammy, became a memento of the antebellum South, her product became a taste of France and French Louisiana, linked by the exiled chevalier to a time before the French revolutionaries emancipated the empire's slaves.

Marie Louise Points, the key figure in fictionalizing the praline mammy and promoting the praline as symbolic of the Creole past during the 1890s, also heralded the confection and offered her own invented history for the praline. One account from 1896, apparently written by Points, stresses that "the taste for this dainty Creole confection is spreading all over the south [*sic*]." She continued, "Strangers visiting New Orleans, stop and buy, and then pay a fee for the recipe, which the old praline makers are loth [*sic*] to give." Points presented interviews, though heavily fictionalized, with several "old negro women, who have been selling pralines since war times." One praline vendor expressed a coyness about the recipes she used: "For praline, you see, mam'zelle, dat is one Creole dish and we no want dose Americains come steal dat from us, too." Black cooks were known for their reluctance to share their recipes, thereby protecting their skilled labor and thus their employment prospects. Yet the popularity of the praline continued to grow. Points wrote, "In almost every home in New Orleans the lady of the house now knows how to make pralines, and the writer has often assisted at a praline party even in the American quarter." Across the city the "knowledge of concocting pralines is more general than before."[5]

Points offered a clear lineage for the pecan praline in December 1897 when the *Daily Picayune* carried the first published recipe for the confection. Although no author is given, the article and instructions were probably written by Points, who was employed as editor of the newspaper's women's section. Raised in a household with a deep commitment to the Lost Cause and to a glorified French Creole heritage, Points overlooked Castellanos's recent publication to propose a different history. She relayed that the confection came from "the great Viart, 'Homme de Bouche,' as he called himself, who tickled the palates of Louis XVIII and Charles X, in the jocund days of the Bourbon restoration." The chef André Viart, also sometimes published as Viard, had authored *Le Cuisinier Impérial* in Paris in 1806. The encyclopedic book gathered recipes from the court of Louis XVI and Napoleon Bonaparte.

This cookbook, along with several others, set the parameters for French cuisine during the nineteenth century, though with title changes to *Le Cuisinier Royal* in 1817 after the restoration of the French monarchy following Waterloo and to *Le Cuisinier National* in 1852 after a wave of political reforms swept Europe during the Revolutions of 1848. Viart's recipe supposedly found its way to New Orleans where the Creoles substituted pecans for almonds sometime after the 1830s. Further strengthening the ties to royalty, the *Daily Picayune* noted that the word *praline* according to "an ancient French dictionary in the writer's home . . . derived from the Marechal Plessin-Pralin whose butler one day advised him to have his almonds prepared after this fashion.'"[6]

Points's publication of the first recipe for pecan pralines reflected her understanding of white southern women's reluctance to engage in kitchen work. As editor of the women's section of the *Daily Picayune,* she needed to ennoble the recipe to mitigate against the racial connotations of cooking. The confection required a preface. By inventing a culinary tradition, she legitimized the home production of pralines by white housewives, who thereby would need not fear treading into kitchen work associated with African American domestics. Postbellum white families even with meager financial resources often hired Black women to prepare meals, sparing white housewives of that task. In the late 1890s when a wave of legislation mandating segregation swept southern states, white women might hesitate to replicate a recipe associated with African American cooks. But, in Points's telling, the recipe permitted southern white women to honor both their French ancestors and antebellum New Orleanians. The heightened racism of the era impelled them to guard their perceived culinary heritage, much as they mobilized to erect Confederate monuments, draft schoolbooks, or create historical archives. Points channeled not only the Lost Cause fixation with preserving antebellum Creole Louisiana but also a similar trend in France after its disastrous defeat in the Franco-Prussian War of 1870–1871, a fate of which she was keenly aware given that at least one sister studied music in Paris. Historian Priscilla Ferguson labels the French focus during the late nineteenth and early twentieth centuries on cultivating attachment to the land and local history through food "culinary republicanism." Points's origin story for the New Orleans praline merged the confection's French past with Louisianans' embellishment. As a recipe author in 1907 declared in the press, "The 'praline' is distinctly a Creole confection."[7]

Tellingly, the first local cookbook to herald the praline rolled off the press in 1900 after the narrative of the noble praline had been firmly established by Castellanos and Points. The *Daily Picayune*'s landmark *Creole Cook Book* became a touchstone for chefs and home cooks. Marie Louise Points served as its primary ghostwriter. The *Creole Cook Book* underwent multiple editions into the twenty-first century, becoming a cherished recipe trove in New Orleans. The editor, echoing Points's 1896 article, boasted of sending a reporter to "interview the old Creole 'mammies,' and to take down from their lips the exact formulae by which the famous Creole dishes are prepared." With the heritage of the praline firmly rooted in France, white New Orleanians could claim the recipes of Black cooks because they served as mere conduits of white Creole culture. Readers could thus gain access to "directions for making pralines and other Creole candies" at an affordable price that brought the book "within the means even of the poorest." They could re-create the Creole past because those Creoles' supposedly faithful former slaves longed to preserve the society that had enslaved them.[8]

As the praline grew in popularity within the tourist trade, New Orleanians leaned on Castellanos's account because it dated the recipe much earlier to colonial Louisiana. This made the praline more exotic and reinforced promotional efforts that enhanced New Orleans as a destination akin to Paris. Businesses tapping the predominantly white marketplace exploited the confection as a prestigious treat. The *Daily Picayune* by 1911 reiterated the story promoted by Castellanos on several occasions.[9] This "mysterious little old aristocrat" who remained unidentified "will live forever in the memory of New Orleans for inventing the luscious combination of pecans and cane sugar that we know as pralines," declared the *Times-Picayune* in 1919. Flo Field, a local historian celebrated for her walking tours of the French Quarter, wrote a pamphlet in the 1920s for the St. Charles Hotel titled "Where and How 'Ole Mammy' Pralines Are Made: A Story of the Candy of the South." Field credited the French nobleman for introducing the praline but, unusually, also recognized that African Americans were the creators of the flat, round patty. As a New Orleanian born in 1876, Field bridged the disconnect between Castellanos's improbable tale and the role of the enslaved by redefining the chevalier's candy: "The Chevalier's pralines were a sugar pocketbook of nut meats. As the slaves of Creole families made them, they became round, flat, and in all grande families, pralines were the confection. The recipe was handed from generation to generation."[10]

Businessmen, led by Theodore Grunewald, seized on the chevalier to package the praline as more than humble street food. Born in the 1870s, Grunewald at 17 years old worked in a music store before launching his own shop. He entered the hotel business in 1893. Gathering investors, he constructed the Grunewald Hotel in 1908 at a cost of $2.5 million. Growing rich from tourists, he soon recognized the additional profits to be reaped from cleverly marketed pralines.[11]

The Grunewald Hotel, labeling its candy kitchen the "Headquarters for Original Creole Pralines," referenced the mysterious chevalier as the hotel moved into the lucrative souvenir market by opening a grocery and delicatessen department in the 1910s. The chevalier myth allowed the hotel and its confectioners to claim an aristocratic heritage. The promoters, declaring that a "Vast Span of Years Bridge the Chevalier's Shop and the Hotel Grunewald Caters," boasted of the candy's regal origins: "Bound up in the traditions of old New Orleans is the story of M'Sieu le Chevalier, French Noble and exile. He, who so cautiously preserved his incognito during the turbulent times of the Eighteenth Century and all the while merrily held court in his tiny shop of the Vieux Carre de la Ville and made a certain confection of sugar and pecan, which, 'tis said, is how the 'praline' originated." The Grunewald's confectioners preserved this noble recipe. The labeling of the praline boxes ignored mammy imagery, instead celebrating "The South's Most Famous Confection" with a side panel that read "Cleanliness Purity."[12]

Wrapping the praline in the garb of French nobility paid hefty dividends for Grunewald. He owned the hotel until the early 1920s and maintained a range of complementary businesses, including a dairy, laundry, and various farms, until his death in 1949. Grunewald's obituary noted that his mail-order business for pralines, nothing less than a "gigantic" success for decades, was the foundation of his financial empire.[13]

The fabricated links to French nobility, the alleged popularity of the confection among antebellum Creoles, and the appearance of published recipes led some white housewives to muscle into the market. A resident of 723 Toulouse Street in the French Quarter advertised in 1903 seeking shops and peddlers willing to sell pralines. In 1904, Emily Clark, a single woman marketing under the homespun name "Aunt Milly," solicited Christmas orders for her packages of a dozen pecan pralines ready to mail nationwide.[14] Such classified ads became common during the twentieth century. Another homemaker, a Mrs. Daniel Jayes, pursued customers near Christmas 1945 by appealing to tradition: "MRS. JAYES Delicious Old Tyme Pecan Pralines." Subsequently interviewed, Jayes declared, "I've been swamped!" During the first month of advertising, she sold 200 dozen pralines at $1.20 to $1.50 a dozen, which she packed into miniature cotton bales. Even the wife of Louisiana governor Jimmie Davis placed an order.[15] Jayes was far from alone. By 1948, Mrs. Jules Seymour Gaiennie, another housewife, was promoting her "home-made confections-catering" featuring pralines and sundries under a clever name that exposed the mythos of the Black mammy, the white southern belle, the revered Old South, and deliciousness: "Aunty-Belle-Umm."[16]

Other white New Orleanians felt comfortable pushing into the fiercely competitive street trade. Sometimes individuals were hired, usually on commission, to walk the streets soliciting sales for confectionary firms and home producers entering the market. Cheap sugar and improved pecans facilitated this widening of praline production into white-owned candy factories and home kitchens. To sell this flood of pralines, businessmen and housewives looked for any means of unloading the confection, even hiring old men and boys of any race to peddle the candy. A praline maker at 735 St. Peter Street in a series of classified ads from 1905 and 1906 sought two elderly men, then a boy, and later elderly men and women to sell pralines for $3 a week.[17] A seller advertised in the classified ads in 1916, "TRAVELING men to sell genuine Creole pralines, side line to retail druggists, confectioners, grocers, news, cigar stands." An establishment on Exchange Alley in the French Quarter in 1926 hired "MEN and boys to sell pecan pralines, make $2 to $3 a day, good hustlers make more."[18] The J. Brown Candy Company on Conti Street in the French Quarter pursued "HUSTLERS. . . . Can make $10 to $15 per day by selling our special home made pralines and all kinds of candies." Another producer sought "3 MEN to sell pralines, commission basis" in 1934.[19]

This "fringe" street economy, as described by the *Item* in 1908, represented "hundreds of thousands of dollars annually," with a population of hawkers recognized as a "peculiar conglomeration of races and tongues." The influx of immigrants, especially from Sicily, Eastern Europe, Greece, Syria, and Bengal, in the late nineteenth and early twentieth centuries crowded New Orleans's streets with a new wave of vendors, predominantly male. These persons of "small capital, considerable thrift and some ambition," like the Black praline hawker, fought a fierce battle for consumer dollars. Fruit peddlers with stalls shouted out their wares. Chili con carne, waffle, and ice cream vendors toiled from pushcarts. Candy hawkers also worked from pushcarts with glass showcases displaying assorted treats, directly challenging the praline seller for customers. The newspaper commented, "Sometimes he places his stock of candies in a smaller showcase, resting on a table, and becomes a fixture at a certain corner. Sometimes he places it in a wheelbarrow, and may be found at any hour of the day extracting the delicious meat from the pecan nuts, which later reappear in 'pralines.'" Like the praline seller, these candy men followed the foot traffic. In the mornings, they gathered near Canal Street "awaiting the crowds hurrying to work" or going shopping. By noon, they congregated "in the vicinity of the big office buildings, where messenger and errand boys constitute a profitable and never-ending source of business." Schools also proved lucrative around noon as students reached the lunch hour. These men encroached on the circuit pioneered by Black women. Such competition further pressured Black woman under Jim Crow to conform to the mammy stereotype. Doing so allowed them to claim authenticity as imagined by white society and to gain access to areas potentially hostile to the presence of African Americans.[20]

Although these early twentieth-century white male vendors remain largely anonymous in the historical record, a few examples surfaced in press reports. In the late 1890s, Maurice Heymann, the son of a Jewish father from Poland and a Jewish mother from France, abandoned the sixth grade to start hustling pralines and cookies to passengers at the Pontchartrain Railroad's central station. He had learned peddling skills from his dad. The experience informed a profitable career in a range of businesses, including operating a movie theater, nursery, and department store with a grocery in Lafayette, Louisiana. He amassed an extensive real estate empire before his death in the late 1960s. A biographer later called Heymann the "quintessential Jewish businessman of the New South."[21] Twelve-year-old Oliver Fitzmaurice from the Carrollton neighborhood was interviewed in April 1926 as a financially ambitious youth. "I've been going to night school at the Benjamin Franklin school for a good while, and peddling pralines all day," explained Fitzmaurice. Fitzmaurice's earnings covered his tuition and assisted his mother.[22]

Nicholas Souhlas emigrated from Greece, arriving in New Orleans in 1923 at age 27. He soon took a job selling pralines and peanuts from a pushcart in the French Quarter while teaching himself English at night. By 1926, he saved enough to open Nicholson's Restaurant on Chartres Street. Souhlas remained in the restaurant business until 1962.[23] Frank Saitta found praline selling far more lucrative and entertaining than working as an electrician. At 32 years old in 1928, Saitta caught the attention of an *Item* reporter during a murder trial. Sitting in the back of courtrooms and wandering the corridors, Saitta, wearing a suit and tie, carried a large basket and proclaimed loudly during recesses, "Pralines, undoubtedly the finest you have ever eaten, pralines with almonds, pecans, peanuts or corn; pralines with lemon or strawberry flavor." He had been hustling those attending court for the past two years, and he knew his trade: "Society women . . . don't eat candy because they don't want to get fat; gamblers are hard men and they don't eat candy." Thus, Saitta favored rural attendees: "Country people . . . eat more candy than city folks. It's like being wild to eat candy if you're from the country." Major trials drew large crowds. He also favored the night court because he faced no competition from diners that were closed. As for being an electrician, Saitta joked that hustling pralines was a "sweeter racket." He was able to use his whiteness to gain access to literal corridors of power where African Americans faced harassment and exclusion.[24] Across the river in Algiers, the white, middle-aged brothers Louis and Sylvester Gravois, blind since birth, wandered Algiers during the 1920s with a basket of pralines prepared each day by their mother. Selling pralines for five cents a pack, they helped sustain the household, usually selling out each day.[25]

Such home production and direct marketing by white New Orleanians remained common into the late twentieth century.[26] One homemade praline maker in 1949 advertised for a praline distributor "in a convenient French Quarter location, preferably Royal street" in an obvious effort to tap the tourist trade. A female employee at a cigar factory in the 1950s sold homemade pralines to her fellow workers during the lunch hour. She made enough money that she was able to donate significant amounts to charity drives, doing so anonymously because "my boss might not approve" of her successful sales technique. Newspaper classifieds in the 1980s showed locals using new express mail services to distribute their homemade goods.[27]

African American women remained in New Orleans's praline market as home producers. But under Jim Crow, fierce competition mostly pushed them out of the tourist trade. Racism curbed their access to the streets central to white-oriented commerce, including the French Quarter, Canal Street, train stations, and other hubs of activity. These areas were also more closely regulated by the municipal government and packaged by businessmen for the tourism market. Such areas of New Orleans became a "geography full of insults" targeting African Americans, according to historian LaKisha Simmons. African American praline vendors retreated to Black neighborhoods. When a reporter asked Black vendor Doris Singleton about the morality of peddling "50 cent cellophane-wrapped pralines" to African Americans waiting in line outside a foodbank in 1983, she shrugged, "Everybody's got to live."[28]

MANUFACTURED SOUVENIRS

In 1895, the young women at Newcomb College hosted an exhibition of art depicting typical New Orleans scenes. The school and community were abuzz. Several students had recently won a competition by publisher Houghton Mifflin to design book covers, including for Grace King's *New Orleans: The Place and the People* (1895). Local press coverage celebrated these sketches and paintings of "our sunny southland." One artwork received special recognition. The *Daily Picayune* remarked, "An old praline woman . . . was especially noticeable, as the old negress who sits at the gate of the Newcomb College, waiting for the girls to buy her sweet stores." This praline vendor was a popular subject among the students. While the newspaper referenced an oil painting depicting the Black seller Marie Louise, it was a drawing of her by Selina Bres that would shape the international image of New Orleans.[29]

Bres's influence extended over the next generation of New Orleans's artists and the burgeoning tourism industry. She was born in New Orleans in 1870. At age 16, she registered for drawing classes at Tulane University and soon afterward applied to neighboring Newcomb College. In 1895, Bres enrolled in the first class on pottery decoration at the college, for which the school would gain international renown. Bres later entered local lore for selling the first piece of Newcomb pottery. She graduated with a diploma in art in 1896 and married a professor of engineering at Tulane University in 1898. She completed her studies as a graduate student in 1902, later returning as an instructor—and student of voice and piano—until 1910. In subsequent years, she participated in numerous volunteer efforts, raising money for Tulane University and her alma mater. She was a founding member of the Lend-a-Hand Club, a voluntary teaching organization, and the Louisiana Engineering Society, becoming the group's first president. All the while, she raised three children, including renowned sculptor Angela Gregory. Bres died in 1953.[30]

Bres's most influential achievement, however, remained her sketch of the praline woman. The exhibition sketches lived on for decades within the New Orleans tourism industry and took a prominent place in the history of postcards. Bres's rendition of the praline woman became one of the first postcards sold in the United States. More than twenty years later, she proudly noted, "These were not only the first souvenir post-cards ever made in New Orleans, but for three years they were the only ones sold here." Only a set of postcards issued for Chicago's Columbian Exposition in 1893 and another set marketed by Harvard University in 1891 predated the Newcomb students' contribution to this emerging mass-circulation art form. As the United States mobilized for war in April 1917, replicas of these "first 'souvenir postcards' of New Orleans" were reprinted and widely distributed to bookstores and hotels. The sketches of the riverfront, cemeteries, bayous, "and, most popular of all, the old negro mammy . . . who used to sell pralines on the steps of Newcomb college," reappeared to greet a new generation of tourists, who mailed them across the world.[31]

The Newcomb postcards marked a milestone in the commercialization of New Orleans culture for tourists, visually complementing the narratives about praline mammies devoted to white Creole society. Tellingly, King's *New Orleans: The Place and the People,* Castellano's *New Orleans as It Was,* and the Newcomb postcards all debuted in 1895. The year marked a time when state politicians were steadily codifying Jim Crow, a process culminating in the Louisiana Constitution of 1898. In response, Creole of color Homer Plessy appealed to the U.S. Supreme Court to overturn Louisiana's law mandating racial segregation on railways. Plessy's doomed effort ended with the Thibodaux-born sugar planter and future Chief Justice Edward Douglass White joining the 7–1 majority in *Plessy v. Ferguson* (1896), which upheld the legal principle of separate but equal. The work of King, Castellanos, and Bres provided cultural cover for political maneuvers stripping the franchise from African Americans, for social practices that dismissed racial equality, and, especially important to the history of the praline, for economic co-option of the lucrative praline trade from working-class Black women. As tourism developed as a major sector of the New Orleans economy in the early twentieth century, the praline emerged as the most popular souvenir of the Crescent City.

At the dawn of the twentieth century, New Orleans experienced a proliferation of small factories devoted to candy production. The *Item* in 1917 harped, "Few industries of New Orleans have shown the remarkable growth of the candy trade, which is less than two decades old, so far as the manufacture of fine candies is concerned." Combined, the confectioners "forced practically all out-of-town candy jobbers from this market." The oldest manufacturer, Jacobs Candy Company, claimed a national reach. Fuerst & Kraemer, founded around 1902 on Dauphine Street, expanded to a factory on Bourbon Street in 1911 near the French Opera House. By 1917, the firm expanded production again, leasing a building at Claiborne Avenue and Canal Street. The Miller-Elmer Company started around 1910. The city's candy sector during the late 1910s included eight large factories employing more than a thousand workers, "mostly girls" who were white, with an annual payroll close to $250,000. They produced more than $1 million worth of candies.[32] These young white women and children provided low-cost labor for these new confectionary plants.[33] The local press labeled the renamed Elmer Candy Company factory at 541 Magazine Street "one of the largest in the South." Here, visitors could watch "Creole pralines being made according to an 'ol' mammy' recipe."[34] By 1920, numerous other small confectioners had joined the fray, relying on tourists to boost sales of products linked to New Orleans's heritage and locally sourced goods. Albert Kraemer noted that the New Orleans candy industry had reached around three thousand employees by late 1921. A spokesman for the Yorkman Candy Company recognized how saturated the praline market had become. The company founded by World War I veteran Alexander Yorkman, who had previously managed the candy division at the Grunewald Hotel, struggled to gain market share. The company representative lamented in 1924 that even though "New Orleans is the home of the praline, this is the deadest market for that kind of candy. Everybody makes them and only the visitors buy them to any extent."[35]

Candy factories preferred hiring white women to do the labor of praline production. Historian April Merleaux explains, "Confectioners linked candy with the bodies of attractive young white women in order to emphasize the healthfulness and naturalness of sweets."[36] Within white popular culture, their whiteness and youth conveyed purity and cleanliness at a time when African Americans were viewed as unsanitary and prone to disease. In the first published photograph of a praline, budding actress Frances Carson in November 1916 appears in the kitchen of Fuerst & Kraemer, learning to make pralines under the watchful eyes of the white employees. The candy department of the Grunewald Hotel in 1918 sought twelve "neat, clean girls" to wrap pralines, among other tasks. A year later the firm petitioned for an additional fifteen young women: "Girls to wrap pralines. Easy work. Also experienced packers of fancy packages."[37] The J. Brown Candy Company wanted "girls experienced in making pecan pralines."[38] A. G. Williams, a Greek immigrant, employed young white women to prepare candies at his A. G. Williams Home-Made Candy Company on Baronne Street near Poydras. Lucile Godwin, one of his employees from 1917 until 1919, recalled, "He made and packaged his candies on big marble-topped tables in the rear, and did a fantastic mail-order business."[39] Williams in 1921 urged tourists that "your visit to New Orleans will not be complete" without a visit to the company's well-regulated and sanitary facility.[40] Although the Jacobs Candy Company hired African American women experienced at making pecan pralines through the late 1940s, the firm did so to perpetuate the production of pralines via Black labor for visitors to ogle. Visitors were assured that the production process occurred under the strict control of white supervisors.[41]

Confectioners facing stiff competition in selling pralines to tourists used the mails to distribute their confections nationwide. Mail orders brought a piece of the city to friends and family back home and provided tasty reminders of past visits to the Crescent City. Al Kaufman, employed by the candy manufacturing firm Fuerst & Kraemer, one of the earliest companies to mass market pralines, boasted of robust sales during Mardi Gras 1911 as revelers from throughout the United States, and even abroad, flocked to the city. "The buyers have been of a better class than usual and everybody wanted to take away something made in New Orleans," observed Kaufman. He elaborated, "As an illustration, we have sold thousands of Pralines. Our factory has been working a double force and still unable to supply the demand. We have been doing a tremendous out-of-town business, too, in territory as far east as North Carolina, and as far South as Havana." The lesson was clear. "Every merchant ough [*sic*] to create something that would be distinctly a

New Orleans product—it would advertise the city and boost his business," argued Kaufman.[42]

Fuerst & Kraemer seized on the growing popularity of New Orleans fare, including "Creole pralines," even to the point of opening a satellite store on the boardwalk of Atlantic City for the 1914 summer season. This "'Southern headquarters' for Orleans' colony of society folk" also beckoned to bathers along the Jersey shore.[43] Albert Kraemer celebrated the opening of this praline shop, which was operated by three candymakers from New Orleans who used "Louisiana sugar and pecans."[44] The experiment succeeded. At the height of the busy summer season, the firm doubled its workforce and production. The effort also adopted a gimmick promoted by New Orleans's businessmen who called on sellers to advertise goods made or from New Orleans with the label "MINO," an acronym for "Made in New Orleans." Kraemer remarked, "Our store is a good advertisement for New Orleans. 'M.I.N.O.' is pasted on the outside and the inside, and everyone of the thousands who buy the Creole pralines know they are New Orleans sweets even though they are made at the seaside."[45] Sales were so brisk that by 1916 the store doubled in size and the owners installed an onyx and marble fountain costing $5,000.[46] Wage increases as U.S. industry boomed during World War I brought hefty profits, and they grew each year—35 percent in 1917 alone. Demand proved so great that Fuerst & Kraemer ran their New Jersey factory day and night. A bright electric sign heralded "New Orleans Famous Pralines" over the door facing the famed Boardwalk. The *States* bragged, "For the Amalgamated Order of Yum-Yum throughout the North and East has hailed another New Orleans product with superlative delight. This product is the New Orleans praline."[47]

The rise of commercial air shipments bolstered opportunities to sell perishables such as pralines. Virginia Lee Barrow opened the New Orleans Shop in the Palmer House in Chicago in 1927, considered the first store of its kind to feature solely New Orleans-related items. Chicago represented a major focus of tourism promotion efforts by New Orleans boosters, and its residents featured prominently as a percentage of tourists venturing to the city. The shop contained only books by New Orleans authors and goods made in New Orleans, including ample supplies of pralines. In 1932, the *States* announced that the Junior League Coffee Shop had "gone modern." The young businesswomen regularly sent Creole pralines by airplane. The newspaper carried the photograph of two Leaguers placing their first shipment aboard an American Airways flight to Houston as part of a regular consignment of pralines freshly made in New Orleans in the morning to be sold to Texans in the afternoon. Chicago-Southern Airline officials in 1936 selected a photograph of a "Creole mammy by the side of an airplane on which New Orleans pralines were being shipped" as the winner of a competition for an image deemed "as being the most typical of the city from which it was sent." The image was chosen from more than fifty entries.[48]

The growing emphasis on factory production and food purity at the dawn of the twentieth century undermined the independent African American producer-seller. S. W. Clark and Sons advertised in 1899 that their "Home-made Confections" [*sic*] were, ironically, "Made under our own roof, fresh every day—a guarantee for cleanliness and toothsomeness." The owners emphasized "Real old-time Pralines, made of clean materials with clean hands." The firm carried the slogan "You're safe at Clark's." Whites' fears about Blacks' uncleanliness and potential to carry diseases manifested as a wave of white supremacist sentiment swept the nation in the 1890s. In a subsequent ad, the proprietors made their effort to replace the Black cook explicit. They bragged that "no old Creole mammy, anxious to please her young charge, could make a more dainty supply" of Creole pralines.[49] Thus the firm's "Southern delicacies for Northern visitors" balanced the flavorful standards achieved by the praline mammy with the increasingly stringent cleanliness standards demanded by white consumers. Another advertisement was blunter: Clark's pecan, peanut, and coconut pralines were made with "Clean Sugar, Utensils and Hands."[50] D. H. Holmes, a prominent department store on the New Orleans retail landscape since 1842, celebrated its pecan pralines "made on our own premises, thereby guaranteeing purity and freshness."[51]

Though the praline mammy was a revered picturesque figure, businesses stressed sanitation to contain her independence and harness the profitable treat she popularized. Images of caricatured Black women, men, and children proliferated on brands marketed by national corporations in the early twentieth century. African Americans became figurative within the consumer marketplace as canned goods and boxed products replaced the domestic labor they previously provided by making chores such as cooking and cleaning more convenient for white housewives. By likening their products to Black labor, as with the fictional Aunt Jemima, marketers put their brands at the service of white purchasers. This coincided with the peak enforcement of segregation legislation and the perpetration of lynching across the United States. The emphasis on sanitation and white managerial supervision in those same advertising campaigns segregated the brands from the perceived impurity of African Americans.[52]

The concern with cleanliness reflected widespread fears that African Americans potentially spread disease into white communities both directly by their persons and by the things they touched, such as food created by Black hands. Irvin Fuerst and Albert Kraemer took the rare step of crediting Black women for inventing the praline. In an account of their firm's foray into the tourist trade of Atlantic City in 1914, the *Item* remarked, "Obscure genius she was—that unnamed negro mammy, who, a hundred years ago, with her big black hands mixed toothsome nuts and condiments into Orleans molasses and evolved the first morsel of Creole praline." However, this admission highlighted the improvements offered by the company's white candymakers and their sanitary protocols. Its marketing emphasized that the fabled confection was in the hands of white businessmen who ensured quality and safety: "Fuerst & Kraemer is one of the biggest exploiters of this candy since the making of it has been taken largely out of the hands of negro mammies and given over to the scientific and sanitary equipments [*sic*] of the modern factory."[53] For much of the twentieth century, Black bodies, culturally envisioned by whites as brute laborers of the agrarian past, were seen as unsuited for factories equipped with modern technology symbolic of mental ingenuity and sterile environments. The company stressed that a "firm member personally supervises" the production line "in a scrupulously clean factory, where more than 80 workers are employed."[54]

Similarly, Maurice Kreeger of Kreeger's Department Store celebrated the establishment's ninetieth birthday in 1955 with a poem titled "I Remember When," recalling the changed times from his youth:

> I remember when "Mammies" sat at the edge of
> a sidewalk, vending pralines, gingerbread, tarts and
> other sweets—all exposed to dust and flies.
> One wonders how we survived the attack of germs

(then unknown) whose very names today
fill us with dread.

Cordially yours,
Maurice B. Kreeger

A praline mammy's wares might be tasty, but those wares according to some white competitors were potentially deadly.[55]

Updated municipal ordinances and police enforcement of licenses facilitated the takeover of the praline trade by white-owned businesses with financial resources. Although the poverty stricken could receive free or discounted vending licenses, applying for such permits invited scrutiny. Police in December 1898 investigated the free licenses of two competing white men who operated chuck wagons that marketed "cooked food to laborers around the American Sugar Refinery." The officer, after witnessing their sales, reported that they should each pay for a license, given their "good business." A policeman in April 1899 confiscated the license of a candy stand operator after neighbors complained that the display was "not 'under cover,' causing flies to gather in numbers and infest the adjoining residences." Law enforcement denied an African American woman a free license to sell ice cream, cakes, candy, and soda water on the grounds that she was a "young able bodied woman and has a strong able bodied husband who owns and runs two furniture wagons."[56] The process of obtaining a free or discounted license could also put into public record painful matters that families might prefer to keep private, as when a white woman needed to recount that her "husband is now confined in Jackson Insane Asylum & has been for the past four years" or when another woman explained that she cared for a "son named Edward who is in the last stage of consumption & unable to maintain himself."[57]

City officials' focus on bolstering the use of public markets, which provided significant funds to municipal coffers, led to tighter restrictions on street vendors. An ordinance enacted in November 1900 prohibited all street peddling between 6:00 a.m. and noon, the cool morning hours when public markets operated. Street vendors were also banned from crying out about their wares and knocking on doors. The price of a peddling license was increased to an average fee of $40 from $5, a low charge introduced during the hardscrabble years immediately after the Civil War. However, nearly a thousand street vendors operated with free permits awarded through the mayor's office. The license fee for the "crippled and destitute" was determined "in such amount as the mayor sees fit." The cost came in tighter police supervision. The new restrictions pushed many street hawkers, including praline sellers, off the streets and paved the way for the takeover of the trade by white-owned candy firms and tourist shops during the next several decades.[58]

The professionalization of the praline trade by white-owned businesses in the early twentieth century further marginalized many independent street vendors. Working-class Black women did not have the resources to purchase quality pecans and sugar, much less the equipment to scale their production to meet market demand or the criteria for a municipal license. White confectioners created uniform pralines bearing brand names that cultivated consumers' loyalty. They also invested in expensive equipment to produce large quantities of pralines quickly. Copper kettles spread the heat more evenly and caused less sticking. A marble slab covered with wax paper allowed pralines to cool (and thus harden) faster, whereas wood retained heat and slowed the production process. African Americans did not possess the income to purchase marble or copper pots, much less the space necessary to scale production upward. Cookbook writers like Natalie Scott, in her revealingly titled *200 Years of New Orleans Cooking* (1931), repeatedly emphasized the use of marble slabs in replicating fare from the Crescent City, normalizing such equipment as authentic to local culinary customs. Lura Robinson, in the similarly suggestive *It's an Old New Orleans Custom* (1948), recommended that readers, after boiling the brown sugar and pecans, "drop large spoonfuls on greased marble (preferably) or porcelain-top table to form individual pralines." The burgeoning mass market undermined Black entrepreneurs who were dependent on home production. Often stuck in ramshackle, small homes in the poorest areas of the city, many African Americans barely had enough income to cover the necessities. Copper cookware and marble tables—and the space to use them—were luxuries even successful street vendors could ill afford. Canned and packaged goods like shelled pecans, bagged sugar, or store-made candies increased the costs of the ingredients, which years ago were foraged pecans and black-market sugar straight from the levee.[59]

The onset of World War I and the prohibition of alcohol during the 1910s strengthened the candy manufacturing industry in New Orleans. Soldiers received rations of sweets, increasing the hunger for candy among men. The ban on alcohol also led Americans to substitute candy for cocktails. A soldier stationed in Britain pleaded to his father in New Orleans in March 1918: "Send some more pralines over. They're pretty fine. Candy is the dope we can't get over here in England, as they are very strict about sugar."[60] The end of the Great War unleashed a "candy boom" in 1919. Reports from confectioners in New Orleans echoed military studies showing that Americans deprived of alcohol often turned to candy as a substitute. Firms such as Fuerst & Kraemer, the Creole Praline Company, and the Elmer Candy Company reported massive increases in sales. Orders for pralines spiked, with requests coming from across the United States: "The sweeter the confection the quicker its effect was the situation discovered by army officials, hence the favor of New Orleans pralines, which are almost entirely composed of pure Louisiana cane sugar."[61] Interviewed in 1920, Louisiana labor inspector Martha Gould stressed, "The factories of the city all have doubled their capacity in the last ten years. Since prohibition new candy factories have sprung up by the dozens. Pralines seem to be the substitute for cocktails."[62]

The range of branded pralines abounded during the 1920s. The Nutqueet Company hawked its "Perfect Pecan Pralines," featuring both pecan pralines and maple coconut pralines, starting in 1920.[63] Nick Tacko, the nephew of A. G. Williams, served as Williams's chief candymaker for eight years before opening the ironically named Louisiana Home-Made Candy Factory at 1017 Common Street weeks before Christmas 1920. His shop featured "Original Creole Pralines." His wife served as sales manager at the facility, which the public could visit to alleviate any reservations about cleanliness in the kitchen. Tacko eventually took over Williams's business after his uncle's death.[64] The Napoleon Candy Company marketed its "Genuine Mammy's Creole Pralines" described as "The Befo' de Wah Kind." To distance itself from the perception of being mass marketed, the D. H. Holmes department store promoted its "Holmesmade Pralines," each a "flaky round of melting crush sugar filled of halves of real Louisiana pecans, mailed anywhere."[65]

While undercutting the independent Black praline seller, businesses double downed on the mammy image, thereby reassuring customers that mass-produced pralines were as authentic as those sold by Black vendors. Solari's offered pralines described as "Just like mammy used to make" in 1915. An ad from 1918 promised that "Grunewald Creole Pralines" were the "best gift to send out of town" because they were "Real New Orleans old-fashioned

Pralines, like Mammy used to make." Katz and Besthoff, a local retail firm, similarly offered Creole pralines described as "Just Like Ole' Mammy Used to Make" in 1918. These were made "according to the old-time Creole recipe" and were a "most appropriate and delicious souvenir to send of New Orleans—suggestive—and full of 'local color.'"[66] The Creole Praline Company, with a logo featuring a Black woman in a tignon, promised that its confections "Bring Back the Memories of the Good Old Southern Days and the Negro Mammy." The Napoleon Candy Company in 1920 sold "Genuine Mammy's Creole Pralines" featuring in its advertising a mammified Black vendor.[67] The Jacobs Candy Company promised that its pralines "are packed in a way that recalls the French Market and Ol' Mammy."[68]

Increasingly the Black praline vendor was no longer an independent producer and marketer but instead a stereotyped gimmick used by white confectioners. In 1921, the business at 740 St. Ann Street sought ten "colored women, old time Creoles preferred, to sell genuine Creole pralines." The classified ad emphasized, "Right parties can make big money, experience not necessary." Any African American was suited to play the praline mammy shtick. In an article titled "Feud," the *Item* in 1934 recounted the escalation of a rivalry between two women who ran competing gift shops on St. Peter Street in the French Quarter. Deciding to steal customers, one "bought herself a big dressmakers' model, dressed it in mammy clothes with a red tignon, and neatly inserted a little gadget in her stuffed insides which played, over and over, 'Come in and buy some pralines.'" The competitor across the street grew vexed: "True, she had a nice wall inscribed all over with celebrities' signatures, and clever sayings. But she didn't have any mammy." Rankled, she hired a "buxom colored woman, dressed her in mammy clothes with a tignon and everything, and seated her out on the sidewalk with a large tray of pralines (samples!)." The living mammy trumped the mannequin because she "could get up and walk, could hand in [*sic*] delectable bits of candy to passing sightseers on busses, developed a line of sales talk." The other shopkeeper "outdid herself trying to get even again." Quarterites chuckled that "she has rigged up five mechanical mammies, and placed them in various places in and out of her shop." Albert Goldstein, a reporter for the *Times-Picayune,* wrote in 1937, "There used to be a time when the first thing a tourist asked to be shown when he stepped out of his hotel was one of these old Southern mammies. And for the life of you, you couldn't find him one below Canal street, or above it either." Yet that had changed. A "regular plague of mammies" descended on the French Quarter during the interwar years as tourist shops and confectioners proliferated. Mannequins dressed as mammies and costumed African American women abounded. Goldstein added that the "French Quarter tearooms and such which bag the tourist trade, started dressing up their negro waitresses as mammies on the assumption, apparently, that you have to give the customers what they want."[69]

Preservationists during the interwar years encouraged the hiring of African American women garbed according to the mammy stereotype. In May 1935, Helen Pitkin Schertz, a prominent socialite and an advocate for historic preservation, urged New Orleans boosters to promote within the French Quarter "traditional figures and customs of old New Orleans such as the clothes pole man, the mammies selling pralines, outdoor art exhibitions and trained guides for the Vieux Carre . . . as a method of inducing visitors to remain in the city after Mardi Gras." In *Gumbo Ya-Ya* (1945), a collection of folktales gathered by employees of the Louisiana Writers' Project under director Lyle Saxon, the compilers informed readers that pralines "have been sold on New Orleans streets through all the city's history, and always the delicious Creole confections of brown sugar and pecans have been vended by Negresses of the 'Mammy' type." Saxon, a pioneering advocate of historic preservation in the French Quarter and a major booster of New Orleans tourism, gave a veneer of authenticity to the schtick of businesses costuming African American women as mammies. Although "now they represent modern candy shops," readers and tourists could trust the sellers' lineage as saleswomen of color and as welcoming ambassadors of the city. The authors concluded, "Day by day they sit in the shadows of the ancient buildings, fat black faces smiling at the passers-by, fanning their candies with palmetto fans or strips of brown wrapping paper. Usually, besides the pralines, Mammy dolls and other souvenirs are sold." Sitting in the shade and "garbed in gingham and starched white aprons and *tignons*," the saleswomen, like the buildings next to them, harked back to early New Orleans. They served as relics to ogle.[70]

After the 1960s civil rights struggle, shops steered away from hiring Black women to stroll the streets with a basket of pralines while costumed as mammies. The *Times-Picayune* remarked with "nostalgia" in 1974 that Black women in mammy garb hawking pralines in public had disappeared, leaving only the pralines "found in souvenir shops today." However, life-size mannequins dressed as mammies continued to beckon tourists from the front doors of several souvenir shops within the French Quarter into the 1980s. And in a few tourist shops operating in storefronts where visitors could observe praline production, Black employees were still dressed in styles that echoed the mammy stereotype.[71]

African American author and native New Orleanian Fatima Shaik captured the intent of the mannequins in her novel *Mayor of New Orleans,* published in 1987 when the figures still crowded the French Quarter. The book describes the costumed mannequin: "She was stuffed cotton, like a big rag doll or something a taxortionist . . . would do." Shaik's play on the word "taxidermist" cleverly blurs the word with "extortionist," linking nostalgia for servile Black labor with exploitation of Black culinary creativity. Shaik continues, "People from out of town took their pictures with it. Children lifted the woman's dress to see if she had on underwear, or her scarf to see if she had hair." Through her description, Shaik recasts the mammified mannequin as if at a slave auction, meticulously observed and stripped bare. Further, the boundary between object and person blurs as Shaik uses both "it" and "she" to describe the figure.[72]

Pralines too donned costumes via their packaging. The packing of pralines into miniature cotton bales was standard practice from the early through mid-twentieth century. By 1903, small cotton compresses appeared on the market to create hand-sized bales as souvenirs. These became an instant hit among tourists. One visitor chuckled when a relative rushed down Royal Street in the French Quarter to buy a "few more bales of cotton for her Sunday School kids."[73] Frank Kelly, Fair Grounds Race Track superintendent, was said to have "originated the 'cotton bale' package for New Orleans pralines" while operating a "place of business at Spanish Fort in the old days."[74] As part of the massive effort to draw the Jerusalem Temple Shriners to New Orleans, members at the national convention in Indianapolis in 1919 received pralines placed, as described for the first time, in "cotton bales bearing the wording 'Jerusalem Temple, New Orleans.'" The concept quickly took hold.[75]

Recognizing the demand for these containers, Aaron Hirschwitz, a New Orleans inventor, refined the small toy cotton bale he had patented in 1910 by significantly enlarging it to accommodate pralines. His patent from 1920 detailed "a small box made in imitation of a miniature cotton bale forming a souvenir." The new design provided a sturdy container that secured items "against shocks and jars incident to transportation and use," a necessity for protecting delicate pralines on tourists' road or train journeys. The outer burlap and cotton acted as shock absorbers.[76]

Confectioners during the 1920s were regularly placing their pralines in boxes that mimicked a cotton bale. The famed St. Charles Hotel by 1920 opened a souvenir department, named the "'Ole Mammy' Candy Shop," amply stocked with pralines that served "as delightful 'reminders' of New Orleans."[77] These treats were packed inside small cotton bales.[78] Schoolchildren from New Orleans in 1925 gifted New York governor Al Smith a "cotton bale of Creole pralines" along with an invitation to visit the city. Louise Cook by 1929 emphasized how "there is nothing that is more typical of New Orleans than a cotton bale of original creole pralines."[79] Yorkman Candy Company in the 1929 packed its pralines "in attractive cotton bale boxes." Although Solari's in the 1920s placed its Creole pralines in boxes "colored as gaily as a Carnival costume," by the 1930s the firm had switched to cotton bales with "burlap sacking and fluffy white fibres." Betty-Lou Bakeries celebrated its pralines in 1937 as "old Creole candy, made just as it was in the Plantation days" and placed them in a miniature cotton "bale of deliciousness!"[80]

Some stores accompanied praline boxes with small dolls depicting stereotyped Black praline sellers. Such dolls were popularized by the Vargas family. The artist Francisco Vargas and his daughter Concepción had emigrated from Mexico and in 1879 opened a studio in New Orleans crafting wax figures. They gained popularity after receiving the contract to sculpt a large wax display of the state's agricultural and floral abundance for the Louisiana exhibit at the 1884–1885 World's Industrial and Centennial Cotton Exposition. Their success led to contracts for other expositions. After Francisco died in 1915, his daughter Adelina pivoted the family business toward the tourist trade by concentrating on crafting wax dolls of New Orleans's African American street peddlers through the 1940s.[81]

The gimmick quickly spread across the city's tourism industry, often joining the racialized doll with the praline. Opened in 1914, Laura's Fudge and Cake Shop on Canal Street by the 1930s placed its pralines in "attractively decorated cotton bales, with the real cotton sticking out of the ends of the bale wrapped in genuine burlap, and with a rag cut-out of the old Southern 'mammy,' wearing her bandanna, red or blue gingham apron, and everything."[82] Maison Blanche department store strapped a mammy doll to its cotton bales of pralines during the 1950s. The Little Courtyard Shop offered pralines, as well as "Pickaninnies and Mammy Dolls." This included a pairing named "'Emmy Lou' and 'Lasses.'" Tourists were enticed by the uniqueness of each "hand embroidered" figure. They could also personalize the figures by selecting the color of the bright clothes worn by the dolls.[83]

The packaging of pralines into bales fostered a cottage industry. In 1939, forty-two applicants responded to an ad seeking young women to stitch cotton bales and mammy dolls. A reporter commented, "Mammy dolls and miniature cotton bales filled with pralines are an institution and an industry in New Orleans. Down Royal Street you'll see thousands of them. Kerchiefed mammies and pigtailed pickaninnies grin at you also in hotel lobbies, travel agencies and department store gift shops."[84]

Such racialized kitsch remained standard within the New Orleans tourism industry through the 1980s. Cotton bale boxes containing pralines were ubiquitous. So too were dolls depicting African Americans, especially Black street vendors. For instance, D. H. Holmes used faux cotton bales until the 1980s, when the retail chain substituted a "scenic New Orleans box" featuring Jackson Square and St. Louis Cathedral. The blatant racism displayed by the boxes and dolls lost popular appeal among whites after the racial reckoning brought on by the civil rights struggle and the rise to political power of Blacks within New Orleans, who helped elect the city's first mayor of African ancestry in 1977.[85]

A GOLDEN OPPORTUNITY FOR SMALL PRODUCERS

With the surging demand for sweets after World War I, E. E. Smith saw opportunity in promoting the praline as a national treat. Smith came to New Orleans from Charleston, West Virginia, and quickly spied the praline as a way to make significant profits. By selling pralines, anyone could go into business as a proprietor. But rather than sell sweets, Smith sold sweet dreams. He established the Southern Candy Company at 312 St. Louis Street. The company did not sell pralines but instead the means of production to let others make pralines. Smith advertised in the daily newspaper in 1920: "GO into business. Make big money. We start you manufacturing and selling famous Southern pralines. New business. Enormous profits. Tremendous demand.

Wonderful opportunity."[86] For $25, Smith sold the materials and equipment for making pralines. Orders arrived from across the United States, so fast that Smith faltered. He started shipping incomplete orders, with some receiving only a recipe, molds, and a thermometer. Quickly, his customers cried foul. U.S. postal inspector Gilmer Johnson charged Smith with fraud for collecting $11,000 in profits within a few months while not delivering on his promises. The rush had overwhelmed Smith who had operated, according to prosecutors, with good intentions. The debacle ruined him. Smith simply had not anticipated the high American demand for New Orleans's pralines.[87]

Americans pursued pralines as flavorful souvenirs of New Orleans, circulating the confection worldwide. Meyer Bitterman and his wife came to New Orleans for their honeymoon in the late 1920s, returning home to Chicago with twenty-four boxes of pralines.[88] A major convention, such as the National Education Association conference in 1937 with more than 11,000 attendees, amounted to a "land-office business" boom for tourist shops. Local booster Walker Ross, a member of the New Orleans Association of Commerce's Convention and Visitors Committee, remarked, "Why, I saw people ordering dozens of boxes of pralines at a time." He continued, "The amount sold of New Orleans candies, and mammy dolls, and such, although no one will ever know the total, was enormous." The USO provided a shopping service to military personnel stationed in the New Orleans area during World War II, allowing them to place orders for items to send to family members nationwide. A staff member remarked, "They all like to send something characteristic of New Orleans in their remembrances, like pralines, mammy dolls for the children, and sketches or paintings of the French Quarter."[89] In fact, when it came to "remembrances" of New Orleans sent to family and friends back home, pralines were "far and away the favorites" of soldiers based in the city.[90] Furthermore, the influx of mobilized workers from across the United States introduced these Americans to the confection.

Consumption of pralines increased during World War II because they remained widely available at a time when government rationing and purchases of chocolate and sugar for the war effort reduced the supply of branded candy bars.[91] Soldiers in the field craved the sweet disk. Sergeant Anthony Salinger wrote to the New Orleans Association of Commerce, after pooling $12 from his unit, to request a shipment. Salinger wrote, "We have acquired a hunger for real New Orleans pralines and pecan rolls."[92] Marine sergeant Douglas

Cloakey thanked his father in New Orleans for mailing him a package of tobacco and pralines while stationed on an island in the South Pacific in 1943. He elaborated, "The pralines and tobacco are being used to promote American good will. The tobacco goes to one of the native chiefs, who thinks the Marines are the finest fellows in the world. The pralines go to his favorite daughter, who, in return, is doing my laundry." Even Senator Harry Truman, unrecognized despite being the vice-presidential candidate, wandered the French Quarter alone in October 1944 during a stop from campaigning to buy pralines for his wife and daughter.[93]

In addition to the candy factories, department stores, and hotels producing pralines, a range of white-owned tourist shops muscled into the praline market during the interwar years. Most were founded by white women. Located in or near the French Quarter, their businesses stood among the first woman-owned storefronts in New Orleans. A confection that had empowered Black women in the late nineteenth century now empowered white women. The burgeoning mass tourism industry grounded by automobile travel and the cultural association of sweets and dolls with femininity opened opportunities for entrepreneurial white women, as they pushed their way into urban spaces long dominated by men. But they did so by exploiting stereotypes of Black praline vendors and perpetuating stories about the Creole praline that further obscured its origins as a working-class street food linked to the enslaved who had fled Louisiana's sugar plantations.[94]

Louise Cook, a native of Illinois born in 1887, managed the newsstand in the St. Charles Hotel. In 1922, Cook abandoned her job to open a shop "for the distribution of her own Louise Cook Home Made Candies, her Mammy Pralines," and other items right across the street from her former employer.[95] From 1924 until her death, she supplied Southern Pacific Lines with a daily batch of pralines for trains heading westward from New Orleans to El Paso, Oakland, and Portland.[96] She twice moved to larger locations during the mid-1920s. However, in December 1928, Cook died after a brief illness. The *States* mourned, "Mrs. Cook's name was known to almost every tourist who had visited this city in the past fifteen or twenty years." She died without relatives or heirs, leaving her estate and shop under public administration.[97]

Cook's store—and her popular brand name—survived for decades. Paul W. Gorham operated the Louise Cook Praline Shop at 623 St. Peters until 1948, when he sold it to Mrs. Howard N. Spofford and Miss Elizabeth

Walker. They continued the business at the same location and under the same name.[98] Spofford had recently returned from seventeen months in China with the United Nations Relief and Rehabilitation Administration. Walker had for the previous three years worked with the Red Cross in Australia, the Philippines, and Tokyo, among other Pacific locations. The two met in New Orleans while with the Crusade for Children. After purchasing the praline shop, the two opened a neighboring restaurant called the Gumbo Shop after hiring a "Creole cook" to develop the recipes. A specialty was a dessert of ice cream with a sauce of melted pralines.[99]

Kate Latter, born in England in 1902, settled in New Orleans in the early 1920s.[100] She opened a candy shop in January 1926 at 713 Canal Street. The *States* took the occasion of her grand opening to announce Latter's prominence among the upper crust: "She is well known among the younger set of local social ranks." Latter gifted her initial customers a souvenir and held a contest to name the shop.[101] The cash prize of $20 went to the person who proposed banking on Latter's social prominence. The budding confectioner adopted the name Kate Latter's Candy Shop.[102] The *States* noted that Latter's business, located in the same building as the prominent Roosevelt Hotel, carried the "distinction of being one of the few Canal street stores conducted by women." Latter, joined by her sister Sara, experienced a business boom. Celebrating the shop's second anniversary, Latter stated, "Our first year was a most successful one that far exceeded our fondest expectations." She continued, "And our second year took us away over the top." Latter drew a significant share of locals and tourists while maintaining a thriving mail-order business.[103] She opened another outlet at 114 University Place in 1937. In the late 1940s, she employed salesmen to convince chain stores and groceries to carry her pralines. By the 1950s, she regularly hired African American women experienced in praline production to make the confection in view of customers—an idea taken from a competitor.[104] Latter also paid $30 a week for vendors to work the parade routes during Carnival.[105] She invited patrons to her newly opened site at 835 Conti Street in 1955 to watch pralines being made. "We're really in French Quarter style now," quipped Latter, who had married and adopted the surname Lorning though left her business's name unchanged. By 1963 she reported that the best-selling item in her shop was not the candy but the dolls: "We sell almost as many mammy dolls in the gift department as we do pralines in the candy section." She elaborated, "Our main difficulty is keeping enough mammy dolls in stock to satisfy tourists. We have three women making mammies, but that's not enough and we need some new ideas for variety's sake." Latter retired in 1969.[106]

Léda Plauché was Kate Latter's closest competitor in hawking pralines and dolls to tourists. Born in New Orleans in 1887, Plauché, after graduating from Newcomb College, married a Cotton Exchange executive. The couple had two children who, by the early 1930s, were entering adulthood. Plauché had built a reputation as a costume designer for several Carnival organizations. But with her kids leaving home, she opened a retail business. One krewe gifted her a lei of green orchids, inspiring the name for her praline shop.

Plauché started the Green Orchid at the height of the Depression. She explained, "I didn't even begin on a shoestring." She depended on her African American domestic servant Mary Louise to launch her business: "The old mammy who had been in our family for so many years gave me my start. She led me to the attic and showed me scraps of material she had been saving for us, just forever. With these, I made gifts and souvenirs—pin cushions, sewing kits, things like that to sell." Plauché plowed the meager profits from selling these trinkets into purchasing "praline material." Mary Louise again assisted by providing the praline recipe. Plauché admitted, "I stood beside her and watched her make them. . . . But I had to stop her at intervals for measurements." The pralines were branded Ma-Lou, the family nickname for Mary Louise. Census records from 1930 show her name to be Louise Woods, a live-in servant at the Plauché residence born about 1857.[107]

Although popular for its pralines, the Green Orchid offered a unique line of dolls depicting stereotyped African Americans. In May 1935, Plauché traveled to Washington, DC. She visited Eleanor Roosevelt, giving the First Lady a forty-inch handcrafted doll with a brown satin face on which Plauché had painted a broad smile. She intended for the doll to be raffled, with proceeds going to disabled children in Warm Springs, Georgia, a community frequented on holidays by President Franklin Roosevelt. This was good publicity. But Plauché had already arranged another, more important, appointment in the nation's capital: she visited the Patent Office to file the final papers protecting her doll design. The patent granted Plauché the exclusive right to produce brown-colored, rather than black-colored, satin "mammy" dolls with painted faces, wool hair, and her design of apron and tignon.[108] Plauché was renowned for her skill in handcrafting roughly fifteen such dolls per day. "Other gift shop owners and artists can make black-faced cloth mammies, but nobody can make brown ones without paying her a royalty," explained the *States.*[109]

The Green Orchid became a landmark within the French Quarter. In the late 1940s, Plauché pioneered the gimmick of hiring Black women to dress in attire associated with the mammy caricature and have them make pralines in an open kitchen within view of customers. Some 1,500 visitors per day entered the Green Orchid during the summer. Around 3,500 patrons per day dropped in during the winter. Plauché acknowledged, "The ones who are most anxious to see the pralines made and who come back again and again usually aren't the ones who buy." She also noted how some customers still called the treats "plarines." Her two African American employees produced a maximum of eight thousand pralines a day as they continually performed the production process. Plauché's scheme to promote sales by turning her workers into an attraction succeeded, inspiring copycats throughout New Orleans's tourism industry.[110]

Plauché also widely distributed a small booklet titled *Story of the Praline.* The pages celebrated the contrived history of the confection. Yet the booklet did double duty: it promoted the Green Orchid while also serving as a souvenir preserved by tourists as a memento of their visit to New Orleans. Plauché assured readers that the Green Orchid's open kitchen was the "only place in New Orleans where you can see mammy making pralines."[111]

The Green Orchid moved from 630 St. Peter Street to 618 Royal Street, a building Plauché purchased, in 1949. Prominent local editor Hermann Deutsch celebrated her as "one of those bourgeois success stories" who had gone from "capital of no dollars and no cents" to paying "cash for a $38,000 building," all by selling "Mah-Lou pralines to every section of the civilized globe." The Green Orchid operated into the 1970s, dealing "mainly in pralines and 'Mammy' dolls." Léda Plauché died in 1980.[112]

Not to be outdone, Louise Glynn opened the Old Town Pralines shop on Royal Street in 1935, employing Stella Harris—the most prominent performer of the Black praline vendor during the 1930s and 1940s—to advertise the business.[113] Born in New Orleans in 1897, Glynn was the oldest child of parents who emigrated from France in 1888. Her father worked as a hotel pantryman where he was responsible for the stockpile of foods and beverages sold to guests. Her French heritage and the insight into the tourist trade gained from her father encouraged Glynn, though married since 1919, to open her own business, eventually aided by her sisters Renie and Melanie.[114] Glynn hired Stella Harris to perform, in the words of the *States,* the "jolly negro mammy" smoking a corn pipe on Jackson Square with a basket of the store's pralines. On sunny days, Harris sat in the shade under the archways of the Cabildo, a historic museum popular with tourists. In 1937, Oliver Mills of Washington, DC, won the Newspaper National Snapshot Contest with a picture of Harris submitted to the *Washington Star.* Mills took a prize of $100, but the Old Town Praline Shop garnered national publicity through Stella Harris's performance.[115] Harris and her basket bearing the name of Glynn's shop became much sought after by tourists, who often photographed her. By the 1950s, Glynn had cooks open the patio kitchen daily for patrons to view.[116] The business continues to operate at 627 Royal Street, the same location established by Glynn though currently under the name "Old Town Pralines and Parasols" and with the mammy imagery long abandoned.[117]

Although white women asserted considerable influence over the praline market via tourist-oriented shops, several men entered the lucrative trade as well. They used the supposed authenticity of their pralines to launch even more gimmicks that became ubiquitous within the New Orleans tourism industry.

None of these men was as successful as Pierre Bagur. Founders of Aunt Sally's Creole Pralines, Pierre Bagur and his wife Diane were native New Orleanians born in the late 1880s. Pierre Bagur bore the name of a grandfather and father who had carved a niche within the local economy as two of the "best known clothing dealers in the city," according to the *Daily Picayune.* But Pierre ventured into a new trade. Married in 1910, Pierre and Diane had four children over the next decade, supported by Pierre's job as a car dealer. Selling automobiles proved a lucrative business. Like many in the 1920s, the Bagurs used their wealth to invest in real estate, including a lot in the up-and-coming suburb of Lakeview along Lake Pontchartrain and a double shotgun house along Jackson Avenue. By 1929, however, the car market was saturated. The onset of the Great Depression that October tightened access to credit. Consumers' wealth evaporated. In 1930, the Bagurs saw not only car sales plummet but also their investments in real estate vanish as their properties were foreclosed on and put to auction.[118]

Down on his luck, Pierre Bagur redirected his well-honed salesmanship and business experience to enter the praline and sightseeing trade. Bagur recognized how the automobile had transformed American society, bolstering tourism to New Orleans as a cheap but exotic destination for cash-strapped vacationers during the Great Depression. In 1935, Bagur introduced Aunt Sally's Original Creole Pralines, a name he likely invented for its simplicity and racial inference. In 1936, he patented a box designed as a cotton bale featuring the image of a smiling mammy to package his business's pralines, a design he elaborated on over the years.[119] Bagur opened a store at 500 Royal Street with a factory at 511 Chartres Street. He expanded to another store at 134 Royal Street in 1940. By late 1941, Bagur had five praline shops hawking an array of goods targeting tourists.[120] In a highly competitive market, Bagur drew attention with a special gimmick. During the 1940s, brochures promoting the business instructed tourists to look "for Mammy with Blinking Eyes" at each of his stores. The proprietor in 1949 urged, "See them [pralines] made fresh daily in Aunt Sally's Old-Fashioned Creole Praline Kitchen" on Royal Street. These were packed in "attractive boxes and beautiful hand-made souvenir Cotton Bales."[121]

Bagur soon complemented his praline shop chain with New Orleans's first horse-drawn sightseeing carriages. In December 1940, Bagur applied to operate horse-drawn carriages through the French Quarter. The former car salesman whose vehicles had pushed horses from the streets thus capitalized on Americans' nostalgia for literal horsepower. He petitioned, "This service will bring back to New Orleans the historic setting of old-fashioned horse and buggy days for which it is famous and will accommodate tourists who otherwise would walk through the Vieux Carre." For seventy-five cents, his carriages gave visitors the thrill of stepping into the past for a forty-five-minute ride.[122] Bagur purchased approximately thirty carriages and five stagecoaches from New England. He also bought two mules to pull a giant cotton bale through the city featuring advertising for his praline business. As a sideline, he offered to rent his horse-drawn vehicles for private parties or events such as Carnival and the Spring Fiesta.[123]

To appeal to white fantasies of old New Orleans held by "the soldier and tourist trade," Bagur hired African American men to drive the carriages. The onset of World War II bolstered Bagur's various businesses. In 1943, he desperately pursued experienced Black drivers for his various horse-drawn vehicles. Bagur beckoned for more workers in March 1944: "COLORED men to drive horse and carriages, also sight seeing stage coach through French Quarter. Must be neat and have experience in handling horses." The large number of war workers and servicemen passing through New Orleans provided a lucrative opportunity.[124]

Bagur's success made him a prominent business figure and Aunt Sally's outlets the most eye-catching gift shops within New Orleans. Stanton Delaplane, a Pulitzer Prize–winning reporter for the *San Francisco Chronicle,* could not ignore Bagur's business empire during a visit to New Orleans in 1950. Delaplane declared, "Couldn't find out who Aunt Sally is. The chain of shops is marked by a bandannad [*sic*] Negro woman figure whose eyes flash electrically. If you prowl the French quarter [*sic*], you can get them at a much lower price. Aunt Sally is for tourists."[125] Though Pierre Bagur died in 1968, Aunt Sally's remained in operation. The company maintained the practice of placing pralines in cotton bale packaging into the 1970s. After fire gutted the 314 Royal Street location in 1974, the renovated French Market complex near Jackson Square became the main outlet for the firm.[126] Here, pralines were "cooked in the window and may be viewed by everyone starting at 9 a.m. Watch how Mammy does it!"[127] A large window allowed passersby to ogle African American women making pralines in the store's kitchen into the 1980s. By 1987, the company maintained a mailing list of about 25,000 global addresses. Roughly 30 percent of its pralines were shipped. Domestic orders largely went to California, Illinois, Texas, Alabama, and Georgia. Many customers were homesick former New Orleanians. International orders mostly went to Canada, England, France, West Germany, and Australia. Aunt Sally's remains a major marketer of pralines in the twenty-first century, though without the display kitchen, carriage rides, or depictions of African American women as mammies.[128]

As at the end of World War I, the New Orleans candy sector enjoyed a post–World War boom fueled by the end of rationing, the baby boom, and an American population eager to cast off years of economic depression and scarcity. Tourists flocked to New Orleans. Oscar Elmer, of Elmer's Candy Company, announced in August 1945 that the factory would double production while increasing its workforce by 50 percent, of whom 90 percent were white women. A journalist who toured the plant remarked of the employees along the production line, "The bare arms of the girls, who wore neat colorful uniforms and snow white head gear, seemed to be doing a swift dance. . . . The white arms and fingers flew up and down like a bevy of ballet dancers." A varied assortment of candies soon rolled off the line, including pralines produced at a rate of 20,000–25,000 a day. These were placed in boxes depicting "sugar cane fields, a sugar mill, and cane cart and Negro workers in the fields, and also a frolicsome carnival scene." Elmer explained the symbiotic nature of marketing candy and the city by noting how "when we enhance the attraction of New Orleans we help our own business."[129]

Businesses also developed the production of creamy pralines after World War II because they stayed fresh longer than the more brittle traditional pralines. By the 1970s, praline makers also differentiated into a variety of flavors to maximize appeal, including using coffee, buttermilk, or even rum. Laura's Original Praline and Fudge Shop alone sold eight varieties of pralines such as Creole pecan, vanilla, chocolate, maple, rum, coconut, light caramel, and burnt caramel. Jeannie LeBlanc of Creole Delicacies offered chocolate, rum, plantation, and chewy pralines, the latter changing the texture of the confection.[130]

PRALINE CITY IN A PRALINE WORLD

The praline became synonymous with New Orleans in the popular American imagination during the early and mid-twentieth century. Pralines could be found "in every drug store, every grocery, on cigar stands and, frequently, vended along the sidewalks" by the 1920s.[131] Commentators during the interwar years even nicknamed New Orleans after the praline. Yorkman Candies Incorporated in 1925 labeled New Orleans as "The Praline City." To hammer the point, marketers employed by the department store Maison Blanche in 1925 exclaimed, "Say 'Praline' any place in the United States and the next thought is 'The Crescent City.'" Kate Latter in 1927 noted how "New Orleans as the praline city, occupies a distinctive place in the candy market of the country." Chara Monta, who moved to the city in the mid-1930s, observed the extent to which pralines permeated the local culture. When he attended a professional baseball game in 1953, pralines had become as mainstream locally as the great American pastime: "I saw the good old American way of life. Popcorn, pralines, hot dogs, cold drinks, candy and peanuts began to flow."[132]

So strong was the association of pralines with New Orleans that recreations of the Crescent City in performances and fairs regularly included the confection. In 1955, a musical revue organized by the socialite Harlan

Women's Club in Harlan, Kentucky, depicted the French Quarter. Their attention to detail included distributing copies of the *Times-Picayune* to the audience and parading "bandannaed 'mammys' [*sic*] peddling pralines through the aisles." In 1958, the St. Thomas Military Academy in St. Paul, Minnesota, hosted a fundraising festival titled "New Orleans Holiday." The school armory was transformed into a "combination Vieux Carre, Mardi Gras, Mississippi river gambling boat, plantation mansion, French Market coffee stand and cotton field, with beauteous Southern belles, pralines, drip coffee, camellias and magnolias thrown in for lagniappe."[133]

The popularity of such faux New Orleans sites beyond the city, increasingly commonplace over the twentieth century, contributed to the displacement of the confection even while affirming its origins in the Big Easy. For the World's Fair in New York in 1939–1940, boosters constructed a three-acre re-creation of New Orleans that included replicas of French Quarter buildings, the riverfront with cotton bales, a showboat, and famed eateries and bars such as Morning Call Coffee Shop, Café Louisiane, the Absinthe House, and a po' boy stand. Souvenir stands featured pralines and other Louisiana fare.[134] The Orly Airport in Paris adjoined a Hilton Hotel popular with locals and tourists alike for its restaurant La Louisiane, which offered a "French impression of an American river boat setting." Along with "New Orleans jambalaya" and other fare associated with the city, such as softshell crab, gumbo, and "Louisiana pecan pie," the restaurant served Aunt Sally's Creole Pralines. Similarly, when the Foreign Correspondents Club of Japan hosted a "New Orleans Night" in 1972, organizers arranged for Pan American Airways to "ship direct from the Crescent City to Tokyo pralines, chicory coffee, pecans for pecan pie and menus from the famous restaurants in the city to supply the atmosphere." The U.S. Information Agency invited New Orleans mayor Moon Landrieu in 1973 to represent the nation at the Berlin Green Week Fair. A garden-courtyard restaurant serving Creole dishes, a café serving beignets, and a bar serving New Orleans-related cocktails showcased the United States. Sidewalk artists, jazzmen, and wandering vendors of pralines completed the faux Big Easy in Berlin.[135]

The successful and pervasive use of the praline as a marketing gimmick by New Orleanians, along with the proliferation of sugar fields and pecan orchards across the United States, led other communities to claim the confection. By 1924, Florence Stone, leading the Louisiana delegation to the

Business and Professional Women's Clubs conference in Indiana, explained why members shunned praline distribution as a means of publicizing New Orleans, instead opting for locally authored guidebooks. Stone noted that her group "used to take pralines as souvenirs, until other states copied the idea, calling the confection by other names such as 'pecan cakes.'" In 1929, the *Times-Picayune* reprinted copy from the Florida *Times-Union* announcing the Sunshine State's praline gambit: "A new Florida delicacy will be placed on the market this winter when pralines, made by the Southern Sugar Company, will be distributed in the principal cities of the North." The Floridians acknowledged that although "the product will be similar to the popular Louisiana dainty, it is planned to make the Florida praline smaller to distinguish it from that made in Louisiana." The *Item* responded with dismay, labeling the efforts of the Floridians an "invasion" of Louisiana's culinary terrain.[136]

Pralines had saturated the tourism market across the South by the 1950s. They seemed to be everywhere. Boosters in Bay St. Louis, Mississippi, claimed the hamlet to be "the home of the famous Pecan Pralines." Virginia Swain in the travel magazine *Holiday* in 1951 honored the New Orleans praline, but as a Missourian, she preferred the "creamier Ozark praline, rich and racy with black walnuts." In an article aptly titled "They Collect Bits of Dixie," the *Times-Picayune* reported, "Few tourists can pass through Georgia without loading up on pecans and pralines."[137] The confection had traveled far from Louisiana's sugarcane fields and wild pecan stands. As the magazine *Good Housekeeping* in 1955 commented, "In the South, you'll find pralines wherever and whenever candy is sold. Southerners nibble pralines as Northerners nibble candy bars."[138]

Epilogue

During the Cold War, as Americans celebrated the nuclear family, the mythological history of pralines took another turn. According to the *States* in a 1953 article, French colonial housewives had introduced to Louisiana the treat named for Marshal Praslin, substituting the local pecan for almonds. The Old Ursuline Convent Guild members soon inserted the nuns into this narrative. Promoting a new cookbook titled *Recipes and Reminiscences* in 1971, the guild argued that the Ursuline nuns invented the confection in the early 1700s. The nuns came from Orleans, "where the Duke of the region had a great sweet tooth." Without naming Duke Praslin, the guild members claimed that the nuns adapted the recipe developed by the duke's chef to "Louisiana's plentiful supply of pecans." But the nuns did more than invent the pecan praline: they also educated Louisiana's wealthy daughters. "So in this way, the Ursulines passed on their adaptations of native foods," concluded the cookbook compilers. Harriet Cortez, food editor for the *States-Item*, popularized this account through the 1970s.[1]

The shift away from Castellanos's chevalier narrative reflected a more significant move away from the Black praline vendor as the preserver of white Creole culture. Colonial French housewives, courtesy of the Ursulines nuns, had fostered Louisiana cuisine, with the praline a cornerstone. Housewives armed with cookbooks maintained the legacy, leapfrogging the long-lasting role of Black domestics within white households. With increased white flight to suburbia in neighboring Jefferson Parish along with intensifying civil rights protests, the days of Black domestics and blatant racial stereotyping within the tourism market were fading by the 1960s and 1970s.

Also fading away were sugar plantations as a significant living landscape for Louisianans. A 1964 survey of 56 sugar plantations identified 1,269 work-houses, averaging just over 22 dwellings per plantation. Of this total some 231 white families and 1,038 African American families lived in the quarters alongside the cane fields. Over the course of the 1970s and 1980s, all the whites, except for those living in the mansion or managerial house, departed the plantations. By the late 1990s, an even more dramatic population shift had occurred. Historian John Rehder observed, "When plantation owners and their insurance companies realized the liability of maintaining a quarters, they wanted out of the housing business. It was too dangerous." Nearly all Black and white laborers and retirees were pushed out of dwellings on the plantations. "The era of traditional patriarchal concern, care, and oversight for plantation laborers in the quarters was over," concluded Rehder. The result was that only a very few land-owning families still lived on plantations, with many other owners operating the fields as absentee landlords while living in nearby urban centers. Only twenty sugar refineries remained by 1995, roughly half the number operating just two decades earlier. The big houses, when not abandoned, increasingly served as museums, bed-and-breakfasts, event spaces, and movie sets rather than homes.[2]

As Louisianans abandoned the plantations for urban living, they also lost familiarity with pecan trees. Industrialized production involving carefully cultivated trees designed for maximized yield, along with the mechanized shelling operations in major cities, further distanced the tree from consumers increasingly living in cities and suburbs. Nostalgia for the tree waned. The pecan industry of Louisiana, though it was in the native heartland of the tree, fell far behind that of other states. Hurricanes regularly ravaged orchards there, as well as those in Alabama and Mississippi. In the wake of such storms, Louisiana's pecan industry largely consisted of native trees with few orchards of improved cultivars. More than 70 percent of pecans by the twenty-first century came from Georgia, Texas, and New Mexico.[3]

The successful exploitation of the national sweet tooth also carried consequences—a growing obese population. Few understood the challenge better than Richard Simmons, a native New Orleanian born in 1948 and raised in the French Quarter. His first job at Leah's Pralines when he was only seven years old spurred his weight gain. By his teens, Simmons had grown obese. He moved to Los Angeles in his late twenties and soon launched a career as an exercise guru, using his personal example of losing more than one hundred pounds to encourage Americans to shed fat. Stopping in New Orleans in 1983 to record several episodes of his award-winning television show, Simmons quipped, "New Orleans is like a Disneyland of pralines and restaurants now." A calorific food created by the enslaved on sugar plantations and popularized among poor African Americans who were working difficult manual labor after emancipation lost purpose in a world of often sedentary jobs.[4]

Finally, the racial meanings central to the praline's importance within New Orleans and its tourism industry from the 1880s through the 1980s became an unbearable weight after civil rights campaigns ended Jim Crow. Ursula Bernard, a native New Yorker who headed the State Department's Reception Center in New Orleans from 1965 through 1974, reflected on her role organizing itineraries of international visitors to the Crescent City. Those from abroad most frequently shopped for jazz records, Creole pralines, and Confederate flags. Bernard noted, "Many international visitors ask to be taken to a cotton plantation. They are disappointed when they don't see slaves singing and working in the fields. It's like giving up Santa Claus."[5] The linkage of mammy imagery with the praline fell out of favor as southern society strove for greater racial equality. A saleswoman at a French Quarter shop in 1974 acknowledged the seething anger of many African Americans: "Some Negroes get offended about the mammy dolls but most don't, or if they do they keep their mouths shut." The racial kitsch grounding New Orleans tourism receded from view but slowly. Lynnell Thomas, a historian describing her childhood as an African American in New Orleans in the 1970s and 1980s, noted the "disjuncture" she confronted in the city where tourist shops abounded with a "representation of blackness that leaves the actual black New Orleans invisible." She "continually confronted a tourist landscape of black docility, subservience, and stereotypical distortion." Those images lingered into the twenty-first century. Until the late 2010s, the Evans Creole Candy Factory in the French Market still carried a sign depicting a mammified Black praline seller.[6]

But even the Evans Creole Candy Factory drifted away from the narrative of Black women as the preservers of the Creole praline, despite being among the last tourist shops to use the image of the mammy. Perhaps the disconnect between narrative and image allowed the business to be a holdout. Jay Cuccia opened the establishment in 1968. Although ads featured a mammified Black woman, he offered readers of the *Times-Picayune* a different origin for the pralines sold by his shop at 848 Decatur Street in the French Market: "Since 1900, Andre Dulac-Evans has been making pralines and other Creole candies. He had a few treasured recipes, a French Quarter kitchen well equipped with shiny copper utensils, and a ready supply of fresh pecans and sugar cane from the nearby open-air market." Yet, no newspaper or census records corroborate the existence of this supposedly well-known confectioner with an unusual name or even of his shop located on the 1100 block of Decatur Street. Cuccia likely invented the French-sounding name and the origin year of 1900 to give his business a distinguished culinary history seemingly rooted in the Creole past—one that emphasized white men. By hyphenating the surname, he could exploit mammy imagery through the very Anglo-sounding "Evans," despite not mentioning the role of African Americans in making or selling pralines. Cuccia explained that "because the Evans chefs zealously preserve Andre's original recipes and methods, their old fashioned candies are becoming another of the Vieux Carre's cherished traditions." During the 1980s, Cuccia operated three local factories plus the Decatur Street shop.[7] Employing four cooks, two wrappers, and six packers, the business produced more than 32,000 pralines on a normal production day and maintained a mailing list of 26,000 customers.[8]

Finding the right narrative was essential to ensuring such high sales, especially as a latecomer to the tourist-oriented French Quarter praline market. Cuccia's focus on Andre Dulac-Evans, like the narrative about the Ursuline nuns introducing pralines to New Orleans, sidestepped the role of Black women in either creating or perpetuating the confection. Instead, the mammified depiction of a Black praline seller on the business's sign was left unmoored to New Orleans's past or the racial narratives crafted by Grace King, Marie Points, and other writers of the nineteenth century. But with changing times the history of the praline circled back to its origins, with an important twist. The neighboring beignet shop Café du Monde—operated by the Roman family, descendants of Jacques Télésphore Roman who owned Oak Alley sugar plantation where the enslaved Antoine first grafted pecan trees—acquired and rebranded the candy company in 2015, removing the mammified imagery of a Black woman.

Significantly, African Americans after the civil rights movement reclaimed their heritage of being key figures in the production of pralines.

Loretta Harrison pioneered the renaissance. Harrison, working with her mother Loretta Shaw, used her grandmother Lucy Moore's praline recipe to launch her own business in the 1980s. She had begun making pralines at age thirteen as gifts for friends and relatives. While studying political science at Southern University, she marketed her pralines at the 1983 New Orleans Jazz and Heritage Festival to raise income. The massive sales convinced her to set aside college to focus on the business of trading New Orleans's most famous candy, producing 3,500 pralines a day along with a variety of other sweets. Her specialty was even featured at the Folk Art Festival at the Smithsonian Institute in Washington, DC, in 1985. Harrison passed away in 2022. The Lifetime channel that year dedicated its Christmas film *New Orleans Noel* to Harrison, with the family matriarch and successful praline mogul, performed by Patti LaBelle, loosely modeled on her.[9]

Sharing in this revival of African American–made pralines was Eva Louise Perry. Perry honed her skills in the California food industry, where she worked as a private chef in homes and various eateries before returning home to New Orleans in 1987. Perry revived her grandmother's recipes for pralines and other sweets, proud of her family's roots working sugarcane on the Glendale Plantation in St. Charles Parish. She marketed her pralines under the "Tee-Eva" name, a shortened form of "Auntie Eva" that erased the racially derogative "aunt" label often used by whites for Black women during Jim Crow. Perry also reclaimed the dress of early Black women street vendors as part of the African American community's working-class heritage. She celebrated the style's practicality and ability to attract attention in busy spaces. She proved as shrewd as her forebearers, even donning nineteenth-century garb during a 1992 interview when she hawked her wares at a casting call for the film *JFK*, unexpectedly landing an appearance in the movie. Perry chuckled, "I sold my way through the door, then I sold straight on up the line—right to the casting table." Her business drive trumped a desire for a cameo: "I just went there to make my quota for the day." Perry followed in the footsteps of Black praline sellers a century earlier, working streets in the business district and even strolling the hallways of City Hall with her goods. She appreciated the importance of this tradition within the African American community: "I'm very proud to walk the streets with my basket. I strut when I walk the streets with my basket because I'm part of a long tradition of black women who made a living and kept their independence selling pralines this way." With the assistance of her granddaughter Keonna Thornton, she successfully operated Tee Eva's Famous Old Fashion Pecan Pralines and Cookery on Freret Street before moving to Magazine Street, serving up traditional New Orleans dishes like jambalaya and crawfish pie along with sweets. Perry remained active until 2000, handing over the reins to her granddaughter. When Perry passed away in 2018 at age eighty-three, New Orleanians honored her with a second line.[10]

The praline remains culturally prominent even if its importance within the New Orleans tourism industry has lessened due to the troubling narratives long told about the confection. The racial mythologies that enwrapped the praline during Jim Crow linger. But by interrogating the myths and restoring the history of the praline (or plarine), New Orleanians and those visiting the city can cast aside the bitter tales to savor the ingenuity and complexity embodied by the simple treat of brown sugar and pecans.

APPENDIX

EARLY PRALINE RECIPES FROM NEW ORLEANS NEWSPAPERS

·····

PECAN PRALINES

Daily Picayune | DECEMBER 30, 1897

The recipe is as follows: Take a pound of new pecans, shelled so that they have come out unbroken, and rub them well in a linen cloth to take off any lingering dust. Put them into a skillet with a pound of sugar, a little carmin and a half glass of water. Place on the fire until the pecans crackle hard, then take off and work until the sugar becomes quite sandy and well detached from the pecans. Separate one part of the sugar, and again put the pecans or almonds on the fire, stirring them lightly with a spoon, according as they pick up the sugar, paying strict attention that the fire is not too quick. When the pecans have taken up this part of the sugar put in that which you have reserved, and continue to parch them until they have taken up all the sugar. Then place a piece of paper on a sleve and throw the pecans upon it, shaking them around to separate those which still hold together.

·····

CHRISTMAS CANDIES

Item | DECEMBER 9, 1902

Children never enjoy candy so much as the home-made kind. Let them make it themselves if possible for the Christmas festivities. Chocolate taffy is an easy recipe for children to manage. One pound of granulated sugar, half pint of water put over a brisk fire. When the sugar and water are dissolved, add one-fourth teaspoonful of cream of tartar. Do not stir. When "crack" is reached pour into greased pans. While cooling, put in the center of the candy four squares of chocolate that have first been melted. Throw the edges of the candy as it cools, over the chocolate, and let it work in. A cream taffy may be made from a cup of granulated sugar, half a teacup of molasses, one cup of milk or cream and butter the size of an egg. This time stir the mixture all the time to "crack."

Then if desired pour it over chopped nuts. With chopped pecan nuts this makes the famous New Orleans pralines.

•••••

PRALINES

Daily Picayune | JANUARY 6, 1907

Melt a pound of granulated sugar with four tablespoonfuls [*sic*] of water and boil to a syrup; into this stir; into this stir the grated meat of a small, fresh cocoanut and let the whole cook until it will "thread" between thumb and finger. This should not take more than two or three minutes, and a porcelain-lined saucepan should be used; stir constantly, and pour out on a buttered slab or large dish by the spoonful, dropping in cakes and flattening with the spoon.

Pecan Praline—For pralines, crack and extract the meat from enough nuts to make two cups, after cutting some into quarters, some smaller and some into halves. Prepare the syrup exactly as for the cocoanut, with the addition of a tablespoon of butter, stirring constantly. Drop in cakes on a buttered slab. A pound of nuts gives half their weight after shelling.

•••••

HOME-MADE CANDIES

Daily Picayune | JANUARY 6, 1911

Pralines.—One and seven-eighths cups of powdered sugar, one cup of maple syrup, one-half cup of cream, two cups of hickory nuts or pecan meats, cut in pieces.

Boil first three things until, when tried in cold water, a soft ball forms. Remove at once from fire and beat until creamy; add nuts and drop from tip of spoon in small blobs on buttered paper.

.....

PECAN PRALINES

Item | JULY 8, 1914

One pound of white (granulated) sugar, one-half pound shelled pecans, one spoon butter, four tablespoons or less of water. Set the sugar to boil, with just enough of the water to melt it. As it begins to boil add the pecans, stirring constantly till it begins to bubble, and just as the syrup thickens into sugar take off the fire and turn out on a marble slab, in small flat cakes.

Peanut pralines may be made in the same way.

.....

EVE UP-TO-DATE: PECAN PRALINES

Times-Picayune | JANUARY 6, 1915

Pecan pralines: One cup of sugar, one cup of molasses; boil until it begins to thread, then add a cup and a half of pecans, and stir rapidly until it begins to sugar. Pour in rounds on buttered marble or dish.

.....

EVE UP-TO-DATE: OLD-TIME SOUTHERN PECAN "PRALINES"

Times-Picayune | OCTOBER 7, 1915

One way of making old-time Southern pecan "pralines." Place in a saucepan one cupful of new milk, three cupfuls of brown sugar, one tablespoonful of butter, cook to the soft-ball stage; draw the pan aside, and add three cupfuls of pecan meats (as nearly unbroken as possible). Stir until the syrup begins to grain when quickly turn into a buttered pan and cut into squares.

.....

EVE UP-TO-DATE: PECAN PRALINES AND COCOANUT PRALINES

Times-Picayune | DECEMBER 25, 1916

Pecan Pralines—One pound of sugar, one small cup of water, one small cup of molasses, one pound of pecans weighed in shell.

Place the sugar, water and molasses on a slow fire. When partly cooked add the peeled pecans. Have convenient a buttered marble on which to test the candy. When cooked drop from a tablespoon on the marble. The candy should be stirred from time it begins to boil until cooked.

Cocoanut Pralines—One cup and a half of sugar, seven tablespoonfuls of water, one cup of grated cocoanut. Wet the sugar and water and cook until stringy. Remove from the fire and beat in cocoanut until it begins to sugar. Drop from a tablespoon on the marble.

For Chocolate pralines beat in grated chocolate with the cocoanut.

•••••

NEW ORLEANS PRALINES

Item | JANUARY 19, 1919

Dissolve 2 cups brown sugar in ½ cup water and cook gently until syrup candies. Add 1 cup pecan meats and stir until syrup adheres to every nut. Arrange on oiled paper in praline shaped pats.

•••••

EVE UP-TO-DATE: PECAN PRALINES

Times-Picayune | JANUARY 27, 1919

Pecan Pralines—One pound of brown sugar, 1 tablespoon butter, 1–2-pound freshly shelled pecans, 4 tablespoons water.

Set the sugar to boil and as it begins to do so, add the pecans. Let it boil until the mixture begins to bubble, then remove from the stove and drop by spoonfuls on a marble slab or buttered dish. Be careful to stir the mixture constantly until the syrup begins to thicken and turn to sugar.

•••••

EVE UP-TO-DATE: PECAN PRALINES

Times-Picayune | DECEMBER 26, 1919

Pecan Pralines (the kind sold on the streets of New Orleans)—Let two cupfuls brown sugar and half a cupful of water simmer on the fire until it candies. Put in a cupful of carefully peeled pecans, stirring until the sugar adheres to the nuts. Be careful the mixture does not burn. Put in a plate to cool and serve, or put a spoonful at a time in small paper boxes or in pats on a dish.

WHITE PRALINES

States | SEPTEMBER 17, 1921

Put one pound of fine white sugar in a saucepan with 4 tablespoons of water. Boil, when it begins to sirup, [*sic*] remove from the stove and add on freshly grated cocoanut. Mix thoroughly and return to the stove. Let it boil, stirring constantly, until it threads. Remove from stove when it begins to bubble. Have ready a buttered platter and drop candy from a spoon. If you wish you can shape the drops with a fork before they settle.

PRALINES

States | OCTOBER 16, 1921

One pound brown sugar, one cup boiling water and one pound Brazil nuts. Dissolve the sugar in the water and let it boil three or four minutes: put in the nuts and boil until a thick syrup is formed. Remove from fire and stir until the nuts are well sugared. Return to fire and stir until the sugar melts, then remove, stir again and pour onto oiled paper.

NOTES

INTRODUCTION

1. Knapp, "Pralines Are More than just New Orleans' Signature Candy." https://www.eater.com/2016/10/27/13422426/praline-new-orleans-pecan-candy.

2. Rosemary Ruiz, "Souvenir City," *States-Item*, April 11, 1974.

3. Cohen, *Pure Adulteration*, 147. A considerable academic literature has emerged in the twenty-first century analyzing southern foodways and their historical meanings. For works informing this history of New Orleans pralines, see Wallach, *Dethroning the Deceitful Pork Chop* and *Every Nation Has Its Dish;* Stanonis, *Dixie Emporium;* Cooley, *To Live and Dine in Dixie;* Egerton, *Southern Food;* Engelhardt, *A Mess of Greens;* Ferris, *The Edible South;* Moss, *The Lost Southern Chefs;* Sharpless, *Grain and Fire;* Williams-Forson, *Building Houses out of Chicken Legs;* Zafar, *Recipes for Respect.*

4. Etymologies have long recognized the link between "praline" and Marshal du Plessis-Praslin. See Brachet, *Etymological Dictionary of the French Language*, 283.

5. "The History of the Praline," La Maison de la Praline, https://www.maisondelapraline.com/en/la-maison-de-la-praline-our-universe/la-maison-de-la-praline-histoire-de-la-praline-side.

6. Pie Dufour, "New Orleans for Visitors," *Times-Picayune*, February 20, 1955; Stall, *Buddy Stall's Big Easy*, 23.

7. New Orleans stores retained the generic term "praline" for sweets of French origin. A. M. and J. Solari, prominent New Orleans grocers, offered "Pralines Vanille" and "Pralines Louis XV" in 1899. See, Messrs A. M. and J. Solari, LTD, ad, *Daily Picayune*, November 19, 1899. By 1924, the establishment promoted "Pralines Bourbon (Burnt Almonds)" to tease the inclusion of alcohol but with an explanation to be clear that Prohibition was not being violated and that almonds, not pecans, were used. See Solari's ad, *Times-Picayune*, November 30, 1924.

8. Bochet and De Lamarre's ad, *Daily Picayune*, April 30, 1861; D. Lopez ad, *Daily Picayune*, December 17, 1863; J. Villarrubia and Company ad, *Daily Picayune*, May 18, 1870.

9. On the enslaved as cooks, see Deetz, *Bound to the Fire*, 18–23, 28–41, 45–72; Harris, *High on the Hog*, 89–106.

10. Barrow, "The Civil War Diary of Willie Micajah Barrow, Conclusion," 713.

11. Barrow, "The Civil War Diary of Willie Micajah Barrow, I," 449. The authors of this article, reflecting on the rarity of the word "plarines" by the 1930s, made the editorial decision to include the suggestion "[pralines?]" next to the term.

12. "'Praline' Best Known of N. O. Confections," *Item,* February 21, 1941; "Praline Famed N. O. Confection," *Item,* March 6, 1942. The *Item* refers to the pecan praline as approximately fifty years old.

13. "And Now Behold a Momentous Question!" *Daily Picayune,* February 27, 1911; Howard Jacobs, "Remoulade," *Times-Picayune,* February 18, 1958.

14. Beriss, "Authentic Creole," 156.

15. Cram, *Old Seaport Towns of the South,* 272.

1. PRALINES, MADAME?

1. Dunbar-Nelson, *The Goodness of St. Rocque and Other Stories,* 175–177.

2. For background on Dunbar-Nelson and the influence of New Orleans, see Bryan, *Myth of New Orleans in Literature,* 62–74; Green, "Local Color, Social Problems, and the Living Dead," 113–121; Menke, "Behind the 'White Veil,'" 77–87.

3. William Semple to George Bagby, April 5, 1862, George William Bagby Papers, Virginia Historical Society.

4. Mure, "Financial and Economic Disturbance in New Orleans," 33.

5. Cable, *Kincaid's Battery,* 261.

6. Cable, *Kincaid's Battery,* 270–271; J. B. Jourdain to Congressional Committee, December 12, 1866, *Report of the Select Committee on the New Orleans Riots,* 204.

7. Cable, *Kincaid's Battery,* 273–274; Stone, *Brokenburn,* 100.

8. Solomon, *Civil War Diary of Clara Solomon,* 355; Blassingame, *Black New Orleans,* 26–30, 51.

9. Benjamin Butler to Edwin Stanton, May 25, 1862, *Private and Official Correspondence of Gen. Benjamin F. Butler,* vol. I, 520; De Forest, *A Volunteer's Adventures,* 39.

10. W. Mitthoff to Benjamin Butler, May 21, 1862, *Private and Official Correspondence of Gen. Benjamin F. Butler,* vol. I, 509–510; Edward Page to Benjamin Butler, May 27, 1862, *Private and Official Correspondence of Gen. Benjamin F. Butler,* vol. I, 524.

11. Blassingame, *Black New Orleans,* 31, 35–36.

12. William Root, "Private Journal of William H. Root," 654.

13. Corsan, *Confederate States,* 40.

14. "Louisiana," *Lowell (MA) Daily Citizen and News,* January 25, 1864; Hogue, *Uncivil War,* 1–30; James, *A Freedom Bought with Blood,* 34–51; Blassingame, *Black New Orleans,* 36–38.

15. Rousey, *Policing the Southern City,* 106–113; Blassingame, *Black New Orleans,* 31–33.

16. Charles S. Sauvinet to Congressional Committee, December 22, 1866, *Report of the Select Committee on the New Orleans Riots,* 44. The report misspells the surname as Souvinet.

17. *Grand Celebration in Honor of the Passage of the Ordinance of Emancipation,* 15, 31.

18. Henry Houston interviewed by Arene Tarrow, 1935, John B. Cade Slave Narratives, Archives and Manuscripts Department, John B. Cade Library, Southern University and A&M College.

19. Taylor, *Louisiana Reconstructed,* 47–62, 88–104.

20. Hart, "A Boy's Recollection of the War between the States," 258; *The Statistics of the Population of the United States, Ninth Census* (Washington, DC: Government Printing Office, 1872), vol. I, 156. Algiers witnessed a tripling of the black population between 1860 (1,349 persons) and 1870 (3,013 persons). The districts of the former municipality of Jefferson contained 3,126 persons of color in 1870.

21. Thomas Conway to Congressional Committee, January 26, 1867, *Report of the Select Committee on the New Orleans Riots,* 525, 530; O. J. Dunn to Congressional Committee, December 22, 1866, 69; Rousey, *Policing the Southern City,* 114–116.

22. Edward P. Brooks to Congressional Committee, December 13, 1866, *Report of the Select Committee on the New Orleans Riots,* 18.

23. Charles Dallas to Congressional Committee, December 24, 1866, *Report of the Select Committee on the New Orleans Riots,* 75; "New Orleans Riots: Report," February 11, 1867, *Report of the Select Committee on the New Orleans Riots,* 35; Hogue, *Uncivil War,* 31–52.

24. Whitelaw, *After the War,* 240.

25. Trowbridge, *A Picture of the Desolated States,* 414.

26. Blassingame, *Black New Orleans,* 185–186.

27. Taylor, *Louisiana Reconstructed,* 111–113, 128–134.

28. Hogue, *Uncivil War,* 116–148, 165–179; Taylor, *Louisiana Reconstructed,* 276–299, 486–489; Tunnell, *Crucible of Reconstruction,* 193–213.

29. Baker, "*Das Kapital* on Tchoupitoulas Street," 174–191, quote from 176.

30. For the most detailed description and illustration of Comus's 1873 parade, see Young, *Mistick Krewe,* 71, 79, 115–128, 222.

31. For insight on the racial politics of late nineteenth-century Mardi Gras and the celebration's national influence, see Gill, *Lords of Misrule,* 93–107; Mitchell, *All on a Mardi Gras Day,* 65–81; Parsons, "Midnight Rangers," 819–827, 833–836; Stanonis, "Through a Purple (Green and Gold) Haze," 109–131.

32. Stanonis and Wallace, "Tasting New Orleans," 6–20.

33. Marler, *The Merchants' Capital,* 184–230.

34. Blassingame, *Black New Orleans,* 49–50, 60–61, 71; Arnesen, *Waterfront Workers of New Orleans,* 36–46.

35. Charles H. Hughes to Congressional Committee, December 25, 1866, *Report of the Select Committee on the New Orleans Riots,* 105.

36. Elvira Garrett interviewed by Lobe Garrett, no date, circa 1935, John B. Cade Slave Narratives, Archives and Manuscripts Department, John B. Cade Library, Southern University and A&M College.

37. Thomas Harris to Congressional Committee, December 27, 1866, *Report of the Select Committee on the New Orleans Riots,* 201; Hesse-Wartegg, *Travels on the Lower Mississippi,* 184; Hunter, *To 'Joy My Freedom,* 25–26.

38. Blassingame, *Black New Orleans,* 77.

39. Latham, *Black and White,* 150–151; Hickey, *Hope and Danger in the New South City,* 43–53; Hunter, *To 'Joy My Freedom,* 26–27, 50–51, 58, 65; Williams-Forson, *Building Houses out of Chicken Legs,* 32–37. For a broad contextualization of African American women's lives from

the Civil War into the early decades of Jim Crow, see Berry and Gross, *A Black Women's History of the United States,* 87–106.

40. Latrobe, *Impressions Respecting New Orleans,* 22, 47.

41. "Sunday Market in New Orleans," *Daily Picayune,* February 19, 1911; Sitterson, *Sugar Country,* 190.

42. Baker, "Fires on Shipboard," 601–624, quote from 603; Baker, "*Das Kapital* on Tchoupitoulas Street," 186–189; Williams-Forson, *Building Houses out of Chicken Legs,* 25–36.

43. Rousey, *Policing the Southern City,* 157–169, 188–196, newspaper quoted from page 160.

44. Latham, *Black and White,* 150; Sparling, *Under the Levee,* 106–107.

45. Captain George Long to Police Commissioner William O'Connor, Police Report, January 27, 1910, Police Reports to Mayor Martin Behrman, New Orleans Police Department Correspondence and Reports, City Archives, Louisiana Division, New Orleans Public Library, hereafter cited as Police Reports to Mayor Behrman-NOPL; Captain Joseph Jagot to Police Commissioner William O'Connor, Police Report (February 18, 1910), Police Reports to Mayor Behrman-NOPL.

46. Captain George Long to Police Commissioner William O'Connor, Police Report (February 19, 1910), Police Reports to Mayor Behrman-NOPL; Report on Application of Antonia Retteo (April 21, 1899), Police Department: Investigation by Police of Various Business Permits, New Orleans Police Department Correspondence and Reports, City Archives, Louisiana Division, New Orleans Public Library, hereafter cited as Police Department Permits-NOPL; Report on Application of Emma Morgan (March 4, 1899), Police Department Permits-NOPL; Report on Application of Providenzia Puccia (April 8, 1899), Police Department Permits-NOPL.

47. Fogel and Engerman, *Time on the Cross,* 49–102; Johnson, *Soul by Soul,* 32, 113–114, 138–158.

48. Augustin, *General Digest of the Ordinances and Resolutions of the Corporation of New-Orleans,* 155, 157; Young, "Nourishing Networks," 119–124.

49. Creecy, *Scenes in the South,* 39; Dabel, "'My Ma Went to Work Early Every Morning,'" 217–229.

50. Morrison, "'Big Businesswoman,'" 61–78.

51. Willink, "An Old Lady's Gossip of Life in Louisiana," 382.

52. Hall, *The Manhattaner in New Orleans,* 70.

53. Corsan, *The Confederate States,* 20.

54. Blassingame, *Black New Orleans,* 92–94, 100–103, 163.

55. For background on Hearn, see Collins, "Under Reconstruction: Lafcadio Hearn in New Orleans (1877–1887)," 35–48; Loichot, "Cooking Creoleness," 3–8; Cott, *Wandering Ghost,* 117–205.

56. Hearn, *Inventing New Orleans,* 102–103.

57. Jamison, *Lady Jane,* 37–38, 41.

58. *Lady Jane* received considerable attention in the New Orleans press, which published readers' reviews promoting the book throughout the twentieth century. See Olga Daste, "Lady Jane," *Times-Picayune,* April 4, 1926; Emily Alice Blomquist, "Lady Jane," *Times-Picayune,* June 24, 1945.

59. *1900 United States Federal Census.*

60. "Old Praline Woman Buried," *Item,* March 9, 1908.

61. *Louisiana, U.S., Statewide Death Index, 1819–1964.*

62. According to the 1908 city directory, New Orleans contained at least three women named Elizabeth Carter. See *U.S., City Directories, 1822–1995*.

63. *Louisiana, U.S., Wills and Probate Records, 1756–1984*; Blassingame, *Black New Orleans*, 60, 120–121.

64. G. William Nott, "Tante Clementine," *Times-Picayune*, April 30, 1922. Nott offered a similar nostalgic account of Tante Clementine of Chartres Street in "The Charm of Old New Orleans," *The Mentor*. February 1925.

65. Olga Kaufmann, "Here and There about New Orleans," *Item*, February 10, 1924; "Old Praline Woman Is Missing," *States*, February 17, 1925.

66. "Antoine Araguel," *Times-Picayune*, December 29, 1918; *1910 United States Federal Census; U.S., City Directories, 1822–1995*.

67. *1900 United States Federal Census; 1910 United States Federal Census; 1920 United States Federal Census.*

68. *1900 United States Federal Census; 1910 United States Federal Census; 1920 United States Federal Census.*

69. "City of New Orleans," *Daily Picayune*, February 10, 1889; Nellie Conner McCay, "When Carnival Holds Sway," *Times-Picayune*, February 27, 1927.

70. Ethel Willia Perkins, "Calliope Depot of '78 and Union Station," *Times-Picayune*, April 28, 1954.

71. Bremer, *Homes of the New World*, 15; Porter, "Miss Martin," 799; McCulla, "Consumable City," 87–104.

72. Marie L. Points, "Petit Girard," *Daily Picayune*, April 6, 1890; Millie Ball, "Gospel Soul Children," *Times-Picayune*, May 16, 1982.

73. "All Saints' Day," *Daily Picayune*, November 1, 1887. For other descriptions of praline mammies outside cemeteries on All Saints' Day, see "By-the-Way Chat," *Daily Picayune*, November 4, 1894; "All Saints' Day," *Daily Picayune*, October 31, 1899; and "Saints' Day of the Purchase Centennial," *Daily Picayune*, November 2, 1903.

74. "New Orleans Pays Its Devoirs to the Dead," *Daily Picayune*, November 2, 1899. In 1983, Save Our Cemeteries, a charity dedicated to preserving New Orleans's tombs, proposed placing stands outside St. Louis Cemetery No. 2 so, according to journalist David Leser, "people would come to picnic and to buy pralines, cotton candy and balloons as they did during the 19th century." The organization also proposed a "Spring Sundays" schedule of jazz performances at the cemeteries. See David Leser, "Picnics, Jazz May Bring Life to Cemeteries," *Times-Picayune*, January 14, 1983. Facing criticism for disrespecting the gravesites, Save Our Cemeteries director Mary Louise Christovich argued for the "revival" of the New Orleans "custom" of serving food at cemeteries. See Mary Louise Christovich, "Your Opinions: Cleaning up the Cemeteries," *Times-Picayune*, January 20, 1983.

75. Lily Jackson, "'A Very Important Day' in the Creole Calendar," *Times-Picayune*, October 31, 1984; Stanonis, *Creating the Big Easy*, 28–69; Stanonis, *Faith in Bikinis*, 39–67.

76. "Personal and General Notes," *Daily Picayune*, February 14, 1889.

77. Ruth McEnery Stuart, "A People of Romance," *Daily Picayune*, December 31, 1896. On how African Americans subverted racism while seemingly satisfying whites' expectations, see Williams-Forson, *Building Houses out of Chicken Legs*, 57–65.

78. "Cookery at Newcomb," *Daily Picayune,* June 15, 1900; "With the Colleges during the Week," *Daily Picayune,* November 17, 1900. For further coverage of this seller, see "Tulane and Newcomb," *Daily Picayune,* December 23, 1905.

79. "A Delightful Affair of the Week," *Item,* November 20, 1904.

80. Nunez, "'Just Like Ole' Mammy Used to Make,'" 162-165; "Jerusalem Nobles Are off to Capture Shrine Convention or 'Bust,'" *Item,* June 9, 1919; "Shriners off to Land Convention for New Orleans," *States,* June 9, 1919.

81. *1900 United States Federal Census; 1920 United States Federal Census.*

82. *1910 United States Federal Census; 1920 United States Federal Census.*

83. "Coffee and Pralines Given All Comers," *Times-Picayune,* June 11, 1919; *1870 United States Federal Census; 1880 United States Federal Census; 1900 United States Federal Census.*

84. "Shriners' 1921 Meet May Be Held Here," *Times-Picayune,* June 14, 1919.

85. "Howell to Invite Legion South," *Times-Picayune,* October 14, 1921; Lyle Saxon, "Thousands Visit Old Part of City," *Times-Picayune,* October 17, 1922; Meigs O. Frost, "What 60 Years Can Do!" *Times-Picayune,* October 25, 1936.

86. "Trumpet Notes," *Item,* April 23, 1922.

87. "Thousands Crowd to Canal Street for Elks' Circus," *Times-Picayune,* December 22, 1918; Mary Louise Guild, "Rue Royale's Valentine," *Times-Picayune,* February 8, 1931.

88. "Steal So Gently," *Daily Picayune,* September 24, 1876.

89. Blight, *Race and Reunion,* 98–139; Foner, *Reconstruction,* 460–563; Summers, *Railroads, Reconstruction, and the Gospel of Prosperity,* 108–117; Wang, *Trial of Democracy,* 134–146.

90. Gottschall, *Travels from Ocean to Ocean and from the Lakes to the Gulf,* 38, 44.

91. "Epicureans Dedicate Ball to Bicen," *Times-Picayune,* February 14, 1976.

2. WHY DO YOU TASTE SO GOOD?

1. Twain, *Life on the Mississippi,* 419, 476, 479.

2. Sutton, *Remembrance of Repasts,* 88–89.

3. Ripley, *Social Life in Old New Orleans,* 25; Sitterson, *Sugar Country,* 191.

4. Stokes and Atkins-Sayre, *Consuming Identity,* 30–31, 112–118; Merleaux, *Sugar and Civilization,* 102, 108, 118.

5. Rost, *Oration Delivered before the Agricultural and Mechanics' Association of Louisiana,* 16; Rehder, *Delta Sugar,* 43.

6. Rehder, *Delta Sugar,* 42; Sitterson, *Sugar Country,* 4–11.

7. Sitterson, *Sugar Country,* 147–150, quote from 150; Rehder, *Delta Sugar,* 57–58, 62, 134–138; Follett, *The Sugar Masters,* 22–25; Heitmann, *Modernization of the Louisiana Sugar Industry,* 10–40.

8. Onebane, *House That Sugarcane Built,* 17; Follett, *Sugar Masters,* 18–21; Rehder, *Delta Sugar,* 12–19, 43–51; Sitterson, *Sugar Country,* 13–20, 26, 44.

9. Lavinia Trowbridge to Elizabeth Smith (April 11, 1847), Trowbridge Family Papers, Louisiana Research Collection, Howard-Tilton Memorial Library, Tulane University.

10. Follett, *Sugar Masters,* 21; *Historical Statistics of the United States: Colonial Times to 1970,* 8.

11. Onebane, *House That Sugarcane Built,* 33; Follett, *Sugar Masters,* 28–30; Moody, "Slavery on Louisiana Sugar Plantations," 233–234; Rehder, *Delta Sugar,* 18–19.

12. Prichard, "A Tourist's Description of Louisiana in 1860," 119; Richard Follett, *Sugar Masters,* 24–33, quote from 117.

13. Willink, "An Old Lady's Gossip of Life in Louisiana," 383.

14. Sylvia Handely interviewed by John Banks, Date Unknown [circa 1935], John B. Cade Slave Narratives, Archives and Manuscripts Department, John B. Cade Library, Southern University and A&M College; Olmsted, *Journey in the Seaboard Slave States,* 660; Cartwright, "Curative Virtues of the Sugar-House for Bronchial, Dyspeptic and Consumptive Complaints," 598.

15. "Extension of the Sugar Region of the United States," 200.

16. Stowe, *Key to Uncle Tom's Cabin,* 41.

17. Douglass, *My Bondage and My Freedom,* 447.

18. V. C. Macon to William Macon Waller (July 24, 1847), William Macon Waller Papers, Virginia Historical Society; Mintz, *Sweetness and Power,* 43–73; Grant, *A Civilised Savagery,* 21–37, 84–85, 109–134; Higgs, *Chocolate Islands,* 10–14, 24, 74–76, 86–88, 160–164.

19. *Population of the United States in 1860,* 193; Johnson, *Soul by Soul,* 47–63, 88, 136–161.

20. Woodbury, *Writings of Levi Woodbury,* 438.

21. "A Bavarian Organist Comes to New Orleans," 31–32.

22. Johnson, "Speech on the State of the Union," 187.

23. Onebane, *House That Sugarcane Built,* 41–42.

24. King, *Great South,* 79.

25. Blassingame, *Black New Orleans,* 73.

26. Rodrigue, *Reconstruction in the Cane Fields,* 159–188; Hogue, *Uncivil War,* 188–192.

27. "Concerning Candy," *States,* September 15, 1927.

28. Mintz, *Sweetness,* 117–130, quotes from 95 and 122; Sitterson, *Sugar Country,* 186, 190.

29. Merleaux, *Sugar and Civilization,* 18; Mintz, *Sweetness,* 108; Sitterson, *Sugar Country,* 186–190; Ballinger, *History of Sugar Marketing,* 7, 17.

30. Heitmann, *Modernization of the Louisiana Sugar Industry,* 184–207, 251–255; Onebane, *House That Sugarcane Built,* 78–79; Sitterson, *Sugar Country,* 252–255, 301–307.

31. Onebane, *House That Sugarcane Built,* 50–51, 78–79, 126–129; Hollander, *Raising Cane in the 'Glades,* 23–25, 52–61, 79–103.

32. Heitmann, *Modernization of the Louisiana Sugar Industry,* 249–251; Kramer, *Blood of Government,* 393–397; Merleaux, *Sugar and Civilization,* 28–54.

33. Woloson, *Refined Tastes,* 31; Cohen, *Pure Adulteration,* 155.

34. Schloss, *Sweet Liberty,* 1–45; Dubois, *Colony of Citizens.*

35. Geggus, "Louisiana Purchase and the Haitian Revolution," 117–129, quote of Napoleon from 124.

36. Clark, *Strange History of the American Quadroon,* 21–57; Dessens, *From Saint-Domingue to New Orleans.*

37. "Beet Sugar—Progress of Its Manufacture in France and Germany," 147–148.

38. "Beet Sugar—Progress of Its Manufacture in France and Germany," 147–148; Heitmann, *Modernization of the Louisiana Sugar Industry,* 50–64; Zimmerman, *Alabama in Africa,* 56–67, 101–109, 207–211.

39. Parsons, "Sorghum as a Source of Sugar," 629, 635; *Fourth Biennial Report of the Bureau of Labor Statistics of the State of California for the Years 1889–1890*, 47–48.

40. Abel, "Sugar as Food," 11; Warner, *Sweet Stuff*, 85–108.

41. Cohen, *Pure Adulteration*, 161–170; Warner, *Sweet Stuff*, 133–144.

42. Onebane, *House That Sugarcane Built*, 99, 105; Warner, *Sweet Stuff*, 7–24.

43. Onebane, *House That Sugarcane Built*, 104–105, 109–113; Sitterson, *Sugar Country*, 358–359.

44. Kane, *Deep Delta Country*, 148; Stanonis, *Faith in Bikinis*, 20–21.

45. Hearn, *La Cuisine Creole*, introduction.

46. *Creole Cookery Book*, iii. For context on southern cookbooks of the Jim Crow era, see Tipton-Martin, *The Jemima Code*, 6–13; Sharpless, "The Women of St. Paul's Episcopal Church Were Worried," 32–51; Stanonis, "Just Like Mammy Used to Make: Foodways in the Jim Crow South," 209–216.

47. Blight, *Race and Reunion*, 211–254, 353–366; Foster, *Ghosts of the Confederacy*, 63–75, 145–158.

48. H. Chapman Williams, "Louisiana's Display at the Jamestown Exposition," *Item*, July 11, 1907; Mount, *Some Notables of New Orleans*, 138. For perspective on agricultural displays and product gimmickry, see Marling, "'She Brought Forth Butter in a Lordly Dish,'" 219–228.

49. Nutqueet ad, *States*, March 30, 1919; "Let's Go Shopping," *Item*, April 7, 1929; Sitterson, *Sugar Country*, 297.

50. Warner, *Sweet Stuff*, 22–24.

51. Aryan, *The Aryans and Mongrelized America*, 29; Merleaux, *Sugar and Civilization*, 3, 51; Tompkins, *Racial Indigestion*, 96–101.

52. Hyatt, *Hoodoo-Conjuration-Witchcraft-Rootwork*, 1402; Pérez, *Religion in the Kitchen*, 71–72, 96–98, 183; Stanonis, "Feast of the Mau Mau," 101–103.

53. Wallach, *Every Nation Has Its Dish*, 117; McKenzie's ad, *Times-Picayune*, March 7, 1958.

54. King, *Southern Ladies and Gentlemen*, 11–12; Stanonis, "Feast of the Mau Mau," 93–106; Stanonis, "Just like Mammy Used to Make," 216–224; Tompkins, *Racial Indigestion*, 90–98, 169–170.

55. Buechner, *Daniel Anton Buechner*, 50. These labels were often designed by master lithographer Daniel Buechner, who also designed Mardi Gras krewe invitations and other Carnival-associated artwork.

56. Woodard, *The Delectable Negro*, 65–68, quote from 66; Tompkins, *Racial Indigestion*, 8, 30–31, 90–98, 169–170, quotes from 90 and 161. The 1920s film and music star Josephine Baker exemplifies how African Americans subverted cultural cannibalism by lampooning racialized jungle and sugar tropes, as in the all-African American production of the Broadway play *Chocolate Dandies* (1924) in which she dons blackface, perpetually grins, and performs cross-eyed. See, Bogle, *Brown Sugar*, 42–52.

57. Warner, *Sweet Stuff*, 7–25; Day, "Sugar Sculpture," 689–693.

58. St. Félix, "Kara Walker's Next Act." Also see Loichot, "Kara Walker's Blood Sugar."

59. S. W. Clark and Sons ad, *Daily Picayune*, February 12, 1899.

60. Thomas H. Handy and Company ad, *Item*, December 11, 1917. The company juxtaposed the ad for pralines with an offer for shipments of pecans, an "always appreciated gift for friends in the North, East, and West."

61. Grunewald ad, *Times-Picayune,* December 15, 1918; Grunewald ad, *Times-Picayune,* September 22, 1919.

62. Yorkman Candy Company ad, *Item,* March 30, 1919; Solari's ad, *Item,* February 9, 1928.

63. "My Diary: A Panorama of the Shops," *Item,* March 16, 1919; Elmer Candy Company ad, *Item,* February 23, 1930.

64. Cocks, *Tropical Whites,* 110–123; Stanonis, *Faith in Bikinis,* 116–119.

65. Corinne Lowe, "We're Rounding the Cape of Good Fashion," *Item,* November 8, 1925; Holland ad, *Item,* February 12, 1928; Marks Isaac Company ad, *States,* September 22, 1938.

66. "Colors Will Betray Milady's Fancies under Shades Decreed for Spring and Summer Wear," *Times-Picayune,* March 7, 1926; Marjorie H. Roehl, "Louisiana Styles to Rule the Nation," *Item,* March 23, 1941.

67. Amanda, "New York Designers Cap Climax," *States,* January 17, 1952.

68. Ladies Refreshment Saloon flier (circa 1890s), minute book, p. 56, Firemen's Charitable Association of the Seventh District Collection, Special Collections, Earl K. Long Library, University of New Orleans; Brent Manley and Ed Anderson, "Ford Notes Need for Strong Military," *Times-Picayune,* May 14, 1974. On the relationship between femininity and sugar in popular culture, see Dusselier, "Bonbons, Lemon Drops, and Oh Henry! Bars," 15–40; Cooper, "Love, War, and Chocolate," 68–88; Sutton, *Remembrance of Repasts,* 6; Woloson, *Refined Tastes,* 225–227.

69. "Southern Industrial Convention," *Daily Picayune,* December 5, 1900; "Purchase Centennial Exposition at St. Louis," *Daily Picayune,* September 1, 1904.

70. Woloson, *Refined Tastes,* 226.

71. John Lester, "Pola Negri Will Talk," *Item,* April 4, 1945.

72. G. B. Sartoris, "History of C. P. 807," *Sugar Bulletin,* December 15, 1930, 1; Rehder, *Delta Sugar,* 18; Sitterson, *Sugar Country,* 380–382.

73. Rehder, *Delta Sugar,* 58; Sitterson, *Sugar Country,* 386, 394.

74. "An Interview with President Pipes," *Sugar Bulletin,* October 15, 1927, 2.

75. Onebane, *House That Sugarcane Built,* 148–150.

76. "Pecan Pralines Ever Popular," *Times-Picayune,* April 4, 1968; Rehder, *Delta Sugar,* 62.

77. Williams-Forson, *Building Houses out of Chicken Legs,* 86; Turner, *Ceramic Uncles and Celluloid Mammies,* 24–25; Witt, *Black Hunger,* 50; Long, *Great Southern Babylon,* 203–214; Landau, *Spectacular Wickedness,* 45–76, 109–131.

3. WHAT SHALL WE DO?

1. King, "Madrilène; or, the Festival of the Dead," 870–871.

2. Cable, *Grandissimes,* 329; Cable, "Dance in Place Congo," 528; Turner, *Cable,* 93–102, 199–204, 227.

3. King, *Memories of a Southern Woman of Letters,* 60. For background on Gayarré, King, Cable, and debates over Creole culture in New Orleans, see Bush, *Grace King,* 55–58, 262–263; Fertel, *Imagining the Creole City,* 11–30, 101–117; Taylor, *Gender, Race, and Region,* 28–83; Turner, *George W. Cable,* 90–102, 153–159, 168–170, 194–223, 349–351. With Francophone Creoles dying out, tourism growing in economic importance, and New Orleanians waxing nostalgic for the city's French heritage as France itself bled from the Great War, the Louisiana Historical Society,

of which King served as secretary, invited Cable in 1915 to speak in a display of reconciliation with the author who had made the city so familiar to millions of Americans.

4. The theme of Black eagerness to serve whites is most outrageously presented in King's "Crippled Hope," a short story about a blind African American woman living at a slave trader's office who longs to be purchased so as to be owned by a white master. While she waits and hopes, she nurses sick Black children to health so that they can be sold. For further analysis, see Kuilan, "The 'All Seeing-Eye' in Grace King's Balcony Stories," 99–108.

5. McElya, *Clinging to Mammy,* 13.

6. McElya, *Clinging to Mammy,* 5.

7. On the mammy image, see Deck, "'Now Then—Who Said Biscuits?'" 69–70; Williams-Forson, *Building Houses out of Chicken Legs,* 85–92; Turner, *Ceramic Uncles and Celluloid Mammies,* 23–26. On representations of Black sexuality in New Orleans, see Long, *Great Southern Babylon,* 203–214; Landau, *Spectacular Wickedness,* 45–76, 109–131; Clark, *Strange History of the American Quadroon,* 100–106, 133–159, 162–187; Johnson, *Soul by Soul,* 139–146; Schafer, *Illegal Sex in Antebellum New Orleans,* 39–46.

8. Williams-Forson, *Building Houses out of Chicken Legs,* 86.

9. Geilow, *Old Plantation Days,* 15; Wilkinson, *Plantation Stories of Old Louisiana,* 7–8.

10. Cox, *Dreaming of Dixie,* 3–7.

11. Aunt Jemima ad, *New York Tribune,* November 7, 1909; Aunt Jemima ad, *New York Evening World,* December 10, 1915.

12. Aunt Jemima ad, *Rock Island (IL) Argus,* January 24, 1919.

13. Witt, *Black Hunger,* 25–44, quote from 41. Studies of Aunt Jemima mostly critique the racial stereotypes conveyed by the figure but largely treat Louisiana as interchangeable with any large plantation state in the South. Diane Roberts, for example, describes Aunt Jemima as a "repository of Old South romance." The role and meaning of Louisiana within the Aunt Jemima narrative go largely uninterrogated. Consider Roberts, *Myth of Aunt Jemima,* 157; Manring, *Slave in a Box,* 72–78, 112–129.

14. On white southerners' reaction to Stowe's novel, see Roberts, *Myth of Aunt Jemima,* 57–66, 71–74.

15. Stowe, *Uncle Tom's Cabin,* 463–464.

16. Stowe, *Uncle Tom's Cabin,* 477, 481.

17. Avirett, *Old Plantation,* viii; De Saussure, *Old Plantation Days,* 9, 17–18; Clinkscales, *On the Old Plantation,* foreword, 9.

18. Post, "Truth about Southern Cooking," 32–34.

19. "Open Forum," 374.

20. Stanonis, "Triumph of Epicure," 145–157.

21. Glazier, *Peculiarities of American Cities,* 266; Marler, *Merchants' Capital,* 171–230.

22. Gould, "'Chaos of Iniquity and Discord,'" 232–246; Nunez, "'Just Like Ole' Mammy Used to Make,'" 177–178.

23. Brady, "Mollie Moore Davis," 99–118.

24. Mollie E. Moore, "Keren-Happuch and I," *Daily Picayune,* March 22, 1885.

25. M.G.T., "The Old Tenor," *Daily Picayune,* May 15, 1887.

26. King, "An Interlude," 918.

27. Hunt, *Memoir of Mrs. Edward Livingston,* preface.

28. Hunt, *Memoir of Mrs. Edward Livingston,* 17, 34–35.

29. Hunt, *Memoir of Mrs. Edward Livingston,* 35–37.

30. "100 Pupils to Portray Bombula Dance Chosen," *Item,* March 27, 1920.

31. Mount, *Some Notables of New Orleans,* 116–117.

32. Marie L. Points, "Here at Home," *Daily Picayune,* May 24, 1891.

33. "'Toto,' the Old Praline Woman of Canal Street," *Daily Picayune,* August 5, 1894.

34. Molly Moore Davis, "Keren-Happuch and I," *Daily Picayune,* March 24, 1907.

35. Scogin and Howe, *Down on the Old Plantation,* 9. On women's role in promoting the Lost Cause, see Cox, *Dixie's Daughters;* Whites, *Civil War as a Crisis in Gender,* 132–198.

36. "The Era Club," *Daily Picayune,* November 25, 1900; "Sunshine News and Notes," *Times-Picayune,* March 27, 1916.

37. "Hardware Men," *Daily Picayune,* November 9, 1902.

38. "Hardware Jobbers," *Daily Picayune,* November 20, 1902.

39. "Passenger Chiefs of American Lines Hold Convention," *Daily Picayune,* October 14, 1903; "Kindergarten Convention," *Daily Picayune,* April 3, 1908; "Unitarians and Their Convention," *Daily Picayune,* March 26, 1909; "Real Hospitality for Women Visitors," *Times-Picayune,* September 10, 1919.

40. "Will Erect Booth at Actors' Fund Fair," *Item,* March 29, 1910; "Architects End Convention Here," *Daily Picayune,* December 5, 1913.

41. "Scenes and Memories of Other Days to Live," *States,* March 28, 1920; "100 Pupils to Portray Bombula Dance Chosen."

42. "New Year's Eve Reservation in N. O. Going Fast," *Item,* December 26, 1920; "Featuring Orleans Society," *Item,* September 11, 1921.

43. "Bankers See Paul Morphy's Ghost Emerge from Bath," *Item,* October 31, 1921; "Jenny Lind's Reception Here Is Portrayed in Tableaux as Krewe of Aglaia Gives Annual Ball," *Times-Picayune,* January 28, 1928.

44. Burdette Huggins, "Society," *Item,* March 27, 1941.

45. Burdette Huggins, "Greet Visitors in Hoop Skirts," *Item,* March 23, 1941. For detail on another such parade, see "Parade to Highlight 'A Night in Old N. O.,'" *Item,* March 25, 1948.

46. "Where Are the Bottle Man, Chimney Sweep, Sawyer and Praline Woman?" *Item,* February 29, 1912; Thomas Ewing Dabney, "Snow Law 8 Inches Deep in Canal Street, Blocking Traffic, in Big Snowstorm just 27 Years Ago," *Item,* February 14, 1922.

47. "Women Will Run Lawn Market N.O. Day Nursery Will Benefit," *Item,* May 30, 1919.

48. "On Dit," *Item,* June 8, 1919.

49. "Sidelights of Orleans' Day of Fun Illustrate Whimsical Rule of Rex," *Times-Picayune,* February 14, 1923.

50. "Janvier Counsels Care in Addresses," *Times-Picayune,* January 31, 1923; "Women to Sell Pralines for Club Building Fund," *Item,* January 24, 1923; "Women's Club Members Will Sell Pralines," *Item,* February 11, 1923; "Daily Graphic Review of News Events," *States,* February 13, 1923. According to the *Item,* booths appeared in D. H. Holmes, Lafayette Square, the Grunewald Hotel, Godchaux's Patio Royal, the restaurant Louisiane, the Monteleone Hotel, and the Mayer Israel department store.

51. Maud O'Bryan, "In and about Town," *States*, September 19, 1952; "'Candy' Is Featured in Mid-City Parade," *Item*, February 18, 1955; "Patients Guests at Carnival Ball," *Times-Picayune*, January 30, 1959.

52. "'Gay Old Days Panorama' Theme of Moslem Krewe," *Times-Picayune*, February 12, 1961; "Dental Puppets to Take Bows to Meet," *Times-Picayune*, November 10, 1963; "Visitors Ask for Carnival in July," *Times-Picayune*, June 30, 1968.

53. "First Lady Gets a GFWC Citation," *Times-Picayune*, June 21, 1964.

54. Joseph Gogarty, "Letters to the Editor: A 'New Version,'" *Times-Picayune*, August 5, 1925.

55. Wright, "Vieux Carré," 23.

4. WHY PECANS?

1. Stuart Pecan Company, *The Pecan, and How to Grow It*, 10–11.

2. Stuart Pecan Company, *The Pecan, and How to Grow It*, 85–86.

3. Thomas, *Travels through the Western Country*, 174; J.D.B.S., "Wanderings in the Southwest: No. II," 19; J.D.B.S., "Wanderings in the Southwest: No. V," 65.

4. McWilliams, *The Pecan*, 7–12, 17, quote on 7; Wells, *Pecan*, 3–5, 13, 20.

5. *Forty-First Annual Report of the State Horticultural Society of Missouri*, 296; Colomb, "Lafayette's Visit to Baton Rouge," 179; Firestone, *Flowing South*, 63.

6. Duncan, "Report on the Topography, Climate and Diseases," 195.

7. Peacocke, *The Creole Orphans*, 104; Moody, "Slavery on Louisiana Sugar Plantations," 254–255, 263–264.

8. McWilliams, *The Pecan*, 61; Fogel, *Without Consent or Contract*, 132–145; Ferris, *Edible South*, 77–79; Genovese, *Roll, Jordan, Roll*, 542–549, 603–605.

9. McWilliams, *The Pecan*, 61–62, Wells, *Pecan*, 33, 38–39.

10. Shannon, *Antoine of Oak Alley*, 20, 25–28, 41, 90–91.

11. Shannon, *Antoine of Oak Alley*, 154–158, 178–181, 194, 216.

12. McWilliams, *The Pecan*, 63–64; Wells, *Pecan*, 40.

13. Walworth, *Dead Men's Shoes*, 149; Baker, "'A Recourse That Could Be Depended Upon,'" 21–40.

14. Warner, *Eating in the Side Room*, 33, 49–65, 89, 123–124; William-Forson, *Building Houses out of Chicken Legs*, 92–94; Harris, *High on the Hog*, 95–100.

15. Flo Field, "Remarkable Automatic Machinery to Do This Work Invented by Local Man—How It Operates," *Times-Picayune*, April 18, 1915; *Appendix to the Journals of the Senate and Assembly of the Thirty-First Session of the Legislature of the State of California*, 331; Wells, *Pecan*, 44.

16. Buckley, S. B.,"The Pecan," 349; *Bulletin of the Experiment Stations of Louisiana State University and A & M College*, 878; "Pecan Culture," 134.

17. "Plant Paper-Shell Pecans," *New Orleans Pecan Nursery* (1917), Henry G. Gilbert Nursery and Seed Trade Catalog Collection, National Agricultural Library.

18. "1917 Price List," *Jennings Nursery* (1917), Henry G. Gilbert Nursery and Seed Trade Catalog Collection, National Agricultural Library.

19. *Bulletin of the Experiment Stations of Louisiana State University and A & M College*, 879.

20. Robb and Travis, "Rise and Fall of the Gulf Coast Tung Oil Industry," 14–22; Rucker, "Satsumaland," 60–77.

21. Coen, *Forest Hill, Louisiana*, 59–64, 127; Mozo, "McMinnville, Tennessee: Nursery Capital of the World." https://tnhomeandfarm.com/agriculture/mcminnville-nursery-capital/.

22. McWilliams, *The Pecan*, 106–107.

23. Wells, *Pecan*, 46–52, quote from 46; "Pecan Breeding Cultivars," College of Agriculture, University of Georgia, https://pecanbreeding.uga.edu/cultivars/alphabetical-list/candy.html; Ray Bellande, "Pabst Family," Ocean Springs Archives, https://oceanspringsarchives.net/pabst-family; Ray Bellande, "Bechtel Family," Ocean Springs Archives, https://oceanspringsarchives.net/bechtel-family.

24. Wells, *Pecan*, 42–45.

25. McWilliams, *The Pecan*, 8–9, 81–97; Wells, *Pecan*, 41.

26. "Plant Pecans and Prosper," *J. B. Miller* (Baconton, GA: 1917), Henry G. Gilbert Nursery and Seed Trade Catalog Collection, National Agricultural Library; McWilliams, *The Pecan*, 77–78.

27. McWilliams, *The Pecan*, 96; Wells, *Pecan*, 102, 130–131.

28. "A Crop That Pays: Paper Shell Pecans," *Thomas Kane and Company* (Chicago: 1907), Henry G. Gilbert Nursery and Seed Trade Catalog Collection, National Agricultural Library.

29. "Home-Made Candies," *Daily Picayune*, December 23, 1907.

30. Field, "Remarkable Automatic Machinery to Do This Work Invented by Local Man."

31. Jaffa, *Nuts and Their Uses as Food*, 7, 26.

32. Menefee and Cassmore, *Pecan Shellers*, 5–6.

33. Menefee and Cassmore, *Pecan Shellers*, 14, 66.

34. R. C. Wright, *Investigations on the Storage of Nuts*, 1; Menefee and Cassmore, *Pecan Shellers*, 65.

35. Jamison, *Lady Jane*, 37–38, 41.

36. Menefee and Cassmore, *Pecan Shellers*, xv–xvi, 2–3, 6–7; McWilliams, *The Pecan*, 113–114; Henderson, *History of Mexican Migration to the United States*, 15–57; Johnston, *Revolution in Texas*, 71–88.

37. Menefee and Cassmore, *Pecan Shellers*, xvii, 5, 8–10, 54, quote on xvii.

38. Menefee and Cassmore, *Pecan Shellers*, 17–19, Kilday quoted on 17.

39. Menefee and Cassmore, *Pecan Shellers*, x–xi, 14, 19–22, 55; Fichtenbaum, *Funsten Nut Strike*, 15–17, 34–38.

40. Murphy, "Old Pecan Tree on 'Eureka Plantation,'" 625–627, 630.

41. "S. W. Clark and Sons ad, *Daily Picayune*, December 8, 1901; Solari's ad, *Daily Picayune*, January 31, 1904; Solari's ad, *Daily Picayune*, December 31, 1905.

42. Solari's ad, *Daily Picayune*, October 11, 1908; Katz and Besthoff ad, *Item*, February 17, 1918; D. H. Holmes ad, *States*, October 30, 1919.

43. Yorkman Candy Company ad, *Item*, December 2, 1919.

44. Yorkman Candy Company ad, *Item*, December 4, 1919; "The Pecan Is King of Nuts in Cooking Art," *Times-Picayune*, November 14, 1948.

45. "Tourist-Races Rush Begins Early Here," *States*, November 18, 1917; Helene Robbins, "Speaking of Christmas," *Times-Picayune*, December 20, 1922.

46. "Answers to Questions," *Times-Picayune,* January 14, 1922; "Pecan Pie Leads Recipes for Sunday Nut Dessert," *Times-Picayune,* September 19, 1931.

47. "Children to Send Praline Making to Far Vermont," *Times-Picayune,* December 15, 1925.

48. Alice Terry, "Rogers School Sends Exhibit," *Item,* December 20, 1925; "Products Exhibit Made by School," *Times-Picayune,* April 9, 1926.

49. "Children Advertise City," *Times-Picayune,* March 20, 1926.

50. McWilliams, *The Pecan,* 120–124, quote from 120.

51. Mack's Bakery ad, *States,* August 10, 1954; Courrégée, *Pecans,* preface; McWilliams, *The Pecan,* 120–121; Wells, *Pecan,* xx.

52. "What's Cookin,'" *Times-Picayune,* October 3, 1947; "What's Cookin,'" *States,* October 2, 1947; Rees, *Refrigeration Nation,* 174–177.

53. Pie Dufour, "A La Mode: Gastronomic Map of N.O. in Making," *States,* March 24, 1950.

54. Borden ad, *Life,* November 12, 1951, 137.

55. Borden ad, *Life,* March 9, 1953, 58.

56. Borden ad, *Life,* March 22, 1963, R8.

57. Baskin-Robbins ad, *Times-Picayune,* October 14, 1976; Baskin-Robbins ad, *Times-Picayune,* February 10, 1980.

58. Nancy Rivera, "Ice Cream Cold War Erupts," *Times-Picayune,* March 3, 1985; "Ice Cream Suit Ruling," *Times-Picayune,* August 21, 1985.

59. Crown Buick-Opel ad, *Times-Picayune,* August 6, 1976.

60. Marjorie Roehl, "Praline Liqueur Sales Turn Sour despite Keeping New Orleans Connotations," *Times-Picayune,* July 17, 1983.

61. Marjorie Roehl, "Praline Liqueur Falls Short," *Times-Picayune,* December 9, 1984.

62. Hermann Deutsch, "Gulf Coasting," *Item,* November 21, 1951; Kim Chatelain, "Selling Nuts a Break for Programmer," *Times-Picayune,* November 17, 1988.

63. McWilliams, *The Pecan,* 136, 143–144; Wells, *Pecan,* 102, 124, 154–161, 213.

5. LIKE A DISNEYLAND OF PRALINES?

1. "'Praline' Woman and Clown," *Item,* February 21, 1912; "Society," *Daily Picayune,* January 1, 1914; "Chief Statewide School Campaign Moving Smoothly," *Times-Picayune,* September 24, 1915.

2. "'Praline' Woman and Clown"; Haas, *Mayor Victor Schiro,* 16–20, 23–24, 35–41, 96–101, 145–159, 330; Rogers, *Righteous Lives,* 74–109.

3. Castellanos, *New Orleans as It Was,* 64–65.

4. Zafar, *Recipes for Respect,* 18–28, quote from 20; Tipton-Martin, *Jemima Code,* 23–30, 39–52.

5. "Are Pralines Losing Ground?" *Daily Picayune,* September 13, 1896.

6. "Pecan Pralines," *Daily Picayune,* December 30, 1897. On the development and meanings of French cuisine during the nineteenth century, see Trubeck, *Haute Cuisine,* 11–13, 35–41, 55–59; Spang, *Invention of the Restaurant,* 149–177; Ferguson, *Accounting for Taste,* 71–76, 143–146, quote from 146.

7. "Pralines," *Daily Picayune,* January 6, 1907; Ferguson, *Accounting for Taste,* 146; Cox, *Dixie's Daughters,* 50–72, 97–98, 122–128. On southern white women's views on kitchen work

and the role of cookbooks in easing their concerns with kitchen labor during the early twentieth century, see Tipton-Martin, *Jemima Code*, 6–8, 39–41; Cooley, *To Live and Dine in Dixie*, 20–42; Sharpless, *Cooking in Other Women's Kitchens*, 2–7, 14–31, 129–151.

8. "Creole Cookery," *Daily Picayune*, April 15, 1900. This cookbook remained popular with a national audience. See "The Picayune's Creole Cook Book," *Daily Picayune*, February 26, 1902. Historian Rien Fertel identifies Marie Louise Points as the likely author of the *Picayune Creole Cook Book*. Fertel, "'Everybody Seemed Willing to Help,'" 10–27.

9. S. B. Elder, "The Chevalier," *Daily Picayune*, February 27, 1911; S. B. Elder, "Lakanal and His Lost Work," *Daily Picayune*, March 20, 1911.

10. "Ancient Game of Racquette Revived by New Orleanians," *Times-Picayune*, August 19, 1919; Flo Field, "Where and How 'Ole Mammy' Pralines Are Made," Rare Vertical Files: St. Charles Hotel, Handbills-21, Louisiana Division, New Orleans Public Library.

11. "Grunewald, 76, Former Market Director, Dies," *States*, July 25, 1949.

12. Hotel Grunewald Caterers ad, *Times-Picayune*, September 22, 1919. For items available in the Grunewald Hotel grocery store, see Hotel Grunewald Caterers ad, *Times-Picayune*, September 24, 1919.

13. Meigs O. Frost, "Grunewald to Go Back to the Hotel He Built," *Times-Picayune*, October 31, 1948; "Grunewald Rites Slated Thursday," *Times-Picayune*, July 26, 1949.

14. "For Sale," *Item*, September 2, 1903; "Delicious Christmas Gifts," *Daily Picayune*, December 27, 1904. Emily Clark cannot be further identified in census records or city directories.

15. "Good Things to Eat," *Times-Picayune*, December 5, 1945; "Up and down the Street," *Times-Picayune*, December 19, 1945. Her success led Jayes to continue her home production through Mardi Gras 1946: "Up and down the Street," *Times-Picayune*, March 1, 1946.

16. "Good Things to Eat," *Times-Picayune*, November 20, 1948.

17. "Help Wanted—Male," *Item*, October 17, 1905; "Help Wanted—Male," *Item*, October 29, 1905; "Help Wanted," *Item*, January 26, 1906.

18. "Help Wanted—Sale," *Times-Picayune*, March 29, 1916; "Help Wanted—Male," *Times-Picayune*, October 23, 1926.

19. "Help Wanted—Male," *Times-Picayune*, February 26, 1927; "Help Wanted—Male," *Times-Picayune*, October 25, 1934.

12. "Busy 'Fringers' in Commerce of New Orleans," *Item*, March 31, 1908. On immigrants in New Orleans, see Bald, *Bengali Harlem*, 26–93; Jackson, *Dixie's Italians*, 13–48; Nystrom, *Creole Italian*, 1–33; Gualtieri, "Strange Fruit?" 63–85; 118–120.

21. "Merchant, 81, Taken by Death," *Times-Picayune*, July 26, 1967; Garber, "Maurice Heymann and the Development of the Lafayette Oil Center," 237; Encyclopedia of Southern Jewish Communities—Lafayette, Louisiana, https://www.isjl.org/louisiana-lafayette-encyclopedia.html.

22. "Ambitious Boy to Seek Wealth in Real Estate," *Times-Picayune*, April 11, 1926.

23. "Nicholas Souhlas Dies at 90; Was Retired Restaurant Owner," *Times-Picayune*, January 16, 1982.

24. Bruce Mack-Manning, "Too Many Jellybeans at Sara's Trial; Praline Business Slow!" *Item*, October 18, 1928.

25. "Mother and Two Blind Sons in Business," *Item*, December 2, 1928.

26. "Ad Spotlight: In the Want Ads," *Times-Picayune*, June 1, 1983.

27. "Business Opportunities," *Times-Picayune*, October 19, 1949; Howard Jacobs, "Remoulade," *Times-Picayune*, November 4, 1955.

28. John Pope, "Pot of Gold at End of Long Line Was a Box of Surplus Cheese," *Times-Picayune*, February 25, 1983; Simmons, *Crescent City Girls*, 59–81, quote from 61.

29. "The Newcomb Art Exhibit," *Daily Picayune*, June 4, 1895..

30. Ormand and Irvine, *Louisiana's Art Nouveau*, 152; "Selected Newcomb Artisan Bios," Newcomb Art Museum of Tulane, https://newcombartmuseum.tulane.edu/portfolio-item/artisans/.

31. "Copies of First Newcomb Post Cards to Aid Funds," *Item*, April 8, 1917. The article misidentifies Marie Louise by referencing her daughter Azelie, who continued selling pralines at Newcomb College into the 1920s.

32. "New Orleans Greatest Industrial City in All South Doing More Business than Any Six Southern Cities," *Item*, June 24, 1917.

33. Marguerite Samuels, "Would Raise Working Age of Boys and Girls of City," *Times-Picayune*, April 28, 1920.

34. "My Pre-Easter Diary," *Item*, April 6, 1919.

35. "Saturday Chosen to Be Candy Day," *States*, October 7, 1921; "Business Day by Day," *Item*, May 27, 1924.

36. Merleaux, *Sugar and Civilization*, 137–140, quote from 137.

37. "Miss Carson Makes Pralines for Orphans," *Item*, November 8, 1916; "Help Wanted—Female," *Item*, October 20, 1918; "Help Wanted—Female," *Times-Picayune*, October 19, 1919; "Help Wanted—Female," *Item*, November 23, 1919.

38. "Help Wanted—Female," *Times-Picayune*, November 18, 1928.

39. Howard Jacobs, "Remoulade: A Heavenly Hash Candymaker Cited," *Times-Picayune*, January 8, 1976.

40. A. G. Williams Home-Made Candy Company ad, *Times-Picayune*, February 8, 1921.

41. "Help Wanted—Female," *States*, August 3, 1948.

42. "Carnival Profits Are Tremendous," *Item*, March 2, 1911.

43. "Invade the East," *Daily Picayune*, March 27, 1914.

44. "Creole Pralines Now Purchasable on Famous Board Walk," *Item*, April 28, 1914.

45. "Creole Pralines Are Hit at Atlantic City," *Item*, July 12, 1914.

46. "F. & K. Put in $5000 Fountain at Seaside," *Item*, June 19, 1916.

47. "Kraemer Says All East Trade Is Good," *States*, August 30, 1917.

48. "New Orleans in Trade," *States*, November 30, 1927; "Pralines by Air to Distant Markets," *States*, December 4, 1932; "Winner," *Item*, February 15, 1936; Stanonis, *Creating the Big Easy*, 56–60.

49. S. W. Clark and Sons, *Daily Picayune*, October 30, 1899; "Christmas Cheer in a Food Palace," *Daily Picayune*, December 16, 1900.

50. S. W. Clark and Sons ad, *Daily Picayune*, February 26, 1900; Clark's ad, *Daily Picayune*, November 22, 1901.

51. D. H. Holmes ad, *Daily Picayune*, January 20, 1901.

52. Hale, *Making Whiteness*, 151–168; Turner, *Ceramic Uncles and Celluloid Mammies*, 49–56.

53. "Atlantic City to Have Something New," *Item*, March 27, 1914; Hunter, *To 'Joy My Freedom*, 188–191, 207–210; Deck, "Now Then—Who Said Biscuits?" 70–86.

54. Fuerst & Kraemer ad, *Item,* November 8, 1916.

55. Maurice B. Kreeger, "I Remember When," *Times-Picayune,* October 14, 1955. On cultural links between race, the body, and technology in the United States of the nineteenth and twentieth centuries, see De la Peña, *The Body Electric,* 23–25, 28–32, 44–49, 98–125; Rice, *Minding the Machine,* 14–33.

56. Report Relative to J. E. Marshall Peddling Cooked Food from Wagon without a License (December 14, 1898), Police Department Permits-NOPL; Complain of Candy Stand in Front of #829 Burgundy Street (April 28, 1899), Police Department Permits-NOPL; Report on Application of Sallie Gaines for Free Permit to Sell Ice Cream Corner 6th & Laurel Street (April 6, 1899), Police Department Permits-NOPL.

57. Report of Investigation as to Whether Mrs. Paul Maggio Corner Spain and Urquhart Street Is Entitled to Free Permit (January 26, 1899), Police Department Permits-NOPL; Report Relative to Free Permit Applied for by Mrs. E. Groscha of 516 Constantinople Street (July 3, 1899), Police Department Permits-NOPL.

58. "The Market Question Plainly Set Forth," *Daily Picayune,* January 8, 1901; Young, "Nourishing Networks," 178–187.

59. Scott, *200 Years of New Orleans Cooking,* 218–219; Robinson, *It's an Old New Orleans Custom,* 266; Jennifer Quale, "Vivant," *Times-Picayune,* May 2, 1976; Hunter, *To 'Joy My Freedom,* 111–112.

60. "Fate and Pralines," *Item,* March 30, 1918; Merleaux, *Sugar and Civilization,* 68–71, 81–84.

61. "Candy Man Is Sweetening Bitterness of Arid Days," *Times-Picayune,* July 9, 1919; Dusselier, "Bonbons," 31–40.

62. Marguerite Samuels, "Would Raise Working Age of Boys and Girls of City," *Times-Picayune,* April 18, 1920.

63. Nutqueet ad, *Times-Picayune,* August 7, 1920.

64. Louisiana Home-Made Candy Factory ad, *Times-Picayune,* December 24, 1920; "Nick Tacko Reports His Business Big," *States,* April 10, 1922; Jacobs, "Remoulade."

65. Napoleon Candy Company ad, *Times-Picayune,* February 1, 1920; D. H. Holmes ad, *Times-Picayune,* December 20, 1923.

66. Solari's ad, *Times-Picayune,* December 12, 1915; Hotel Grunewald Caterers ad, *Item,* December 22, 1918; Katz and Besthoff ad, *Item,* February 17, 1918.

67. Creole Praline Company ad, *Item,* December 1919; Napoleon Candy Company, *Times-Picayune,* February 1, 1920.

68. "Twixt You and Me," *Item,* March 9, 1919.

69. "Help Wanted—Female," *Times-Picayune,* January 15, 1921; Sue Bryan, "Feud," *Item,* October 28, 1934; Albert Goldstein, "Page Mr. Jolson: Mammy Situation in Vieux Carre Begins to Puzzle Citizens," *Times-Picayune,* October 25, 1937.

70. "Revival of Old New Orleans Life Urged," *Times-Picayune.* May 30, 1935; Saxon et al., *Gumbo Ya-Ya,* 37.

71. Stella Pitts, "Echoes of the Past Linger in Remaining Street Vendors," *Times-Picayune,* May 12, 1974; Quale, "*Vivant.*"

72. Shaik, *Mayor of New Orleans,* 16.

73. Telling-Grandon Scrapbook, entry for February 25, 1903, Louisiana and Special Collections, Earl K. Long Library, University of New Orleans; Maud O'Bryan, "Up and down the Street," *Times-Picayune,* May 15, 1962.

74. William Wiegand, "Down the Spillway," *Item,* November 3, 1942.

75. "Mayor Declines Invitation to Fly," *Times-Picayune,* May 39, 1919.

76. Aaron Hirschwitz, Toy Bale, U. S. Patent 960922, filed March 10, 1909, and issued June 7, 1910, https://patents.google.com/patent/US960922A; Aaron Hirschwitz, Miniature-Cotton-Bale Box, U. S. Patent 1357866, filed February 27, 1920, and issued November 2, 1920, https://patents.google.com/patent/US1357866A.

77. St. Charles Hotel ad, *Item,* March 23, 1920; St. Charles Hotel ad, *Item,* December 11, 1921.

78. St. Charles Hotel ad, *Times-Picayune,* April 25, 1922.

79. "Children Fill Miniature Trunk with Louisiana Products to Send with Invitation to 'Al' Smith," *Times-Picayune,* December 13, 1925; "Let's Go Shopping," *Item,* April 21, 1929.

80. Yorkman Candy Company ad, *Item,* December 23, 1929; Solari's ad, *Times-Picayune,* January 29, 1929; Solari's ad, *Item,* October 30, 1935; Betty-Lou ad, *Times-Picayune,* January 25, 1937.

81. McCulla, "Consumable City," 205–218. McCulla stresses that the appeal of these wax figures partly reflected the similarities between wax and brown sugar.

82. "Laura's Creole Praline, Fudge, Cake, Heavenly Hash Candy Sold only at 928 Canal Street, New Location," *Times-Picayune,* October 21, 1937. The business was sold to Meddie Crawford in the early 1940s and became known as Laura's Original Praline and Fudge Shop. Crawford sold the business in 1972, and it remains in operation today. See Quale, "Vivant."

83. Maison Blanche ad, *Item,* February 24, 1952; Little Courtyard Shop, J. R. Abbot and H. R. Abbot scrapbook, 1953, Anthony Stanonis Travel Scrapbook and Diary Collection, Special Collections and Archives, J. Edgar and Louise S. Monroe Library, Loyola University New Orleans.

84. "Up and Down the Street," *Times-Picayune,* January 26, 1939.

85. D. H. Holmes ad, *Times-Picayune,* December 21, 1929. Holmes continued to use cotton bale-style packaging into the 1970s: D. H. Holmes ad, *Times-Picayune,* December 1, 1968; D. H. Holmes ad, *Times-Picayune,* February 16, 1969; D. H. Holmes ad, *Times-Picayune,* December 16, 1971; D. H. Holmes ad, *Times-Picayune,* February 22, 1982. On the rise of Black political power in New Orleans, see Hirsch, "Simply a Matter of Black and White," 273–319; Moore, *Black Rage in New Orleans,* 140–163, 203–219.

86. "Business Chances," *Times-Picayune,* May 30, 1920.

87. "Praline Maker Failed to Make Good, Charge," *Item,* July 31, 1920.

88. Ed Anderson, "Near Half-Century Later, How's the Old Burg Look?" *Times-Picayune,* September 29, 1974.

89. "NEA Convention Added Thousands to City's Coffers," *Item,* February 26, 1937; "Shopping Service Has a Birthday," *Times-Picayune,* October 1, 1944.

90. Marjorie Roehl, "Get Girl, Soldier, They'll Do the Rest," *Item,* August 31, 1943.

91. Wiegand, "Down the Spillway."

92. "Boys in England Ask for Pralines," *States,* February 4, 1944.

93. "Pralines Pay for Marine's Wash," *Item,* March 10, 1943; "Truman Scoffs, Says South Is Still Solid," *Item,* October 11, 1944.

94. Tipton-Martin, *Jemima Code,* 40–41; McCulla, "Consumable City," 211–227. For context on southern tourism, gender, and race within the regional consumer market, see Hale, *Making Whiteness,* 125–168, 182–194.

95. Miss Louise Cook ad, *Times-Picayune,* March 25, 1922; *1920 United States Federal Census.*

96. "Your City Is Growing," *States,* July 24, 1927.

97. "Mrs. Louise Cook Famed for Creole Pralines, Dies," *States,* December 19, 1928.

98. "Dissolution Notices," *Item,* June 16, 1948; "Dissolution—New Firms," *States,* June 17, 1948.

99. Marjorie Roehl, "Gumbo Is Their Dish," *Item,* May 12, 1949.

100. "Kate Latter Lorning," *Times-Picayune,* March 16, 1990.

101. "Miss Kate Latter," *States,* January 30, 1926.

102. "Mrs. C. H. Goldstein Wins Better Candy Prize," *States,* January 31, 1926.

103. "Kate Latter Shop Is Celebrating Its Anniversary," *States,* January 27, 1928.

104. Maud O'Bryan, "More Sweets," *States,* October 7, 1937; "Help Wanted—Male," *States,* May 11, 1949; "Help Wanted-Female," *States,* February 21, 1951.

105. "Up and down the Street," *Times-Picayune,* February 4, 1950.

106. "Up and down the Street," *Times-Picayune,* October 28, 1955; Maud O'Bryan, "Up and down the Street," *Times-Picayune,* March 25, 1963. In the early 1970s, John Randazza purchased Kate Latter's. See Quale, "Vivant."

107. Marjorie Roehl, "Her Record Is 8000 Pralines," *Item,* May 19, 1949; *1930 United States Federal Census.*

108. Elizabeth Kell, "In Society," *States,* May 27, 1935; Léda Hincks Plauché, Design for a rag doll, U.S. Patent 97092, filed May 28, 1935, and issued October 1, 1935, https://patents.google.com/patent/USD97092S.

109. Maud O'Bryan, "Now She Can Breathe," *States,* January 29, 1936.

110. Roehl, "Her Record Is 8000 Pralines."

111. Green Orchid, Story of the Praline, circa 1940s, Anthony J. Stanonis Pamphlet Collection, Special Collections and Archives, J. Edgar and Louise S. Monroe Library, Loyola University New Orleans.

112. Roehl, "Her Record Is 8000 Pralines"; Hermann Deutsch, "Problem for Joe," *Item,* August 28, 1950; Stella Pitts, "It Takes Imagination to Name a Shop," *Times-Picayune,* December 14, 1975.

113. "Help Wanted—Female," *Times-Picayune,* October 12, 1952; Old Town Pralines and Parasols, https://www.oldtownpraline.com/about-us/. The shop was located at 721 Royal Street in the 1930s before moving to 627 Royal Street by 1952.

114. Louise Glynn was born Louise Sireix. Frank Gagnard, "Quintessentially the Quarter," *Times-Picayune,* August 16, 1991; *1930 United States Federal Census; New Orleans, Louisiana, U.S., Marriage Records Index, 1831–1964; New Orleans, Louisiana, U.S., Birth Records Index, 1790–1915.*

115. Maud O'Bryan, "Bandannaed Mammy," *States,* September 29, 1936; "Local Photographers Scooped on This, for $100," *Item,* November 11, 1937.

116. Quale, "Vivant."

117. Old Town Pralines and Parasols, https://www.oldtownpraline.com/about-us.

118. "Pierre Bagur," *Daily Picayune,* May 17, 1910; "Sale by Civil Sheriff Judicial Advertisement," *Item,* June 9, 1930; "Sale by Civil Sheriff Judicial Advertisement," *States,* August 4, 1930; *New Orleans, Louisiana, U.S., Marriage Records Index, 1831–1964; 1920 United States Federal Census; 1930 United States Federal Census.*

119. Pierre Eugene Bagur, Design for a Box, U.S. Patent 98472, filed December 3, 1935, and issued February 4, 1936, https://patents.google.com/patent/USD98472S; Pierre Eugene Bagur, Miniature Cotton Bale Receptacle, U.S. Patent 2584414, filed March 2, 1950, and issued February 5, 1952, https://patents.google.com/patent/US2584414A; "Patents Granted," *Times-Picayune,* February 7, 1936; "Patents Granted in Bi-State Area," *Times-Picayune,* March 10, 1952.

120. "36 Parcels of Realty Sold," *States,* June 4, 1940; "Levee Board Sells 2 Sites," *Item,* August 7, 1941.

121. Aunt Sally's, circa 1947, Anthony J. Stanonis Pamphlet Collection, Special Collections and Archives, J. Edgar and Louise S. Monroe Library, Loyola University New Orleans; "For Added Cheer," *Times-Picayune,* November 27, 1949.

122. "Return to Horse, Buggy Days in Vieux Carre Awaits OK," *Item,* December 23, 1940.

123. Quale, "Vivant"; "Tally-Ho, away We Go," *Times-Picayune,* January 29, 1941.

124. "Up and down the Street," *Times-Picayune,* April 17, 1943; "Help Wanted—Male," *Item,* March 9, 1944.

125. Stanton Delaplane, "An Outsider Looks at Us," *Item,* September 21, 1950.

126. "Good Things to Eat," *Times-Picayune,* November 18, 1974; Anita Shrodt, "Praline Shop Lease Is Signed," *Times-Picayune,* July 3, 1974; "Investigation Continues at Fire Site in Quarter," *Times-Picayune,* August 7, 1974.

127. Maud O'Bryan, "Pralines Shipped in Cotton Bales," *Times-Picayune,* November 21, 1974.

128. Quale, "Vivant"; Margaret Fuller, "Christmas Catalogs: Seasonal Sales Power," *Times-Picayune,* December 1, 1987.

129. Carter Stevens, "Candy Plant Plans to Double Capacity after War," *Item,* July 26, 1945; "Elmers Prepare for Postwar Growth in Sales of Quality Candies, Food," *Times-Picayune,* August 23, 1945. On the New Orleans tourism industry after World War II, see Souther, *New Orleans on Parade,* 1–37; Gotham, *Authentic New Orleans,* 69–115.

130. Quale, "Vivant"; Maud O'Bryan, "Advertising Reporter," *States-Item,* December 18, 1975.

131. "Praline at Home When Served Here," *Times-Picayune,* February 11, 1926.

132. "Golden Box Product of Yorkman," *States,* April 12, 1925; Maison Blanche ad, *Times-Picayune,* February 12, 1925; "Miss Latter Home from Candy Markets," *States,* August 30, 1927; Chara Monta, "Simple Fun," *Times-Picayune,* July 16, 1953.

133. "Times-Picayune Flown to Revue," *Times-Picayune,* November 20, 1955; Jacobs, "Remoulade."

134. "'Gay New Orleans' to Be Great Attraction at World's Fair," *Item,* April 18, 1940. For a history of faux-New Orleans constructed outside New Orleans, see Stanonis, "Through a Purple (Green and Gold) Haze," 109–131.

135. Horace Sutton, "Airport Is French Showcase," *Times-Picayune,* December 31, 1967; "Fool, [sic] Other Items Will Go to Japan," *Times-Picayune,* October 26, 1972; Ed Lepoma, "N.O. Exhibit to Represent U.S. at Berlin Fair," *States-Item,* September 12, 1973.

136. "Business Women Seek to Have Towns Organized," *Times-Picayune,* July 20, 1924; "What Our Neighbors Are Saying," *Times-Picayune,* January 16, 1929; "Poaching," *Item,* January 20, 1929.

137. "Welcome to Bay St. Louis, Mississippi," *Times-Picayune,* January 25, 1953; Thomas Griffin, "Oh, Yeah!" *Item,* November 14, 1951; "They Collect Bits of Dixie," *Times-Picayune,* May 18, 1958.

138. "Down Yonder . . . Pralines Lead the Candy Caravan," *Item,* October 23, 1955. Article reprints "Cook's Heaven" from *Good Housekeeping.*

EPILOGUE

1. "How Pralines Got Name," *States,* October 16, 1953; Harriett Cortez, "Recipes and Reminiscences," *States-Item,* November 4, 1971; Harriett Cortez, "Those Jazz Fair Pralinieres," *States-Item,* April 27, 1972.

2. Rehder, *Delta Sugar,* 119–122, 128, 179–190, 294–302, quotes from 121 and 122.

3. Wells, *Pecan,* 164–165, 168.

4. Millie Ball, "Richard Returns," *Times-Picayune,* May 1, 1983; Nancy Schoeffler, "He Thinks Big," *Times-Picayune,* November 24, 1984.

5. Rose Kahn, "She's Been the City's No. 1 Hostess," *States-Item,* December 9, 1974.

6. Rosemary Ruiz, "Souvenir City," *States-Item,* April 11, 1974; Thomas, *Desire and Disaster in New Orleans,* 8–11, quote from 8.

7. Evans Creole Candy Factory ad, *Times-Picayune,* January 29, 1978; "Ad Spotlight: Official," *Times-Picayune,* November 30, 1983; "Café Du Monde to Buy Evans Candy Space in French Market and Expand Operations," *Advocate,* May 27, 2015. The newspaper account from 1983 states that Cuccia bought the business "26 years ago," while a later account states the year as 1968.

8. Jennifer Quale, "Vivant," *Times-Picayune,* May 2, 1976. Jay Cuccia used white instead of brown sugar, noting that the "flavor is better—otherwise it's too rich."

9. Christine Lacoste Bordelon, "Advertising Key: Something Delicious," *Times-Picayune,* March 23, 1986; Leslie Cardé, "Lifetime's 'New Orleans Noel' Is a Sweet Christmas Tribute to Love, Memory and Pralines," *Times-Picayune,* November 28, 2022.

10. Constance Snow, "Carrying on a Sweet Tradition," *Times-Picayune,* September 25, 1992; Todd Price, "Tee Eva, Pie Baker, Baby Doll, and Back-Up Singer to Ernie K-Doe, Dies at 83," *Times-Picayune,* June 8, 2018; Kolb, *New Orleans Memories,* 56.

Bibliography

ARCHIVAL SOURCES

Loyola University New Orleans, J. Edgar and Louise S. Monroe Library, Special Collections and Archives
Anthony J. Stanonis Pamphlet Collection
Anthony Stanonis Travel Scrapbook and Diary Collection

National Agricultural Library
Henry G. Gilbert Nursery and Seed Trade Catalog Collection

New Orleans Public Library, City Archives and Special Collections
New Orleans Police Department Correspondence and Reports
Rare Vertical Files

Southern University and A&M College, John B. Cade Library, Archives and Manuscripts Department
John B. Cade Slave Narratives

Tulane University, Howard-Tilton Memorial Library, Louisiana Research Collection
Trowbridge Family Papers

University of New Orleans, Earl K. Long Library, Louisiana Collection and Special Collections
Firemen's Charitable Association of the Seventh District Collection
Telling-Grandon Collection

Virginia Historical Society
George William Bagby Papers
William Macon Waller Papers

GOVERNMENT DOCUMENTS

The Statistics of the Population of the United States, Ninth Census, vol I. Washington, DC: Government Printing Office, 1872.

1870 United States Federal Census (online database). Provo, UT: Ancestry.com. Operations, 2009.

1880 United States Federal Census (online database). Lehi, UT: Ancestry.com. Operations, 2010.

1900 United States Federal Census (online database). Provo, UT: Ancestry.com. Operations, 2004.

1910 United States Federal Census (online database). Lehi, UT: Ancestry.com Operations, 2006.

1920 United States Federal Census (online database). Provo, UT: Ancestry.com Operations, 2010.

1930 United States Federal Census (online database). Provo, UT: Ancestry.com Operations, 2002.

Appendix to the Journals of the Senate and Assembly of the Thirty-First Session of the Legislature of the State of California, vol. v. Sacramento: State Office, 1895.

Bagur, Pierre Eugene. Design for a Box, U.S. Patent 98472, filed December 3, 1935, and issued February 4, 1936. https://patents.google.com/patent/USD98472S.

———. Miniature Cotton Bale Receptacle. U.S. Patent 2584414, filed March 2, 1950, and issued February 5, 1952. https://patents.google.com/patent/US2584414A.

Ballinger, Ray. *A History of Sugar Marketing: Agricultural Economic Report No. 197.* Washington, DC: U.S. Department of Agriculture Economic Research Service, February 1971.

Bulletin of the Experiment Stations of Louisiana State University and A & M College. Baton Rouge: Truth and Job Office, 1898.

Fourth Biennial Report of the Bureau of Labor Statistics of the State of California for the Years 1889–1890. Sacramento: State Office, 1890.

Hirschwitz, Aaron. Toy Bale. U.S. Patent 960922, filed March 10, 1909, and issued June 7, 1910. https://patents.google.com/patent/US960922A.

———. Miniature-Cotton-Bale Box. U.S. Patent 1357866, filed February 27, 1920, and issued November 2, 1920. https://patents.google.com/patent/US1357866A.

Historical Statistics of the United States: Colonial Times to 1970. Washington, DC: Department of Commerce, 1975.

Louisiana, U.S., Statewide Death Index, 1819–1964 (online database). Provo, USA: Ancestry.com Operations, 2002.

Louisiana, U.S., Wills and Probate Records, 1756–1984 (online database). Lehi, USA: Ancestry.com Operations, 2015.

New Orleans, Louisiana, U.S., Birth Records Index, 1790–1915 (online database). Provo, UT: Ancestry.com Operations, 2002.

New Orleans, Louisiana, U.S., Marriage Records Index, 1831–1964 (online database). Provo, UT: Ancestry.com Operations, 2002.

Plauché, Léda Hincks. Design for a Rag Doll. U.S. Patent 97092, filed May 28, 1935, and issued October 1, 1935. https://patents.google.com/patent/USD97092S.

Population of the United States in 1860; Compiled from the Original Returns of the Eighth Census. Washington, DC: Government Printing Office, 1864.

Report of the Select Committee on the New Orleans Riots. Washington, DC: Government Printing Office, 1867.

U.S., City Directories, 1822–1995 (online database). Lehi, UT: Ancestry.com Operations, 2011.

Wright, R. C. *Investigations on the Storage of Nuts.* Technical Bulletin No. 770. Washington, DC: Government Printing Office, 1941.

NEWSPAPERS AND PERIODICALS

New Orleans

Advocate

Daily Picayune

Item

States

States-Item

Times-Picayune

Other

Life

Lowell (MA) Daily Citizen and News

New York Evening World

New York Tribune

Rock Island (IL) Argus

Sugar Bulletin

BOOKS, ARTICLES, AND DISSERTATIONS

Abel, Mary Hinman. "Sugar as Food." *Farmer's Bulletin No. 93.* Washington, DC: Government Printing Office, 1899.

Arnesen, Eric. *Waterfront Workers of New Orleans: Race, Class, and Politics, 1863–1923.* Urbana: University of Illinois Press, 1994.

Aryan, Junius. *The Aryans and Mongrelized America: The Remedy.* Philadelphia: Eagle Printing Press, 1912.

Augustin, Donatien. *A General Digest of the Ordinances and Resolutions of the Corporation of New-Orleans.* New Orleans: Jerome Bayon, 1831.

Avirett, James Battle. *The Old Plantation: How We Lived in Great House and Cabin before the War.* New York: F. Tennyson Neely, 1901.

Baker, Bruce. "'A Recourse That Could Be Depended Upon': Picking Blackberries and Getting by after the Civil War." *Southern Cultures* (Winter 2010): 21–40.

———. "*Das Kapital* on Tchoupitoulas Street: The Marketing of Stolen Goods and the Reserve Army of Labor in Reconstruction-Era New Orleans." In *Southern Scoundrels: Grifters and Graft in the Nineteenth Century*, edited by Jeff Forret and Bruce E. Baker, 174–195. Baton Rouge: Louisiana State University Press, 2021.

———. "Fires on Shipboard: Sandbars, Salvage Fraud, and the Cotton Trade in New Orleans in the 1870s." *Journal of Southern History* (August 2020): 601–624.

Bald, Vivek. *Bengali Harlem and the Lost Histories of South Asian America*. Cambridge, MA: Harvard University Press, 2013.

Barrow, Willie Micajah. "The Civil War Diary of Willie Micajah Barrow, I." Edited by Wendell Holmes Stephenson and Edwin Adams Davis. *Louisiana Historical Quarterly* (July 1934): 436–451.

"Beet Sugar—Progress of Its Manufacture in France and Germany." Edited by Wendell Holmes Stephenson and Edwin Adams Davis. *Sorgo Journal and Farm Machinist 4, no. 7* (July 1866): 712–731.

Beriss, David. "Authentic Creole: Tourism, Style, and Calamity in New Orleans Restaurants." In *The Restaurants Book: Ethnographies of Where We Eat, edited by David Beriss and David Sutton*, 151–166. New York: Berg, 2007.

Berry, Daina Ramey, and Kali Nicole Gross. *A Black Women's History of the United States*. Boston: Beacon Press, 2020.

Blassingame, John. *Black New Orleans, 1860–1880*. Chicago: University of Chicago Press, 1973.

Blight, David. *Race and Reunion: The Civil War in American Memory*. Cambridge, MA: Belknap Press, 2001.

Bogle, Donald. *Brown Sugar: Over One Hundred Years of America's Black Female Superstars*, rev. ed. New York: Continuum International Publishing, 2007.

Brachet, A. *Etymological Dictionary of the French Language*. Translated by G. W. Kitchin. London: MacMillan, 1873.

Brady, Patricia. "Mollie Moore Davis: A Literary Life." In *Louisiana Women Writers: New Essays and a Comprehensive Biography*, edited by Dorothy Brown and Barbara Ewell, 99–118. Baton Rouge: Louisiana State University Press, 1992.

Bremer, Fredrika. *The Homes of the New World: Impressions of America*, vol. III. Translated by Mary Howitt. London: Arthur Hall, Virtue and Company, 1853.

Bryan, Violet Harrington. *The Myth of New Orleans in Literature: Dialogues of Race and Gender*. Knoxville: University of Tennessee Press, 1993.

Buckley, S. B. "The Pecan." *Southern Cultivator* 27, no. 11 (November 1868): 349.

Buechner, Howard. *Daniel Anton Buechner: Master Lithographer of Old New Orleans*. Metairie, LA: Thunderbird Press, 1983.

Bush, Robert. *Grace King: A Southern Destiny*. Baton Rouge: Louisiana State University Press, 1983.

Butler, Benjamin. *Private and Official Correspondence of Gen. Benjamin F. Butler,* vol. I. Norwood, MA: Plimpton Press, 1917.

Cable, George Washington. *The Grandissimes: A Story of Creole Life.* New York: Charles Scribner's Sons, 1880.

———. *Kincaid's Battery.* New York: Charles Scribner's Sons, 1908.

———. "The Dance in Place Congo." *Century Magazine* (February 1886): 517–532.

Cartwright, S. A. "The Curative Virtues of the Sugar-House for Bronchial, Dyspeptic and Consumptive Complaints." *DeBow's Review* 13 (December 1852): 598–602.

Castellanos, Henry. *New Orleans as It Was: Episodes of Louisiana Life.* New Orleans: L. Graham and Son, 1895.

Clark, Emily. *The Strange History of the American Quadroon: Free Women of Color in the Revolutionary Atlantic World.* Chapel Hill: University of North Carolina Press, 2013.

Clinkscales, John George. *On the Old Plantation: Reminiscences of His Childhood.* Spartanburg, SC: Band and White, 1916.

Cocks, Catherine. *Tropical Whites: The Rise of the Tourist South in the Americas.* Philadelphia: University of Pennsylvania Press, 2013.

Coen, Cheré Dastugue. *Forest Hill, Louisiana: A Bloom Town History.* Charleston: History Press, 2014.

Cohen, Benjamin. *Pure Adulteration: Cheating on Nature in the Age of Manufactured Food.* Chicago: University of Chicago Press, 2019.

Collins, Richard. "Under Reconstruction: Lafcadio Hearn in New Orleans (1877–1887)." In *Songs of the Reconstructing South: Building Literary Louisiana, 1865–1945,* edited by Suzanne Disheroon-Green and Lisa Abney, 35–48. Westport, CT: Greenwood Press, 2002.

Colomb, R. W., ed. "Lafayette's Visit to Baton Rouge, April, 1825." *Louisiana Historical Quarterly* (January 1931): 178–181.

Cooley, Angela Jill. *To Live and Dine in Dixie: The Evolution of Urban Food Culture in the Jim Crow South.* Athens: University of Georgia Press, 2015.

Cooper, Gail. "Love, War, and Chocolate: Gender and the American Candy Industry, 1880–1930." In *His and Hers: Gender, Consumption, and Technology,* edited by Roger Horowitz and Arwen Mohun, 67–94. Charlottesville: University Press of Virginia, 1998.

Corsan, William. *The Confederate States, Including a Visit to New Orleans under the Domination of General Butler.* London: Richard Bentley, 1863.

Cott, Jonathan. *Wandering Ghost: The Odyssey of Lafcadio Hearn.* New York: Alfred Knopf, 1991.

Courrégée, Keith. *Pecans: From Soup to Nuts.* Natchitoches, LA: Cane River Pecan Company, 1984.

Cox, Karen. *Dixie's Daughters: The United Daughters of the Confederacy and the Preservation of Confederate Culture.* Gainesville: University Press of Florida, 2003.

———. *Dreaming of Dixie: How the South Was Created in American Popular Culture.* Chapel Hill: University of North Carolina Press, 2011.

Cram, Mildred. *Old Seaport Towns of the South.* New York: Dodd, Mead & Company, 1917.

Creecy, James R. *Scenes in the South, and Other Miscellaneous Pieces.* Washington, DC: Thomas McGill, 1860.

Creole Cookery Book, edited by the Christian Woman's Exchange. Gretna, LA: Pelican Publishing, 2005.

Dabel, Jane. "'My Ma Went to Work Early Every Morning': Color, Gender, and Occupation in New Orleans, 1840–1860." *Louisiana History* (Spring 2000): 217–229.

Day, Ivan. "Sugar Sculpture." In *The Oxford Companion to Sugar and Sweets,* edited by Darra Goldstein, 689–693. New York: Oxford University Press, 2015.

Deck, Alice. "'Now Then—Who Said Biscuits?': The Black Woman Cook as Fetish in American Advertising, 1905–1953." In *Kitchen Culture in America: Popular Representations of Food, Gender, and Race,* edited by Sherrie Inness, 69–94. Philadelphia: University of Pennsylvania Press, 2001.

Deetz, Kelley Fanto. *Bound to the Fire: How Virginia's Enslaved Cooks Helped Invent American Cuisine.* Lexington: University Press of Kentucky, 2015.

De Forest, John William. *A Volunteer's Adventures: A Union Captain's Record of the Civil War,* edited by James Croushore. New Haven: Yale University Press, 1946.

De La Peña, Carolyn Thomas. *The Body Electric: How Strange Machines Built the Modern American.* New York: New York University Press, 2003.

De Saussure, N. B. *Old Plantation Days: Being Recollections of Southern Life before the Civil War.* New York: Duffield and Company, 1909.

Dessens, Nathalie. *From Saint-Domingue to New Orleans: Migration and Influences.* Gainesville: University Press of Florida, 2007.

Douglass, Frederick. *My Bondage and My Freedom.* New York: Miller, Orton, and Mulligan, 1855.

Dubois, Laurent. *A Colony of Citizens: Revolution and Slave Emancipation in the French Caribbean, 1787–1804.* Chapel Hill: University of North Carolina Press, 2004.

Dunbar-Nelson, Alice. *The Goodness of St. Rocque and Other Stories.* New York: Dodd, Mead and Company, 1899.

Duncan, James. "Report on the Topography, Climate and Diseases of the Parish of St. Mary, La." *Southern Medical Reports* 1 (1850): 190–196.

Dusselier, Jane. "Bonbons, Lemon Drops, and Oh Henry! Bars: Candy, Consumer Culture, and the Construction of Gender, 1895–1920." In *Kitchen Culture in America: Popular Representations of Food, Gender, and Race,* edited by Sherrie Inness, 13–50. Philadelphia: University of Pennsylvania Press, 2001.

Egerton, John. *Southern Food: At Home, on the Road, in History.* Chapel Hill: University of North Carolina Press, 1993.

Engelhardt, Elizabeth. *A Mess of Greens: Southern Gender and Southern Food.* Athens: University of Georgia Press, 2011.

"Extension of the Sugar Region of the United States." *DeBow's Review* 14 (March 1853): 197–208.

Ferguson, Priscilla. *Accounting for Taste: The Triumph of French Cuisine.* Chicago: University of Chicago Press, 2004.

Ferris, Marcie Cohen. *The Edible South: The Power of Food and the Making of an American Region.* Chapel Hill: University of North Carolina Press, 2014.

Fertel, Rien. "'Everybody Seemed Willing to Help': The Picayune Creole Cook Book as Battleground, 1900–2008." In *The Larder: Food Studies Methods from the American South,* edited by John T. Edge, Elizabeth Engelhardt, and Ted Ownby, 10–31. Athens: University of Georgia Press, 2013.

———. *Imagining the Creole City: The Rise of Literary Culture in Nineteenth-Century New Orleans.* Baton Rouge: Louisiana State University Press, 2014.

Fichtenbaum, Myrna. *The Funsten Nut Strike.* New York: International Publishers, 1991.

Firestone, Clark. *Flowing South.* New York: National Travel Club, 1941.

Fogel, Robert, and Stanley Engerman. *Time on the Cross: The Economics of American Negro Slavery.* New York: Norton, 1974.

———. *Without Consent or Contract: The Rise and Fall of American Slavery.* New York: Norton, 1989.

Follett, Richard. *The Sugar Masters: Planters and Slaves in Louisiana's Cane World, 1820–1860.* Baton Rouge: Louisiana State University Press, 2005.

Foner, Eric. *Reconstruction: America's Unfinished Revolution, 1863–1877.* New York: Harper and Row, 1988.

Forty-First Annual Report of the State Horticultural Society of Missouri. Jefferson City, MO: Tribune Printing Company, 1898.

Foster, Gaines. *Ghosts of the Confederacy: Defeat, the Lost Cause, and the Emergence of the New South.* New York: Oxford University Press, 1987.

Garber, Andrew. "Maurice Heymann and the Development of the Lafayette Oil Center." *Louisiana History* (Summer 1999): 327–354.

Geggus, David. "The Louisiana Purchase and the Haitian Revolution." In *The Haitian Revolution and the Early United States,* edited by Elizabeth Dillon and Michael Drexler, 117–129. Philadelphia: University of Pennsylvania Press, 2016.

Geilow, Martha. *Old Plantation Days.* New York: R. H. Russell, 1902.

Genovese, Eugene. *Roll, Jordan, Roll: The World the Slaves Made.* New York: Pantheon Books, 1974.

Gill, James. *Lords of Misrule: Mardi Gras and the Politics of Race in New Orleans.* Jackson: University Press of Mississippi, 1997.

Glazier, Willard. *Peculiarities of American Cities.* Philadelphia: Hubbard Brothers, 1883.

Gotham, Kevin Fox. *Authentic New Orleans: Tourism, Culture, and Race in the Big Easy.* New York: New York University Press, 2007.

Gottschall, Amos. *Travels from Ocean to Ocean and from the Lakes to the Gulf: Being a Narrative of a Twelve Years' Ramble and What Was Seen and Experienced.* Harrisburg, PA: Amos H. Gottschall, 1882.

Gould, Virginia. "'A Chaos of Iniquity and Discord': Slave and Free Women of Color in the Spanish Ports of New Orleans, Mobile, and Pensacola." In *The Devil's Lane: Sex and Race in the Early South,* edited by Catherine Clinton and Michele Gillespie, 232–246. New York: Oxford University Press, 1997.

Gualtieri, Sarah. "Strange Fruit? Syrian Immigrants, Extralegal Violence and Racial Formation in the Jim Crow South." *Arab Studies Quarterly* (Summer 2004): 63–85.

Grand Celebration in Honor of the Passage of the Ordinance of Emancipation. New Orleans: H. P. Lathrop, 1864.

Grant, Kevin. *A Civilised Savagery: Britain and the New Slaveries in Africa, 1884–1926.* New York: Routledge, 2005.

Green, Tara. "Local Color, Social Problems, and the Living Dead in the Late-Nineteenth Century Short Fiction of Alice Dunbar Nelson." In *New Orleans: A Literary History,* edited by T. R. Johnson, 113–121. New York: Cambridge University Press, 2019.

Haas, Edward. *Mayor Victor Schiro: New Orleans in Transition, 1961–1970.* Jackson: University Press of Mississippi, 2014.

Hale, Grace Elizabeth. *Making Whiteness: The Culture of Segregation in the South, 1890–1940.* New York: Pantheon Books, 1998.

Hall, A. Oakey. *The Manhattaner in New Orleans; or, Phases of "Crescent City" Life.* New York: J. S. Redfield and Clinton Hall, 1851.

Harris, Jessica. *High on the Hog: A Culinary Journey from Africa to America.* New York: Bloomsbury, 2011.

Hart, W. O. "A Boy's Recollection of the War between the States." *Louisiana Historical Quarterly* (April 1928): 253–260.

Hearn, Lafcadio. *Inventing New Orleans: Writings of Lafcadio Hearn,* edited by S. Frederick Starr. Jackson: University Press of Mississippi, 2001.

———. *La Cuisine Creole: A Collection of Culinary Recipes,* 2nd ed. New Orleans: F. F. Hansell and Brother, circa 1910.

Heitmann, John. *The Modernization of the Louisiana Sugar Industry.* Baton Rouge: Louisiana State University Press, 1987.

Henderson, Timothy. *A History of Mexican Migration to the United States.* Malden, MA: Wiley-Blackwell, 2011.

Hesse-Wartegg, Ernst von. *Travels on the Lower Mississippi, 1879–1880,* translated by Frederic Trautmann. Columbia: University of Missouri Press, 1990.

Hickey, Georgina. *Hope and Danger in the New South City: Working-Class Women and Urban Development in Atlanta, 1890–1940.* Athens: University of Georgia Press, 2003.

Higgs, Catherine. *Chocolate Islands: Cocoa, Slavery, and Colonial Africa.* Athens: Ohio University Press, 2012.

Hirsch, Arnold. "Simply a Matter of Black and White: The Transformation of Race and Politics in Twentieth-Century New Orleans." In *Creole New Orleans: Race and Americanization,* edited by Arnold Hirsch and Joseph Logsdon, 262–319. Baton Rouge: Louisiana State University Press, 1992.

Hogue, James. *Uncivil War: Five New Orleans Street Battles and the Rise and Fall of Radical Reconstruction.* Baton Rouge: Louisiana State University Press, 2006.

Hollander, Gail. *Raising Cane in the 'Glades: The Global Sugar Trade and the Transformation of Florida.* Chicago: University of Chicago Press, 2008.

Hunt, Louise Livingston. *Memoir of Mrs. Edward Livingston with Letters Hitherto Unpublished.* New York: Harper and Brothers, 1886.

Hunter, Tera W. *To 'Joy My Freedom: Southern Black Women's Lives and Labors after the Civil War.* Cambridge, MA: Harvard University Press, 1997.

Hyatt, Harry Middleton. *Hoodoo-Conjuration-Witchcraft-Rootwork,* vol. II. Cambridge, MA: Western Publishing, 1970.

J. D. B. S. "Wanderings in the Southwest: No. II." *The Crayon* (July 11, 1855): 17–20.

———. "Wanderings in the Southwest: No. V." *The Crayon* (August 1, 1855): 105–107.

Jackson, Jessica Barbata. *Dixie's Italians: Sicilians, Race, and Citizenship in the Jim Crow South.* Baton Rouge: Louisiana State University Press, 2020.

Jaffa, M. E. *Nuts and Their Uses as Food.* Washington, DC: Government Printing Office, 1908.

James, Jennifer. *A Freedom Bought with Blood: African American War Literature from the Civil War to World War II.* Chapel Hill: University of North Carolina Press, 2007.

Jamison, Cecilia Viets. *Lady Jane.* New York: Century, 1916.

Johnson, Andrew. "Speech on the State of the Union." (February 5–6, 1861). In *Speeches of Andrew Johnson, President of the United States,* 176–289. Boston: Little, Brown, 1865.

Johnson, Walter. *Soul by Soul: Life inside the Antebellum Slave Market.* Cambridge, MA: Harvard University Press, 1999.

Johnston, Benjamin. *Revolution in Texas: How a Forgotten Rebellion and Its Bloody Suppression Turned Mexicans into Americans.* New Haven: Yale University Press, 2003.

Kane, Harnett. *Deep Delta Country.* New York: Duell, Sloan, and Pearce, 1944.

King, Edward. *The Great South.* Harford, CT: American Publishing Company, 1875.

King, Florence. *Southern Ladies and Gentlemen.* New York: St. Martin's, 1993.

King, Grace. "An Interlude." *Harper's New Monthly Magazine.* (November 1894): 918–920.

———. "Madrilène; or, the Festival of the Dead." *Harper's New Monthly Magazine* (November 1890): 869–886.

———. *Memories of a Southern Woman of Letters.* New York: Macmillan, 1932.

Kolb, Carolyn. *New Orleans Memories: One Writer's City.* Jackson: University Press of Mississippi, 2013.

Kramer, Paul. *The Blood of Government: Race, Empire, the United States, and the Philippines.* Chapel Hill: University of North Carolina Press, 2006.

Kuilan, Susie Scifres. "The 'All Seeing-Eye' in Grace King's Balcony Stories." In *Songs of the Reconstructing South: Building Literary Louisiana, 1865–1945,* edited by Suzanne Disheroon-Green and Lisa Abney, 99–108.Westport, CT: Greenwood Press, 2002.

Landau, Emily. *Spectacular Wickedness: Sex, Race, and Memory in Storyville, New Orleans.* Baton Rouge: Louisiana State University Press, 2013.

Latham, Henry. *Black and White: A Journal of a Three Months' Tour in the United States.* London: MacMillan and Co., 1867.

Latrobe, Benjamin. *Impressions Respecting New Orleans.* New York: Columbia University Press, 1951.

Loichot, Valérie. "Cooking Creoleness: Lafcadio Hearn in New Orleans and Martinique." *Journal of French and Francophone Philosophy* (August 2012): 1–21.

Long, Alecia. *The Great Southern Babylon: Sex, Race, and Respectability in New Orleans, 1865–1920.* Baton Rouge: Louisiana State University Press, 2004.

Manring, M. M. *Slave in a Box: The Strange Career of Aunt Jemima.* Charlottesville: University Press of Virginia, 1998.

Marler, Scott. *The Merchants' Capital: New Orleans and the Political Economy of the Nineteenth-Century South.* New York: Cambridge University Press, 2013.

Marling, Karal. "'She Brought Forth Butter in a Lordly Dish': The Origins of Minnesota Butter Sculpture." *Minnesota History* (Summer 1987): 218–228.

McCulla, Theresa. "Consumable City: Race, Ethnicity, and Food in Modern New Orleans." PhD diss., Harvard University, 2017.

McElya, Micki. *Clinging to Mammy: The Faithful Slave in Twentieth-Century America.* Cambridge, MA: Harvard University Press, 2007.

McWilliams, James. *The Pecan: A History of America's Native Nut.* Austin: University of Texas Press, 2013.

Meade, Anna Hardeman. *When I Was a Little Girl: The Year's Round on the Old Plantation.* Los Angeles: Fred S. Land, 1916.

Menefee, Selden, and Orin Cassmore. *The Pecan Shellers of San Antonio.* Washington, DC: United States Government Printing Office, 1940.

Menke, Pamela Glenn. "Behind the 'White Veil': Alice Dunbar-Nelson, Creole Color, and *The Goodness of St. Rocque.*" In *Songs of the Reconstructing South: Building Literary Louisiana, 1865–1945,* edited by Suzanne Disheroon-Green and Lisa Abney. Westport, CT: Greenwood Press, 2002.

Merleaux, April. *Sugar and Civilization: American Empire and the Cultural Politics of Sweetness.* Chapel Hill: University of North Carolina Press, 2015.

Mintz, Sidney. *Sweetness and Power: The Place of Sugar in Modern History.* New York: Viking, 1985.

Mitchell, Reid. *All on a Mardi Gras Day: Episodes in the History of New Orleans Carnival.* Cambridge, MA: Harvard University Press, 1995.

Moody, V. Alton. "Slavery on Louisiana Sugar Plantations." *Louisiana Historical Quarterly* (April 1924): 191–301.

Moore, Leonard. *Black Rage in New Orleans: Police Brutality and African American Activism from World War II to Hurricane Katrina.* Baton Rouge: Louisiana State University Press, 2010.

Morrison, Janet. "'Big Businesswoman' Eulalie Mandeville and the World of Female Free Black Entrepreneurs in Antebellum New Orleans." *Louisiana History (*Winter 2021): 61–86.

Moss, Robert. *The Lost Southern Chefs: A History of Commercial Dining in the Nineteenth-Century South.* Athens: University of Georgia Press, 2022.

Mount, May. *Some Notables of New Orleans: Biographical and Descriptive Sketches of the Artists of New Orleans and Their Work.* New Orleans: May Mount, 1896.

Mure, William. "Financial and Economic Disturbance in New Orleans on the Eve of Secession." Edited by Milledge Bonham. *Louisiana Historical Quarterly* (January 1930): 32–36.

Murphy, W. M. "The Old Pecan Tree on 'Eureka Plantation,' East Carroll Parish, LA." *Louisiana Historical Quarterly* (October 1934): 625–630.

Nott, G. William. "The Charm of Old New Orleans." *The Mentor* (February 1925): 28–46.

Nunez, Chanda. "'Just Like Ole' Mammy Used to Make': The History of the New Orleans Praline Woman." In *Working in the Big Easy: The History and Politics of Labor in New Orleans,* edited by Thomas Adams and Steve Striffler, 163–189. Lafayette: University of Louisiana at Lafayette Press, 2014.

Nystrom, Justin. *Creole Italian: Sicilian Immigrants and the Shaping of New Orleans Food Culture.* Athens: University of Georgia Press, 2018.

Olmsted, Frederick Law. *A Journey in the Seaboard Slave States with Remarks on Their Economy.* New York: Dix & Edwards, 1856.

Onebane, Donna McGee. *The House That Sugarcane Built: The Louisiana Burguiéres.* Jackson: University Press of Mississippi, 2014.

"The Open Forum." *American Mercury* (March 1939): 370–383.

Ormand, Suzanne, and Mary Irvine. *Louisiana's Art Nouveau: The Crafts of the Newcomb Style.* Gretna, LA: Pelican Publishing, 1976.

Parsons, Elaine. "Midnight Rangers: Costume and Performance in the Reconstruction-Era Ku Klux Klan." *Journal of American History* (December 2005): 811–836.

Parsons, Henry. "Sorghum as a Source of Sugar." *Popular Science Monthly* (September 1884): 627–636.

Peacocke, James. *The Creole Orphans; or Lights and Shadows of Southern Life.* New York: Derby and Jackson, 1856.

"Pecan Culture." *Irrigation Age* 7, no. 3 (September 1894): 134.

Pérez, Elizabeth. *Religion in the Kitchen: Cooking, Talking, and the Making of Black Atlantic Traditions.* New York: New York University Press, 2016.

Porter, Annie. "Miss Martin." *Atlantic Monthly* (June 1879): 797–805.

Post, Isabelle. "The Truth about Southern Cooking." *American Mercury* (January 1939): 30–34.

Prichard, Walter, "A Tourist's Description of Louisiana in 1860." *Louisiana Historical Quarterly* (October 1938): 1110–1214.

Rees, Jonathan. *Refrigeration Nation: A History of Ice, Appliances, and Enterprise in America.* Baltimore: Johns Hopkins University Press, 2013.

Rehder, John. *Delta Sugar: Louisiana's Vanishing Plantation Landscape.* Baltimore: Johns Hopkins University Press, 1999.

Rice, Stephen. *Minding the Machine: Languages of Class in Early Industrial America.* Berkeley: University of California Press, 2004.

Ripley, Eliza. *Social Life in Old New Orleans: Being Recollections of My Girlhood.* New York: D. Appleton, 1912.

Robb, Jeffrey, and Paul Travis. "The Rise and Fall of the Gulf Coast Tung Oil Industry." *Forest History Today* (Spring/Fall 2013): 14–22.

Roberts, Diane. *The Myth of Aunt Jemima: Representations of Race and Region.* New York: Routledge, 1994.

Robinson, Lura. *It's an Old New Orleans Custom.* New York: Vanguard Press, 1948.

Rodrigue, John. *Reconstruction in the Cane Fields: From Slavery to Free Labor in Louisiana's Sugar Parishes, 1862–1880.* Baton Rouge: Louisiana State University Press, 2001.

Rogers, Kim Lacy. *Righteous Lives: Narratives of the New Orleans Civil Rights Movement.* New York: New York University Press, 1993.

Root, William H. "Private Journal of William H. Root, Second Lieutenant, Seventy-Fifth New York Volunteers, April 1–June 14, 1863." Edited by L. Carroll Root. *Louisiana Historical Quarterly* (July 1936): 637–667.

Rost, P. A. *Oration Delivered before the Agricultural and Mechanics' Association of Louisiana on the 12th of May, 1845.* Philadelphia: J. Van Court, 1845.

Rousey, Dennis. *Policing the Southern City: New Orleans, 1805–1889.* Baton Rouge: Louisiana State University Press, 1996.

Rucker, Brian. "Satsumaland! A History of Citrus Culture in West Florida." *Gulf Coast Historical Review* (Fall 1996): 61–77.

Saxon, Lyle, Edward Dreyer, and Robert Tallant, eds. *Gumbo Ya-Ya.* Gretna, LA: Pelican Publishing, 1945, 1998.

Schafer, Judith. *Illegal Sex in Antebellum New Orleans: Brothels, Depravity, and Abandoned Women.* Baton Rouge: Louisiana State University Press, 2009.

Schloss, Rebecca. *Sweet Liberty: The Final Days of Slavery in Martinique.* Philadelphia: University of Pennsylvania Press, 2009.

Scogin, Samuel Martha, and John Dicks Howe. *Down on the Old Plantation: Original Sketches of Every-Day Life on a Mississippi Cotton Plantation.* San Francisco, 1908.

Scott, Natalie. *200 Years of New Orleans Cooking.* New York: Jonathan Cape & Harrison, 1931.

Shaik, Fatima. *The Mayor of New Orleans: Just Talking Jazz.* Berkeley, CA: Creative Arts Book Company, 1987.

Shannon, Katy. *Antoine of Oak Alley.* New Orleans: Pelican Publishing, 2021.

Spang, Rebecca. *The Invention of the Restaurant: Paris and Modern Gastronomic Culture.* Cambridge, MA: Harvard University Press, 2000.

Sharpless, Rebecca. *Cooking in Other Women's Kitchens, Domestic Workers in the South, 1865–1960.* Chapel Hill: University of North Carolina Press, 2010.

———. *Grain and Fire: A History of Baking in the American South.* Chapel Hill: University of North Carolina Press, 2022.

———. "The Women of St. Paul's Episcopal Church Were Worried: Transforming Domestic Skills into Saleable Commodities in Texas." In *The Larder: Food Studies Methods from the American South,* edited by John T. Edge, Elizabeth Engelhardt, and Ted Ownby, 32–56. Athens: University of Georgia Press, 2013.

Simmons, LaKisha. *Crescent City Girls: The Lives of Young Black Women in Segregated New Orleans.* Chapel Hill: University of North Carolina Press, 2015.

Sitterson, J. Carlyle. *Sugar Country: The Cane Sugar Industry in the South, 1753–1950.* Lexington: University of Kentucky Press, 1953.

Solomon, Clara. *The Civil War Diary of Clara Solomon: Growing up in New Orleans, 1861–1862,* edited by Elliot Ashkenazi. Baton Rouge: Louisiana State University Press, 1995.

Souther, Mark. *New Orleans on Parade: Tourism and the Transformation of the Crescent City.* Baton Rouge: Louisiana State University Press, 2006.

Sparling, E. Earl. *Under the Levee.* New York: Charles Scribner's Sons, 1925.

Stanonis, Anthony J. *Creating the Big Easy: New Orleans and the Emergence of Modern Tourism, 1918–1945.* Athens: University of Georgia Press, 2006.

———, ed. *Dixie Emporium: Tourism, Foodways, and Consumer Culture in the American South.* Athens: University of Georgia Press, 2008.

———. *Faith in Bikinis: Politics and Leisure in the Coastal South since the Civil War.* Athens: University of Georgia Press, 2014.

———. "Feast of the Mau Mau: Christianity, Conjure, and the Origins of Soul Food," In *Dethroning the Deceitful Pork Chop: Rethinking African American Foodways from Slavery to Obama, edited by Jennifer Jensen Wallach, 93–106.* Fayetteville: University of Arkansas Press, 2015.

———. "Just Like Mammy Used to Make: Foodways in the Jim Crow South." In *Dixie Emporium: Tourism, Foodways, and Consumer Culture in the American South,* edited by Anthony J. Stanonis, 208–233. Athens: University of Georgia Press, 2008.

———. "Through a Purple (Green and Gold) Haze: New Orleans Mardi Gras in the American Imagination." *Southern Cultures* (Summer 2008): 109–131.

———. "The Triumph of Epicure: A Global History of New Orleans Culinary Tourism." *Southern Quarterly* (Spring 2009): 145–161.

Stanonis, Anthony J., and Rachel Wallace, "Tasting New Orleans: How the Mardi Gras King Cake Came to Represent the Crescent City." *Southern Cultures* (Winter 2018): 6–23.

Stall, Gaspar "Buddy." *Buddy Stall's Big Easy.* Detroit: Harlo Printing, 1994.

Stokes, Ashli Quesinberry, and Wendy Atkins-Sayre, *Consuming Identity: The Role of Food in Redefining the South.* Jackson: University Press of Mississippi, 2016.

Stone, Kate. *Brokenburn: The Journal of Kate Stone, 1861–1868,* edited by John Anderson. Baton Rouge: Louisiana State University Press, 1972.

Stowe, Harriet Beecher. *A Key to Uncle Tom's Cabin.* Boston: John P. Jewett and Company, 1853.

———. *Uncle Tom's Cabin; or, Life among the Lowly.* Philadelphia: Henry Altemus, 1894.

Stuart Pecan Company. *The Pecan, and How to Grow It.* Chicago: Woman's Temperance Publishing Association, 1893.

Summers, Mark. *Railroads, Reconstruction, and the Gospel of Prosperity: Aid under the Radical Republicans, 1865–1877.* Princeton: Princeton University Press, 1984.

Sutton, David. *Remembrance of Repasts: An Anthropology of Food and Memory.* New York: Berg, 2001.

Taylor, Helen. *Gender, Race, and Region in the Writings of Grace King, Ruth McEnery Stuart, and Kate Chopin.* Baton Rouge: Louisiana State University Press, 1989.

Taylor, Joe. *Louisiana Reconstructed, 1863–1877.* Louisiana State University Press, 1974.

Thomas, David. *Travels through the Western Country in the Summer of 1816.* Auburn, NY: David Rumsey, 1819.

Thomas, Lynnell. *Desire and Disaster in New Orleans: Tourism, Race, and Historical Memory.* Durham: Duke University Press, 2014.

Tipton-Martin, Toni. *The Jemima Code: Two Centuries of African American Cookbooks.* Austin: University of Texas Press, 2015.

Tompkins, Kyla. *Racial Indigestion: Eating Bodies in the 19th Century.* New York: New York University Press, 2012.

Trowbridge, John Townsend. *A Picture of the Desolated States; and the Work of Restoration, 1865–1868.* Hartford, CT: L. Stebbins, 1868.

Trubeck, Amy. *Haute Cuisine: How the French Invented the Culinary Profession.* Philadelphia: University of Pennsylvania Press, 2000.

Tunnell, Ted. *Crucible of Reconstruction: War, Radicalism, and Race in Louisiana, 1862–1877.* Baton Rouge: Louisiana State University Press, 1984.

Turner, Arlin. *George W. Cable: A Biography.* Baton Rouge: Louisiana State University Press, 1966.

Turner, Patricia. *Ceramic Uncles and Celluloid Mammies: Black Images and Their Influence on Culture.* New York: Anchor, 1994.

Twain, Mark. *Life on the Mississippi.* Boston: James R. Osgood and Company, 1883.

Wallach, Jennifer Jensen, ed. *Dethroning the Deceitful Pork Chop: Rethinking African American Foodways from Slavery to Obama.* Fayetteville: University of Arkansas Press, 2015.

———. *Every Nation Has Its Dish: Black Bodies and Black Food in Twentieth-Century America.* Chapel Hill: University of North Carolina Press, 2019.

Walworth, Jeannette. *Dead Men's Shoes.* Philadelphia: J. B. Lippincott, 1872.

Wang, Xi. *The Trial of Democracy: Black Suffrage and Northern Republicans, 1860–1910.* Athens: University of Georgia Press, 1997.

Warner, Deborah. *Sweet Stuff: An American History of Sweeteners from Sugar to Sucrose.* Washington, DC: Smithsonian Institution Scholarly Press, 2011.

Warner, Mark. *Eating in the Side Room: Food, Archaeology, and African American Identity.* Gainesville: University Press of Florida, 2015.

Weiss, Carl Theodor. "A Bavarian Organist Comes to New Orleans." Edited by Robert Clark. *Louisiana Historical Quarterly* (January 1946).

Wells, Lenny. *Pecan: America's Native Nut Tree.* Tuscaloosa: University of Alabama Press, 2017.

Whitelaw, Reid. *After the War: A Southern Tour, May 1, 1865 to May 1, 1866.* Cincinnati: Moore, Wilstach, and Baldwin, 1866.

Whites, Leeann. *The Civil War as a Crisis in Gender: Augusta, Georgia, 1860–1890.* Athens: University of Georgia Press, 1995.

Wilkinson, Andrews. *Plantation Stories of Old Louisiana.* Boston: Page Company, 1914.

Williams-Forson, Psyche. *Building Houses out of Chicken Legs: Black Women, Food, and Power.* Chapel Hill: University of North Carolina Press, 2006.

Willink, Cecile, ed. "An Old Lady's Gossip of Life in Louisiana in the Middle of the Last Century." *Louisiana Historical Quarterly* (July 1923): 380–387.

Witt, Doris. *Black Hunger: Food and the Politics of U.S. Identity.* New York: Oxford University Press, 1999.

Woloson, Wendy. *Refined Tastes: Sugar, Confectionary, and Consumers in Nineteenth-Century America.* Baltimore: Johns Hopkins University, 2002.

Woodard, Vincent. *The Delectable Negro: Human Consumption and Homoeroticism with U.S. Slave Culture.* New York: New York University Press, 2014.

Woodbury, Levi. *Writings of Levi Woodbury, LL.D.: Political, Judicial and Literary*, vol. III. Boston: Little, Brown and Company, 1852.

Wright, George. "Vieux Carré." *Scribner's Magazine* (January 1928): 17–23.

Young, Ashley Roe. "Nourishing Networks: The Public Culture of Food in Nineteenth-Century America." PhD diss., Duke University, 2017.

Young, Perry. *The Mistick Krewe: Chronicles of Comus and His Kin*. New Orleans: Carnival Press, 1931.

Zafar, Rafia. *Recipes for Respect: African American Meals and Meaning*. Athens: University of North Carolina Press, 2019.

Zimmerman, Andrew. *Alabama in Africa: Booker T. Washington, the German Empire, and the Globalization of the New South*. Princeton: Princeton University Press, 2010.

WEBSITES

Bellande, Ray. "Bechtel Family." Ocean Springs Archives. *https://oceanspringsarchives.net/bechtel-family*.

———. "Pabst Family." Ocean Springs Archives. https://oceanspringsarchives.net/pabst-family.

Encyclopedia of Southern Jewish Communities—Lafayette, Louisiana. https://www.isjl.org/louisiana-lafayette-encyclopedia.html.

"History of the Praline," La Maison de la Praline. https://www.maisondelapraline.com/en/la-maison-de-la-praline-our-universe/la-maison-de-la-praline-histoire-de-la-praline-side.

Knapp, Gwendolyn. "Pralines Are More than just New Orleans' Signature Candy." https://www.eater.com/2016/10/27/13422426/praline-new-orleans-pecan-candy.

Loichot, Valerie. "Kara Walker's Blood Sugar: A Subtlety or the Marvelous Sugar Baby." *Southern Spaces*. https://southernspaces.org/2014/kara-walkers-blood-sugar-subtlety-or-marvelous-sugar-baby/.

Mozo, Jessica. "McMinnville, Tennessee: Nursery Capital of the World." *Tennessee Home and Farm*. https://tnhomeandfarm.com/agriculture/mcminnville-nursery-capital/.

Old Town Pralines and Parasols. https://www.oldtownpraline.com/about-us/.

"Pecan Breeding Cultivars," College of Agriculture, University of Georgia. https://pecanbreeding.uga.edu/cultivars/alphabetical-list/candy.html.

St. Félix, Doreen. "Kara Walker's Next Act," *Vulture*. https://www.vulture.com/2017/04/kara-walker-after-a-subtlety.html.

Index

Note: Italicized page numbers refer to images in the text.